In Pursuit of
Great AND Godly
Leadership

Other Books by Mike Bonem

Leading from the Second Chair: Serving Your Church, Fulfilling Your Role, and Realizing Your Dreams (with Roger Patterson)

Leading Congregational Change: A Practical Guide for the Transformational Journey (with Jim Herrington and James H. Furr)

Leading Congregational Change Workbook (with James H. Furr and Jim Herrington)

IN PURSUIT OF GREAT AND GODLY LEADERSHIP

Tapping the Wisdom of the World for the Kingdom of God

Mike Bonem

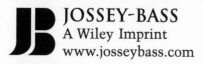
A Leadership ❊ Network Publication

JOSSEY-BASS
A Wiley Imprint
www.josseybass.com

Published by Jossey-Bass
A Wiley Imprint
One Montgomery Street, Suite 1200, San Francisco, CA 94104-4594—www.josseybass.com

All scripture quotations, unless otherwise indicated, are taken from the Holy Bible, New International Version®, NIV®. Copyright ©1973, 1978, 1984, 2011 by Biblica, Inc.™ Used by permission of Zondervan. All rights reserved worldwide. www.zondervan.com. The "NIV" and "New International Version" are trademarks registered in the United States Patent and Trademark Office by Biblica, Inc.™

Scripture quotations marked "ESV" are from The Holy Bible, English Standard Version® (ESV®), copyright © 2001 by Crossway, a publishing ministry of Good News Publishers. Used by permission. All rights reserved.

Scripture quotations marked "NASB" are taken from the New American Standard Bible®, Copyright © 1960, 1962, 1963, 1968, 1971, 1972, 1973, 1975, 1977, 1995 by The Lockman Foundation. Used by permission. (www.Lockman.org)

Excerpts from Kouzes, James M., and Barry Z. Posner. *The Leadership Challenge, 4th ed.* San Francisco: Jossey-Bass, 2007. Reprinted with permission of John Wiley and Sons, Inc.

Jossey-Bass books and products are available through most bookstores. To contact Jossey-Bass directly call our Customer Care Department within the U.S. at 800-956-7739, outside the U.S. at 317-572-3986, or fax 317-572-4002.

Wiley also publishes its books in a variety of electronic formats and by print-on-demand. Some material included with standard print versions of this book may not be included in e-books or in print-on-demand. If the version of this book that you purchased references media such as CD or DVD that was not included in your purchase, you may download this material at http://booksupport.wiley.com. For more information about Wiley products, visit www.wiley.com.

Library of Congress Cataloging-in-Publication Data

Bonem, Mike, date.
  In pursuit of great and godly leadership : tapping the wisdom of the world for
the kingdom of God / Mike Bonem. 1st ed.
    p. cm. (The Jossey-Bass leadership network series)
    Includes bibliographical references and index.
  ISBN 978-0-470-94742-5 (hardback); 978-1-118-16259-0 (ebk); 978-1-118-16261-3 (ebk);
978-1-118-16262-0 (ebk)
  1. Christian leadership.   2. Leadership–Religious aspects–Christianity.
3. Leadership.   I. Title.

  BV652.1.B665 2012
  262′.1–dc23   2011034755

Printed in the United States of America
FIRST EDITION
PB Printing 10 9 8 7 6 5 4 3 2 1

Leadership Network Titles

The Blogging Church: Sharing the Story of Your Church Through Blogs, Brian Bailey and Terry Storch

Church Turned Inside Out: A Guide for Designers, Refiners, and Re-Aligners, Linda Bergquist and Allan Karr

Leading from the Second Chair: Serving Your Church, Fulfilling Your Role, and Realizing Your Dreams, Mike Bonem and Roger Patterson

In Pursuit of Great AND Godly Leadership: Tapping the Wisdom of the World for the Kingdom of God, Mike Bonem

Hybrid Church: The Fusion of Intimacy and Impact, Dave Browning

The Way of Jesus: A Journey of Freedom for Pilgrims and Wanderers, Jonathan S. Campbell with Jennifer Campbell

Cracking Your Church's Culture Code: Seven Keys to Unleashing Vision and Inspiration, Samuel R. Chand

Leading the Team-Based Church: How Pastors and Church Staffs Can Grow Together into a Powerful Fellowship of Leaders, George Cladis

Organic Church: Growing Faith Where Life Happens, Neil Cole

Church 3.0: Upgrades for the Future of the Church, Neil Cole

Journeys to Significance: Charting a Leadership Course from the Life of Paul, Neil Cole

Off-Road Disciplines: Spiritual Adventures of Missional Leaders, Earl Creps

Reverse Mentoring: How Young Leaders Can Transform the Church and Why We Should Let Them, Earl Creps

Building a Healthy Multi-Ethnic Church: Mandate, Commitments, and Practices of a Diverse Congregation, Mark DeYmaz

Leading Congregational Change Workbook, James H. Furr, Mike Bonem, and Jim Herrington

The Tangible Kingdom: Creating Incarnational Community, Hugh Halter and Matt Smay

Baby Boomers and Beyond: Tapping the Ministry Talents and Passions of Adults over Fifty, Amy Hanson

Leading Congregational Change: A Practical Guide for the Transformational Journey, Jim Herrington, Mike Bonem, and James H. Furr

The Leader's Journey: Accepting the Call to Personal and Congregational Transformation, Jim Herrington, Robert Creech, and Trisha Taylor

The Permanent Revolution: Apostolic Imagination and Practice for the 21st Century, Alan Hirsch and Tim Catchim

Whole Church: Leading from Fragmentation to Engagement, Mel Lawrenz

Culture Shift: Transforming Your Church from the Inside Out, Robert Lewis and Wayne Cordeiro, with Warren Bird

Church Unique: How Missional Leaders Cast Vision, Capture Culture, and Create Movement, Will Mancini

A New Kind of Christian: A Tale of Two Friends on a Spiritual Journey, Brian D. McLaren

The Story We Find Ourselves In: Further Adventures of a New Kind of Christian, Brian D. McLaren

Missional Communities: The Rise of the Post-Congregational Church, Reggie McNeal

Missional Renaissance: Changing the Scorecard for the Church, Reggie McNeal

Practicing Greatness: 7 Disciplines of Extraordinary Spiritual Leaders, Reggie McNeal

The Present Future: Six Tough Questions for the Church, Reggie McNeal

A Work of Heart: Understanding How God Shapes Spiritual Leaders, Reggie McNeal

The Millennium Matrix: Reclaiming the Past, Reframing the Future of the Church, M. Rex Miller

Your Church in Rhythm: The Forgotten Dimensions of Seasons and Cycles, Bruce B. Miller

Shaped by God's Heart: The Passion and Practices of Missional Churches, Milfred Minatrea

The Missional Leader: Equipping Your Church to Reach a Changing World, Alan J. Roxburgh and Fred Romanuk

Missional Map-Making: Skills for Leading in Times of Transition, Alan J. Roxburgh

Relational Intelligence: How Leaders Can Expand Their Influence Through a New Way of Being Smart, Steve Saccone

Viral Churches: Helping Church Planters Become Movement Makers, Ed Stetzer and Warren Bird

The Externally Focused Quest: Becoming the Best Church for the Community, Eric Swanson and Rick Rusaw

The Ascent of a Leader: How Ordinary Relationships Develop Extraordinary Character and Influence, Bill Thrall, Bruce McNicol, and Ken McElrath

Beyond Megachurch Myths: What We Can Learn from America's Largest Churches, Scott Thumma and Dave Travis

The Other 80 Percent: Turning Your Church's Spectators into Active Participants, Scott Thumma and Warren Bird

Better Together: Making Church Mergers Work, Jim Tomberlin and Warren Bird

The Elephant in the Boardroom: Speaking the Unspoken About Pastoral Transitions, Carolyn Weese and J. Russell Crabtree

CONTENTS

About the Jossey-Bass
Leadership Network
Series

Leadership Network's mission is to accelerate the impact of OneHundredX leaders. These high-capacity leaders are like the hundredfold crop that comes from seed planted in good soil as Jesus described in Matthew 13:8.

Leadership Network...

- explores the "what's next?" of what could be.
- creates "aha!" environments for collaborative discovery.
- works with exceptional "positive deviants."
- invests in the success of others through generous relationships.
- pursues big impact through measurable kingdom results.
- strives to model Jesus through all we do.

Believing that meaningful conversations and strategic connections can change the world, we seek to help leaders navigate the future by exploring new ideas and finding application for each unique context. Through collaborative meetings and processes, leaders map future possibilities and challenge one another to action that accelerates fruitfulness and effectiveness. Leadership Network shares the learnings and inspiration with others through our books, concept papers, research reports, e-newsletters, podcasts, videos, and online experiences. This in turn generates a ripple effect of new conversations and further influence.

In 1996 Leadership Network established a partnership with Jossey-Bass, a Wiley Imprint, to develop a series of creative books that provide thought leadership to innovators in church ministry. Leadership Network Publications present thoroughly researched and innovative concepts from leading thinkers, practitioners, and pioneering churches.

Leadership Network is a division of OneHundredX, a global ministry with initiatives around the world.

To learn more about Leadership Network, go to www .leadnet.org

PREFACE

Less than a year after I completed my M.B.A. in the 1980s, Mark McCormack wrote *What They Don't Teach You at Harvard Business School: Notes from a Street Smart Executive*. It was a hot topic in my business circles, and since he was talking about my alma mater, I decided that I should read it. In essence, McCormack made the argument that business schools were not teaching the practical leadership lessons that up-and-coming executives needed to learn in order to be successful. It wasn't a slap at Harvard specifically but a more general critique of the things that weren't being taught in most M.B.A. programs. That was no surprise to me.

Fast-forward about five years to a time when I became aware that churches across the country were facing a growing leadership crisis. That's when I began to realize that a parallel book could have been written: *What They Don't Teach You at _____ Seminary*. I won't name a specific seminary because this title could have applied to almost any seminary at that time. Today, many seminaries have gradually incorporated leadership training into their programs and pastors have more nonseminary options for developing their skills, but the average spiritual leader still falls far short of the mark in terms of leadership training and effectiveness.

So is this a book to teach M.B.A. principles to pastors? Not really. My journey has taken me from the corporate world into vocational ministry. I have spent the past ten years serving on the staff of a local church and more than two decades as a coach and consultant to congregations and their leaders. In my own church and others, I have seen the dangers of becoming too corporatized. I have observed the struggles and missteps that can occur when marketplace leaders insist on using "best practices" from business in the church. I have experienced the tension that often exists between clergy and lay leaders because each sees the world through such different lenses.

What I have learned in my journey is that we need a diverse mix of talents and perspectives for our churches and Christian organizations to thrive. The M.B.A.'s and other businesspeople have an important contribution to make. So do the seminary-trained leaders and other clergy. Too often, though, they struggle to find a common ground for effective, enduring leadership.

This book is simply an attempt to establish that common ground by examining biblical and marketplace leadership concepts and asking how best to lead any organization that places Christ at the center of its mission. It is a book that will help pastors grow in their leadership and better understand the businesspeople in their congregations. It will help the leaders of denominational bodies and parachurch organizations relate to their boards in more productive ways. It will give a fresh perspective for those who struggle as they make career transitions from business into ministry. And it will give lay leaders, those gifted men and women who are vital to thriving congregations, a new awareness of how they can use their gifts for greater Kingdom impact.

The church in North America still has a long way to go to achieve this impact. My deep desire is for the church and other Christian organizations to be transformed so that they can transform the world. Realizing this kind of God-honoring, Kingdom-expanding potential will require leaders from a variety of backgrounds to come together and courageously follow God using all the tools that are available to them. My knowledge of these tools comes from my own experience and a variety of business experts. Jim Collins, author of several books including *Good to Great*, is one of the most prominent sources, but you will also be introduced to Patrick Lencioni, Robert Quinn, John Kotter, James Kouzes, Barry Posner, and many others. (Some of my favorite resources are listed in the annotated bibliography at the back of the book.)

Having knowledge of secular leadership concepts is only half the battle. The other half is understanding when and how to apply these tools in Christian organizations. In that effort, I have turned to a number of outstanding Christian authors. I have also been helped by personal interviews with more than forty successful leaders who live in the midst of these tensions, and I am deeply grateful that they shared their stories and insights to enrich this book. In the pages that follow, you'll meet men and women who are pastors of a wide variety of congregations. You'll meet people who lead parachurch ministries, denominational bodies, and Christian universities. You'll hear from seminary faculty who teach on leadership. And you'll be introduced to successful Christian businesspeople who are committed to using their gifts for the Kingdom. (See Appendix A for a list of the leaders I interviewed.)

As I have reflected on all that I have learned from experts, practitioners, and my own experiences, I have developed several central convictions that underlie the rest of this book.

The Bible provides the core foundation, but not all the answers, on how to be an effective leader. In the pages that follow, you will be presented with a number of business concepts, but my starting point is Scripture. Our leadership should be shaped by God's Word and should never violate its teachings. My conviction, however, is that the Bible is more descriptive of leadership principles than it is prescriptive of specific leadership models or actions. For example, it is a clear biblical principle that God often calls leaders to take bold steps. In the specific case of a church that is considering a major expansion of its facilities, what does the Bible say? Does it tell the pastor the best way to involve other leaders in the decision, how to raise the funds, whether to use debt, or what to do if an unexpected roadblock arises? We may find additional principles that relate to these questions, but we will find few concrete answers. That is why we start with, but are not limited to, Scripture as the source for leadership wisdom.

Secular leadership principles are not inherently evil or contrary to Scripture. Given my business background, it's probably no surprise that I say this. This conviction, however, is not based solely on my training. As you will see in the following chapters, it is based on biblical teaching, the perspectives of other noted Christian leaders, and the ways in which God seems to be working in many congregations. In fact, you'll find that a number of "business principles" are very consistent with the teachings of Scripture.

Unwillingness to use solid business principles can limit a church's potential. If an anonymous donor calls your church and offers a gift of $100,000, how long will it take you to say yes? As long as the money was obtained legally and does not have strings attached (and sometimes even if there are strings), you will accept in a hurry. But if a faith-filled, highly successful business leader offers to share his or her leadership gifts, many churches are hesitant. The same congregation that accepts a financial gift can take big steps forward if it accepts help with vision-setting, implementation of plans, financial management, personnel practices, or other areas where business leaders can contribute. I am not saying that churches should practice wholesale or unfiltered adoption of business principles. Nor am I saying that this is the solution to everything wrong with the church in America. I am simply saying that ineffective leadership is poor stewardship when great leadership resources are within arm's reach.

Overreliance on business principles can also limit a church's potential. It cuts both ways. Some churches have become so corporatized that it is hard to figure out where the Holy Spirit is moving in their midst. If all directional decisions are driven by logic and analysis, all financial decisions are driven by accounting calculations of affordability, all difficult personnel decisions are driven by a performance evaluation matrix, and all congregational decisions are made by a majority vote, then all you have is a nonprofit corporation with "church" in its name. One successful leader confided to me that he is haunted by the thought that his church could drift to the point where it doesn't rely on God. It is a thought that should haunt all of us. We must recognize that the tools of business are just that—tools—and that our only source of transforming power is the Lord.

We have a tremendous stewardship responsibility and leadership opportunity. We are all called to be stewards of the gifts that God has entrusted to us. As leaders, we feel the weight of responsibility like the man who was given five talents (Matthew 25:15). We have an opportunity to earn a greater return than those who have been given less, but we also have a greater responsibility. Further, the gifts that we have been given extend beyond ourselves. If you are in a position of leadership, whether first chair or some other key role, you have the opportunity to draw out gifts that God has given to others. That includes the leadership talents and the spiritual discernment that sit in the pews of your church every weekend. Leadership is hard work, but God does not give us the option to walk away because of the difficulty or a bruised ego. He calls us to lead with all diligence.

The space in which we lead offers few easy answers. One classic leadership book from the secular arena is Ron Heifitz's *Leadership Without Easy Answers*, a title that certainly describes congregational leadership. Scripture gives us a number of principles and boundaries that must inform our leadership. We are to seek God in all things, treat others with kindness and compassion, not be guided by other people's praise, and be good stewards. Even if we compile a complete list of all these imperatives, we will find plenty of room for interpretation in how we lead our organizations. Business gives us many practical tools, some that conflict with each other and some that contradict Scripture, but many that seem quite applicable. Spiritual leaders spend their lives in the midst of this ambiguity, trying to determine how best to lead. The most effective leaders don't look for simple answers and don't become paralyzed by uncertainty. They sift through as much as they can from spiritual and secular sources and then prayerfully and confidently put into practice whatever fits their circumstances.

This book explores a number of secular and spiritual resources so that you can choose what fits your leadership needs. The first two chapters look further at the philosophical framework and the personal issues every spiritual leader must face. Then Part One turns to a number of practical topics such as planning, personnel management, finance, and measurement. Addressing these matters is important, but it is not enough, so the second part looks at deeper, foundational matters related to team dynamics, culture, and organizational change.

On many of these topics, I was surprised by the variety of opinions expressed in my interviews. In fact, this diversity is what makes spiritual leadership so challenging and interesting. Every person with whom I spoke is deeply committed to loving and serving the Lord with his or her whole heart, soul, mind, and strength. But exercising the gift of leadership looks different for each of them. Some of those differences are driven by the contexts in which they serve, but many of the differences reflect their understanding of what it means to be a Christian leader and how much to tap the wisdom of the corporate world. Be willing to hear the differing perspectives, and as you do so, reflect on how you can be a more effective leader in your own setting.

Several years ago, I had the once-in-a-lifetime opportunity to take a guided rafting trip through the Grand Canyon with my only uncle and one of my sons. It was an incredible week. (It was also the most unplugged I have ever been in my career—there's no cell phone service at the bottom of the canyon!)

Part of what made the week so amazing was our guides. They were experts at steering the rafts through the still waters and the powerful rapids of the Colorado River. That by itself was an impressive feat, but they did much more than that. Throughout the long days of floating on the river and hiking the side trails, they educated us on the geology of the canyon, its plant and animal life, its unique weather patterns, and the historical explorers and older civilizations that had been there. Interestingly, the men and women who led us were not scientists—they were river guides who had learned from others.

That is a lot like the study of leadership and this book. Leadership is a rich topic with myriad dimensions, and my goal is to be a guide who shares what I have learned from experts and personal experience. Of course, such a rich and complex subject cannot be mastered in one book. At the end of my week in the Grand Canyon, my life had been enriched tremendously, but I also thought, "I want to come back. There's so much more to see and learn and experience." I hope you will feel the same about leadership when you get to the last page.

Another reason my trip was so memorable is that I got to spend the week with two people I love dearly. The best leadership is a journey with friends, not a solo venture. So as you reflect on the concepts that follow, I hope you will engage in a broader discussion with your leadership team or with peers. As you do so, my prayer is that God will use my efforts as a guide to enhance your leadership, strengthen your church, and multiply His Kingdom.

To our children—David, Matthew, Jonathan, and Hope. You have been given the gift of leadership. I pray you will use it to bless others and glorify God.

In Pursuit of
Great AND Godly
Leadership

CHAPTER ONE

IS GREAT THE ENEMY
OF GODLY?

"Good is the enemy of great," according to Jim Collins in the well-known opening line of *Good to Great*.[1] Collins's best-selling book has been a favorite guide for business leaders and has been equally influential for many leaders outside of business, including those in the church.

I am one of those leaders who have been greatly influenced by Collins. Having started my career in business, I readily recognized the relevance of *Good to Great* and similar resources for Christian organizations. But over time, I also realized that leaders in these organizations need to consider another question: "Is great the enemy of godly?"

Before answering this, let me step back and explain Collins's assertion that "good is the enemy of great." Many organizations, after having some measure of success, will declare themselves "good" and may not push themselves to become great. Greatness requires hard work, discipline, and intentionality that are not easily achieved. In corporations, making a profit, releasing a blockbuster product, or beating a competitor can lead to satisfaction and complacency.

Far too many churches and Christian enterprises are satisfied with being good. They look at their results at the end of the year and proclaim victory. If they meet their budget or add a few new members or have a couple of ministry highlights, they say this has been a "good" year. In truth, they're saying that this is "good enough." Their standard is doing enough to preserve their comfort and to avoid any dramatic, unsettling changes. It's an internally derived standard that ignores the reality of a world just outside the doors of the church, a world that is desperate to see and experience God's message of hope. Many books have been written to describe the state of the church and the changes in our world, and it's not my intent to add to that discussion. I simply want to affirm what others have said: if we settle for good results, we will fall far short of the mission to which God has called us, and we will continue to slip toward mediocrity and irrelevance. Good is indeed the enemy of both great and godly.

So is God calling us to greatness? Or is great the enemy of godly? Aspiring to greatness is an interesting dilemma for the church. We can agree with Bill Hybels that the "church is the hope of the world."[2] But we know that "the world"—whether we think of the problems at the local or global level—is terribly broken. This means that the challenge before us is huge. It's a challenge that should stir all of us not to accept the status quo. It's a challenge that should inspire us to give our lives for the sake of God's Kingdom and in doing so to do everything within our power to lead our churches toward greatness.

Or should it? If our mind-set is to do everything *within our power*, does that suggest self-reliance rather than dependence on God? Does it mean that we are building our own kingdoms rather than God's? If we charge toward greatness with blind ambition, is it possible that we will overlook biblical principles in the process? Peter Greer of HOPE International says, "If we're not listening to the Lord, we could run fast, we could jump over tall buildings, and we could be a complete failure in terms of any impact for Christ."* If this happens, then great can become the enemy of godly, and the church is no better off being great then being good.

But it is also possible that "godly is the enemy of great." Before you dismiss this statement, consider your experiences around churches and church leaders. Have you ever encountered someone who used a spiritual smoke screen as an excuse for lack of effort or poor results? I am not talking about genuine failures, those times when a well-designed initiative falls short despite prayer and hard work. I am talking about the occasions when leaders take a

---

*All quotations not credited to published sources are from personal interviews conducted by the author. The subjects of these interviews are identified in detail in Appendix A.

lackadaisical approach, expecting God to make up for their poor planning or minimal effort. It is the adult version of the student who didn't study, prayed as the test was handed out, and expected God to give him recall of facts he never learned. Peter Greer balances his earlier statement, noting that "*nonprofit* should not be a synonym for *nonperforming.*"

I believe that great can be the enemy of godly. I also believe that godly can be the enemy of great. And I'm convinced that God wants—in fact, commands—us to lead our churches to be great *and* godly. So how are we to do this?

That is the subject of this book. In particular, we will explore whether and how much we can use the tools and practices and principles of the business world to pursue this twin goal of greatness and godliness. Do we need to learn from secular experts? If so, how can we do so without compromising the call to godliness? Dan Entwistle of the United Methodist Church of the Resurrection in the Kansas City area, answers that "being a well-run organization is not in direct conflict with being a spiritually vital congregation." While not in direct conflict, the techniques of management can seem very unspiritual. It can be difficult to translate them into spiritual settings. Bishop Janice Huie of the Texas Conference of the United Methodist Church says that "Christian leadership begins and ends with God," but she acknowledges that everything in the middle is where leadership gets complicated. It's that middle space that needs to be addressed.

STRADDLING THE FENCE OF SACRED-SECULAR LEADERSHIP

My leadership journey began in the business world. After completing my M.B.A., I went to work for McKinsey & Company, one of the largest and most prominent strategy consulting companies in the world. It was a tremendous experience in which I learned a great deal about strategy, organizational design, change management, leadership, and many other subjects. After several years at McKinsey, I knew that it was time to make some sort of change but was unsure where that might lead.

At the same time, my good friend Jim Herrington had just been chosen as the new leader of Union Baptist Association (UBA), the

Houston-area judicatory body for Southern Baptists and the largest local Baptist association in the country. Over the next several years, I remained firmly planted in the business arena (in several different jobs) but also began to work with Jim and the great team at UBA and then with other Christian organizations, helping congregations apply the many business principles I had learned. My first book, *Leading Congregational Change* (written with Jim Herrington and James Furr), was an outgrowth of this work. The response to the book and the seminars we led confirmed the benefit of using business principles in the church.

One of my favorite business resources was *Built to Last* by Jim Collins and Jerry Porras.[3] I found the concept of "preserve the core and stimulate progress" to be a powerful tool for stimulating discussions about corporate and congregational leadership. So in 2000, when I learned that Collins would be one of the keynote speakers at a Leadership Network event, I eagerly anticipated hearing him describe his latest research.

One topic that he spent a considerable amount of time talking about was the importance of getting "the right people on the bus and the wrong people off the bus." Collins's research, which was the basis for *Good to Great*, showed that strategic direction was secondary to getting the right leadership team. He concluded that executives should focus on senior staff as a top priority. If you have the right people, they will help define the future direction of the organization. If they are in the wrong positions but fit the culture and have great potential, you can move them to a "different seat on the bus." But when someone is wrong for the organization, whether due to lack of ability or personality clashes, retaining them can drag the entire enterprise down.[4]

I remember nodding my head in agreement as I heard this. Even though my primary employment was in the marketplace at the time, a growing amount of my time was spent as a consultant to churches and speaker on congregational leadership. I knew the tendency of many churches to make excuses rather than confront underperforming staff members. I remember thinking, "Wouldn't the church be much more effective and be able to achieve far more for the Kingdom if we got the wrong people off the bus?"

Little did I know that within a year I would leave my corporate career to serve in a vocational ministry role on a church staff and would begin to have first-hand opportunities to test this and other business principles in a congregational setting. And little did I appreciate some of the differences and challenges that I would encounter.

My wife knew how much I was anticipating the publication of *Good to Great*, and when I came home on the date of release in 2001, I found a copy waiting on my desk. I devoured it. But around the same time, I read another book that stood in stark contrast to my business reading. Our senior pastor kept talking about *Fresh Wind, Fresh Fire* by Jim Cymbala, so I picked up a copy in an effort to expand my reading beyond the business sector.

It's hard to get whiplash from reading a book, but that is how it felt as I pored over the powerful story of Brooklyn Tabernacle. The whiplash did not come from the congregation's success but from the simple, faith-filled approach that Cymbala described. He seemed to run from everything that gave a hint of the leadership methods of corporate America, saying things like "We don't need technicians and church programmers; *we need God*. He is not looking for smart people, because he's the smart one. All he wants are people simple enough to trust him."[5]

I wished that I could dismiss Cymbala, but as I turned the last page of his book, I was forced to face a pivotal question: What does it mean to be an effective, biblical leader in a local congregation? It was no longer enough for me to say, "My leadership gift has been shaped in the marketplace, and now God wants me to use this gift in ministry." I needed to take a fresh look at leadership in the local church.

Over the past ten years, the journey of exploration and discovery has continued for me. On the one hand, I have learned to recognize some of the limitations and downsides of my business-oriented bias. I have learned a great deal from Spirit-led pastors and lay leaders who have helped me listen more closely to God and not rely exclusively on analysis. On the other hand, I have seen our church change and thrive over this decade, and I believe that the mix of gifts that God has assembled, including my business skills, have been key ingredients in our success. Beyond my own church, I have encountered many spiritual leaders who have been asking the same question that I've been asking: What is the most effective and God-honoring way to lead our faith-based organizations?

A BIBLICAL FOUNDATION

If we want to honor God with our leadership, then it is appropriate to start with God's Word. What does the Bible teach us about leadership? In one sense, it teaches us a great deal. The Bible gives us many different images of great leaders and what they accomplish. It also gives us vivid portrayals of leadership failures, both by people who love God (think of David and Bathsheba) and by people who oppose God (think of Pharaoh and the Exodus story). It gives timeless principles that can benefit any leader.

We need to glean as much as possible from Scripture about leadership, but in doing so we should recognize that we will discover general principles far more often than specific practices. In fact, if we search the pages of the Bible for an example of how to handle a difficult problem, we might come up with some strange answers. Would any of us really conclude that God wants us to kill (literally) a former ally who had some ruthless, power-grabbing tendencies? Yet we find this in David's final instruction to Solomon regarding Joab. Of course, that is an extreme example, but there are plenty of other stories that may not point us in the right direction for our particular situation.

Ultimately, leadership in Christian organizations is about getting a group of people to discern a God-given direction and commit their lives to accomplish this purpose. Whether that purpose is building a temple, opposing unjust and unbiblical laws, or organizing and discipling a growing body of new believers, leadership stories flow throughout the pages of Scripture. What are the core principles of biblical leadership? For me, there are a handful that transcend individual stories and that are relevant for every Christian leader.

God's purpose is unchanging and nonnegotiable. The metanarrative of the Bible is God's love for humanity and the story of redemption. Christian organizations must align their priorities around the gospel. Leaders may emphasize certain aspects of this purpose in their organization's mission, but they must not create a vision that is disconnected from God's plan.

God chooses to work through human leaders. As flawed and imperfect as we are, God consistently chooses to use men and women with the gift of leadership to organize and mobilize large groups to accomplish His purposes. When we see leaders fail, we may wonder if there is some other way, but this is the way that God has chosen. Until Christ returns, the church will continue to be God's instrument for carrying out the Great Commission, and human beings will be called on to provide the leadership.

Biblical leadership cannot be boiled down to a single model. Whenever someone offers a definitive model of biblical leadership, I quickly dismiss it. Is biblical leadership top-down or collaborative? It can be either—look at Moses leading the people out of Egypt compared to James in the council of Jerusalem. Are godly leaders intuitive and impulsive, or are they deliberate and thoughtful? Again, the answer is either—just compare Peter to Paul. Leaders in Scripture fit a wide variety of profiles that reflect their specific contexts and their unique personalities. The only absolute is that biblical leadership is obedient to God and brings glory to Him. This means that we should be cautious before pronouncing any model or style of leadership as *the* biblical model.

Effective leadership is grounded in healthy relationships. Relationships are the currency of leadership, especially in the church, and the Bible has plenty of instruction on relationships that every leader should heed. Not every biblical leader is a model of relational health, but we see plenty of examples (Joseph forgiving his brothers, David caring for his men while on the run, Paul mentoring Timothy). More than that, the New Testament is full of guidance on how people should relate: do unto others, in humility consider others better than yourself, speak the truth in love. When the relationship between leader and followers is based on trust and integrity and placing God first, great things can happen.

God-honoring leadership is often a hard, lonely journey. In our society, leadership is glamorized. The top business and political leaders are the ones on the covers of magazines. Leaders in Scripture may seem larger than life at times, but they are also burdened, alone, and rejected in many cases. Look at the pain David expresses in some of the Psalms, Paul's anguish for the people in the churches he planted, or the rejection Moses experienced. No one should begin the journey of Christian leadership expecting it to be a bed of roses.

A leader's character and spiritual health are of utmost importance to God. Which do you think matters most to God, the growth in your church's average worship attendance this year or the growth of your soul? The kingdom of Israel was bigger and more prosperous under Solomon, but David was Israel's greatest and most revered king because of his heart for God. That is God's desire for each of us—that we are increasingly shaped into His image. When that happens, our leadership will flow out of lives that are surrendered to Him, and the organizational results will follow in God's time.

This list of principles is not exhaustive. Perhaps you have thought of others to add to your list of key leadership principles in Scripture. Regardless of what you end up with, we should be able to agree on two things: the Bible lays the foundation for leadership, but it is not a comprehensive guide for every leadership need. It is this second truth that leads us to the arena of business leadership practices.

BUSINESS THINKING IS NOT THE ENEMY

When we refer to "business thinking" or "corporate practices," what do we mean? More important, what mental images are stirred up by this terminology? Many people—church leaders and average citizens—have a decidedly negative image of "corporate America." They think of unbridled greed and oversized executive egos. They are aware of the huge disparity between the compensation of top executives and workers on the bottom rungs of the ladder. They know of cases where companies have bent the rules as far as possible to make a little more profit. This thinking is not unjustified—over the past two decades, we have seen a steady stream of headlines that paint this picture of "business."

Does that mean that all businesses are bad? Are corporations and any leadership ideas that emerge from them inherently evil? Before you answer, consider that over those same twenty years, we have also seen a steady stream of unflattering headlines about churches and church leaders. Churches have split in acrimonious debates, funds have been used to build earthly kingdoms and line the pockets of leaders, and prominent pastors have left the ministry after dramatic moral failures. These stories have caused some in the unchurched world to see Christianity as a sham. Do these failures mean that everything done by the church in America is fundamentally bad?

As Christians, our response is a resounding no and a vigorous defense of the church. You might say, "These are just a handful of the many congregations in the country, and they're giving a bad name to all the good, godly work being done in the name of Christ." And you would be exactly right. Perhaps we should think of business the same way: there are some bad apples, but we shouldn't conclude that business thinking is the antithesis of Christian leadership. Instead, we should examine more closely what business might offer to our churches.

NOT ALL BUSINESS PRINCIPLES ARE APPLICABLE

An easy starting point is to acknowledge that some business principles are not applicable for leadership in the church. Some of the methodologies that spur corporate success are either contrary to the teachings of Scripture or simply don't fit with an orthodox understanding of the purpose of the church. For example, some business practices are based on manipulation—convincing potential customers to buy a product that they don't really need or coercing employees to do something that they don't want to do. Manipulating people is clearly not appropriate conduct for Christian leaders. Another widely accepted business mantra is "the customer is always right." While it is important to know and listen to our members and potential members, the church is not a consumer goods company whose goal is to develop products to please its "customers."

Scott Cormode of Fuller Theological Seminary uses a variety of secular resources in his leadership classes. In evaluating whether material is appropriate, he looks at the underlying motive that is espoused. If the author's end goal is profit or personal advancement for the reader, Cormode steers away from it. Such resources may have great nuggets of leadership wisdom to offer, but their basis may be out of line with our purposes in Christian organizations. When in doubt, biblical principles should trump "best practices."

SCRIPTURE IS FULL OF "BUSINESS PRINCIPLES"

I would never suggest that the Bible is a business book. The purpose of Scripture is to teach people about God and point them toward God. It is to communicate God's love for humanity and to offer God's grace to all who will receive it. It is to tell the story of God working in history to redeem His creation.

Within that story, however, we see a surprising number of principles that are applicable for leading any kind of enterprise, whether a corporation, a church, a university, or a governmental agency. A handful of these biblical leadership precepts illustrate the point:

- In Exodus 18, Moses is visited by his father-in-law, Jethro, who recognizes that Moses' "span of command" has gotten too large and is unsustainable. He wisely advises Moses to reorganize the people by appointing second-tier leaders to handle the minor issues so that only the major ones are brought to Moses' attention. It is a classic principle for organizing any growing enterprise.
- The book of Nehemiah is a great picture of a leader who is gripped with a compelling vision, communicates it to the people, and then implements a specific plan to see the vision realized.
- In Acts 6, the early church appoints seven men to oversee the distribution of food so that the apostles can focus on "prayer and the ministry of the word" (Acts 6:4). This passage shows the importance of selecting the right people (making good hiring decisions), putting people into roles that fit their strengths, and organizing a group to accomplish a desired goal.

Of course, plenty of biblical examples are completely contrary to any kind of business logic. Think of Gideon dismissing almost all of his army before going into battle, Joshua marching around Jericho, or Jesus' hard teaching that caused many to turn away. I don't expect corporate executives to throw out all their business books and rely exclusively on the Bible for guiding their companies, but I am not surprised when they find practical wisdom in Scripture.

BUSINESS IS FULL OF SCRIPTURAL PRINCIPLES

If a new concept for leadership emerges in a business leadership book, does that mean that the author is the discoverer? Or is it possible that the core of the concept has much older, deeper roots? In the scientific realm, the breakthrough that wins a Nobel Prize for one person is almost always built on the work of others. The same can be said for some of the well-known leadership concepts from the business world. They are built on or have grown out of biblical origins.

Consider one of the significant findings in Collins's research for *Good to Great*: the Level 5 leader. Collins and his team discovered that the "good to great" companies were not led by larger-than-life, ego-driven CEOs. While this may be the exact image that comes to mind when you think of successful corporate executives, Collins describes this model as a "Level 4" leader. The great companies had Level 5 leaders at the helm. According to Collins, a Level 5 leader is "an individual who blends extreme personal humility with intense professional will."[6] Is this a new insight from the world of business? The "Level 5" terminology is new, but the description fits the best leaders in Scripture. It is what we see in Christ modeling servant leadership but never losing sight of his mission. It is Paul's missionary zeal while at the same time confessing that he is the worst of sinners, unworthy of God's mercy (1 Timothy 1:13–14).

Or consider this finding from *The Leadership Challenge* by Jim Kouzes and Barry Posner: "Exemplary leaders have a passion for something other than their own fame and fortune. They care about making a difference in the world."[7] Isn't this exactly what has always been modeled by great Christian leaders whose passion is not self-directed but is focused on glorifying God and advancing His Kingdom?

The point is that we must not discard a leadership concept just because it is presented as having a secular source. An article in *Forbes*, a flagship magazine in the business community, states, "Many CEOs try to improve their leadership through precepts that ultimately have a biblical bias."[8] Or to quote King Solomon: "There is nothing new under the sun. Is there anything of which one can say, 'Look! This is something new'? It was here already, long ago; it was here before our time" (Ecclesiastes 1:9–10). Many of the leadership debates and solutions that we think are unique to our generation are far older than we ever imagined.

An Organism *and* an Organization

One of the long-running debates is whether the church is an organism or an organization. In recent years, the rise of house churches, organic churches, and cell groups has heightened the issue. Those who say it's an organism focus on the spontaneous, unpredictable movement of God. They argue against planning, against reliance on human techniques and tools, and against being too structured. Advocates for organization focus on the wasted energy and resources that occur when plans are lacking. They believe that any church larger than a cell needs to have order and structure. Rather than taking sides, the better question is whether a church can be both.

Chris Hodges, senior pastor of Church of the Highlands in Birmingham, Alabama, says, "The church is an organism, not an organization. It's the living, breathing body of Christ." But Hodges knows the need to lead with both in mind. He continues, "There is a corporate side to it [the church]. If you turn it into a business, that turns people away; but if it's not run well, like a business, that turns people away as much." Hodges is right. If we squeeze the Spirit of God out of a congregation by becoming overly structured, it's no longer a church.

Every effective leader must balance between the crippling chaos of too little organization and the stifling rigidity of too much. Dan Reiland, executive pastor of 12Stone Church in Lawrenceville, Georgia, addressed this subject in a leadership lesson that he titled "How Do You Lead with Your Heart on Fire When It Feels like Your Hair Is on Fire?" We all want leaders who are passionate, whose hearts are on fire, and who encourage that passion in others. What keeps them from being able to do that? Any number of factors can squelch that passion, but one of the most frequent is the continual firefighting that comes from lack of structure. Paul instructed the church in Corinth to be orderly in worship, so isn't it reasonable that God wants everything in our churches to "be done in a fitting and orderly way" (1 Corinthians 14:40)?

For people to get connected, be discipled, and plug into areas that use their gifts and passions, a certain level of infrastructure and process—in other words, organization—is necessary. Perhaps the problem is that the word *organization* has negative connotations. If organization means "rigid" and "rule-oriented" and "resistant to change," we should run from any hint of it. These are actually characteristics of a bureaucracy, not a thriving entity. In truth, the best companies do not function like this. Collins and Porras found that visionary companies have a "drive for progress" that "is never satisfied with the status quo, *even when the status quo is working well.*"[9] When policies trump purpose, as happens far too often in churches, the result is self-preserving institutionalism, not organization.

If an organization is not a spiritless, inflexible bureaucracy, what is it? What benefits come from being an organization? It is the power of bringing large numbers of people together to work for a greater purpose. God used Healing Place Church in Baton Rouge in incredible ways after Hurricane Katrina. The church, a major hub in a local network called the Pastors Resource Council, served more than one hundred thousand meals, offered temporary lodging to three hundred people for a month, housed a full-service medical clinic, and distributed literally tons of clothing and other necessities to those whose lives were devastated by the storm.[10] Mobilizing thousands of volunteers to do this would not have been possible had the church not functioned as an organization. Its extravagant response would not have been possible had the church not been operating as an organic body led by the Spirit. Organism and organization can work together.

A FALSE DICHOTOMY

In my interviews with Christian leaders, I asked how they reconciled the use of corporate principles in their settings. By far the most frequent answer I heard was "All truth is God's truth." In other words, if a leadership principle is valid and true, it doesn't matter who made the statement because God is the ultimate source of all truth and wisdom.

But what does this mean? Greg Holder, lead pastor of The Crossing in the Saint Louis area, says, "We're not afraid of truth because we know who stands behind all truth. The sacred-secular line, which in some ways goes back to the Middle Ages, is not something we operate under." Holder makes it clear that he and his colleagues don't just "cut and paste" anyone's practices—from business or other churches—into their church, but they're not afraid to adapt any "truth" that they uncover. Judy West, who serves alongside Holder at The Crossing, notes that the staff read Kirk Kazanjian's *Exceeding Customer Expectations* to learn more about hospitality. This book about the history of Enterprise Rent-A-Car provides some powerful lessons about care of the customer. But West is quick to add that The Crossing's interpretation of "care" does not mean "the customer is always right." She points out that a business might tolerate an angry customer who is mouthing off, but the church has an obligation to correct inappropriate behavior.

Rodney Cooper of Gordon-Conwell Theological Seminary proposes that the use of secular leadership concepts is a form of "spoiling the Egyptians."[11] The Hebrew people were instructed to "spoil the Egyptians"—take their gold and jewelry—as they began their exodus. God allowed them to take something of value from ungodly people, and He ultimately used it for a sacred purpose—building the tabernacle. In the same way, Cooper says we should take the best of business and apply it to benefit our churches and glorify God.

Jim Leggett of Grace Fellowship United Methodist Church in Katy, Texas, expands on this by saying, "All truth is God's truth, but the best business practices will only produce 'human temple' results without dependence on God's Spirit. Eternal fruit is not going to happen apart from God's Spirit, even if we're using best business practices." Leggett alludes to the biblical teaching that it is vain to build anything apart from God (Psalm 127:1), yet that is exactly what can happen when leadership principles are adopted without a spiritual context. Christian leaders must guard against using secular leadership resources to make a "golden calf" rather than a God-honoring temple.

Even though Jim Collins is identified as a business expert, he believes that great leadership principles transcend the corporate arena. After the runaway success of *Good to Great*, Collins received many requests to address the "social sectors" (governmental entities, schools, nonprofit organizations, churches, and the like), organizations that do not have profit as their bottom-line motivation. In *Good to Great and the Social Sectors*, he states, "We must reject the idea—well-intentioned, but dead wrong—that the primary path to greatness in the social sectors is to become 'more like a business.' ... We need to reject the naïve imposition of the 'language of business' on the social sectors, and instead jointly embrace a *language of greatness*."[12] So how can we embrace a "language of greatness" in the church in a God-honoring way?

Jim Mellado, president of the Willow Creek Association, simply says, "We don't dichotomize business practices versus spiritual practices." He describes the first time that a case study on Willow Creek Community Church was taught at Harvard Business School, a story that is also told in Bill Hybels's book *Courageous Leadership*. Mellado and Hybels were both in the class that day, and as Hybels notes, "One of the students raised his hand and challenged me. 'Bill, I just don't think you should mix best management practices with spiritual stuff. I'm really uneasy with all this leadership training, leadership development, and managing for results that I see at Willow.'" Hybels, who grew up around his father's business and has always been a student of leadership best practices, responded:

> What you have to understand is that some of us church leaders believe to the core of our beings that the local church is the hope of the world. ... That's why we are so determined to get our visions right and live out our values and come up with effective strategies. We truly believe that it matters that we attain our goals. It matters that we align our staffs and leverage our resources. We believe that the success or failure of our churches directly affects people's lives here today and for eternity. ... That's why we make no apology for learning and applying best practice principles as God leads us in our churches.[13]

ADAPT, NOT ADOPT

As we consider the practices of greatness that we find in business, a simple rule of thumb is to *adapt*, not adopt. We should not adopt these practices wholesale, as they are applied in the corporate world, but instead should adapt them, based on our understanding of Scripture and the unique contexts of our Christian organizations. Of course, this guidance is true for great ideas that we find even in other Christian organizations. A novel ministry may have been very effective in one church, but that doesn't mean it is right for yours. Many churches endure the "program of the month" drill when their pastors bring back the latest new idea from a conference. Dino Rizzo, senior pastor of Healing Place Church, likes to say, "One person's plan is another person's poison."

Adapting rather than adopting is easier said than done. Bishop Andy Doyle of the Diocese of Texas (Episcopal) believes that too many churches "look for the silver bullet" in business tools without understanding how to apply them effectively. Many pastors and Christian ministry leaders have little, if any, training or experience in business or organizational leadership. As a result, they struggle with knowing which business concepts to use and how to put them into practice. The corporate leaders in these same ministries understand the business use of the tool but lack an appreciation for the nuances of church life. If these two groups are unable to work together, they miss the opportunity to strengthen the congregation.

One pastor invited a retired corporate CEO to help rethink the church's staff development systems. The pastor was concerned that the best-performing staff members were not being adequately recognized, so the CEO developed a corporate-style bonus plan. Once the pastor saw the plan, he realized that a system based on financial rewards would not work in the environment of his church, so he abandoned it. He decided that receiving affirmation and playing an important role in a thriving church were the best ways to motivate the staff.

Leading Upside Down

The key to adapting rather than adopting is to run secular leadership concepts through a biblical filter. I rise early in the mornings and make the first pot of coffee in our house. The filter is an essential part of the process. When I put it in the basket correctly, I get a nice cup of coffee. Every once in a while, the filter gets folded over and I get a pot full of grounds. In either instance, the pot looks and smells the same from a distance; but in the latter case, if I actually take a sip, it's gross!

Any leadership or organizational concept that we consider bringing into our churches and Christian entities should be filtered through Scripture. Some ideas may be contrary to our interpretation of God's Word, in which case we should throw them out, no matter how well they work elsewhere. Some, as described earlier, may actually have a basis in Scripture, in which case we have a good starting point for adapting and applying them. And many will fall somewhere in between.

For those in-between cases, it is important to remember that the way we see the world and the things that drive us should be fundamentally different than in business. In *The Divine Conspiracy*, Dallas Willard tells the story of a fighter jet pilot who "turned the controls for what she thought was a steep ascent—and flew straight into the ground. She was unaware that she had been flying upside down."[14] Willard returns to this image later when he reminds us of a core truth of Christianity: "What is truly profound is thought to be stupid or trivial, or worse, boring, while what is actually stupid and trivial is thought to be profound. That is what it means to fly upside down."[15] Greg Surratt, senior pastor of Seacoast Church in Mount Pleasant, South Carolina, echoes this theme when he says, "There is obviously a fundamental difference in the prevailing philosophy of the world than there is in the church." Surratt notes that Jesus' teaching on leadership and servanthood—"whoever wants to become great among you must be your servant" (Matthew 20:26)—is "upside down from the world."

This is just one area where the underlying mind-set of business is upside down from Scripture. Business thinking is dominated by the profit motive, the drive to make more money and earn a larger return for shareholders. Business thinking assumes that people are self-serving, and it works from a self-deterministic belief that individuals must seize the initiative for their career success. This thinking ignores the possibility that God might be at work or that we should seek His will for our lives.

Some secular leadership resources, while very helpful at one level, run counter to a Christian worldview in subtle but significant ways. *The Leadership Challenge* is a great book, full of solid concepts for any leader. In describing the first of five practices for exemplary leaders, Kouzes and Posner emphasize the importance of knowing your own values: "You must know what you care about.... If you don't burn with desire to be true to something you hold passionately, how can you expect commitment from others? And until you get close enough to the flame to feel the heat, how can you know the source?"[16]

From a Christian perspective, that sounds like solid leadership advice. We would identify the source of the heat as God, something that Kouzes and Posner don't acknowledge. They don't prescribe what we should care about, whereas a Christian would say that Scripture gives clear direction on this. Still, it sounds like good advice.

In the same section, however, the authors conclude, "We are much more in control of our own lives ... when we're clear about our personal values."[17] That is where I take exception. I don't think I am in control of my life, and I don't think the Bible says that I should be. If my purpose in clarifying my values is to have better control of my life, I am working against God, who calls me to fully surrender to Him.

This simple example illustrates the subtle challenge in adapting secular leadership principles. These principles, to some degree, turn leaders toward a way of life that is upside down from God's ways. Even if you personally have a solid foundation, there are plenty of other leaders on your board, in key volunteer roles, or serving alongside you who spend (or have spent) much of their lives in the corporate arena. They soak up these great (and sometimes ungodly) ideas every day and then bring them into the church. Their intentions are good, and they genuinely want the church to succeed, but they fail to see the pitfalls of their recommendations. Discovering a common leadership language and approach for Christian organizations is a theme that runs throughout this book and is addressed explicitly in Chapter Nine.

That brings us to one last upside-down mind-set that can undermine Christian leaders: the drive for success. Our society is consumed with success. It is what makes athletes take performance-enhancing drugs to gain an edge. It is what leads "nice" businesspeople to cut ethical corners to beat a competitor. It is what causes some pastors to ignore their families and lose sight of God "for the sake of the church." God wants and deserves our very best. He wants our churches to be "successful," but there is a point at which our pursuit of success is not a pursuit of God. In fact, the drive for ministry success can ultimately run counter to God's desires. Jim Mellado observes that many ministry leaders focus on skill development more than character development. As their leadership skills improve and their ministries grow, the spiritual dimension—becoming more like Christ—fails to keep pace. Mellado concludes, "Great skills [and] more ministry, but flawed character, leads to a crash."[18]

Our congregations need excellent leadership, but every Christian leader should wrestle with what it means to be "excellent." Greg Matte, senior pastor of Houston's First Baptist Church, believes that many of his peers may have "gone too far with [the use of business tools]. They'd rather be seen as great leaders than great theologians." Matte was a business major in college and is an avid student of secular leadership material, but he explains that he sees a theologian as someone who is "learning and leading from a place of spiritual depth. Leadership is by all means important, but at the end of the day, God didn't call me to be a 'C.E.O. for G.O.D.' but to minister to people through leading and loving. Good old Psalm 78:72 ['And David shepherded them with integrity of heart; with skillful hands he led them']."

Therein lies the dilemma for any leader in a Christian organization, whether it is big or small, new or well established, church or parachurch. We are to lead with integrity of heart and with skillful hands. We are to lead from a place of spiritual depth and to lead with all diligence for the glory of God. We are to lead toward greatness *and* godliness.

WHAT ARE YOU PURSUING?

* Describe your philosophy for using secular leadership principles in Christian organizations. What is the basis for your philosophy? Who or what (people, models, reading) have influenced you most in this regard?
* Sit down with someone who has a different background or philosophy from yours. Discuss your differing perspectives. Discuss specific leadership situations and how each of you would handle them.
* What would you add or change in the list of core principles of biblical leadership in "A Biblical Foundation" in Chapter One?
* Over the next week, listen for a secular leadership concept, and consider whether you agree with it. Do you or don't you? Can you explain why? How might it be adapted to fit your organization?
* If Christian leadership should be upside down from secular leadership, which way are you pointed? Head up? Head down? Somewhere in between?

CHAPTER TWO

WHERE SHOULD YOU BEGIN?

If you have read this far, you must be ready to improve your leadership by exploring the best practices that are found outside the Christian arena. But *leadership* is a very broad term, so the next question on your mind may be "Where should I begin?" The answer may surprise you: you should begin by looking in the mirror. You don't need to choose a particular dimension of leadership, such as planning or finance. These are important and will be covered in later chapters, but the specifics are not nearly as important as the core of who you are.

Jim Kouzes and Barry Posner state this clearly in *The Leadership Challenge*: "The instrument of leadership is the self, and mastery of the art of leadership comes from mastery of the self. Self-development is not about stuffing in a whole bunch of new information or trying out the latest technique. It's about leading out of what is already in your soul."[1] When leaders don't truly understand what is in their souls, their leadership is inauthentic and is inappropriately influenced by all sorts of external forces. That is why Reggie McNeal says that self-understanding is the "most important information you will need as a leader"—and then he adds an important qualifier: that "self-understanding begins and ends with God."[2]

If you want to develop into the leader God wants you to be and your ministry needs you to be, you must be honest with yourself. Self-understanding means being confident in the aspects of leadership where you soar and acknowledging the places where you struggle. But self-understanding is more than a skill inventory; it also means recognizing the things in your personality and past that could keep you from becoming an effective leader. It means being willing to say, "I may be part of the problem. I may need to change." You don't have to change who you are or who God made you to be, but you may need to change the way you see yourself and exercise your leadership gifts.

One thought-provoking resource that can help in this discovery process is Robert Quinn's *Deep Change*. In his research, Quinn found that people tend to externalize blame, pointing to factors outside themselves to explain organizational problems. They may blame a culture of mediocrity or a lack of vision for the company's woes. Quinn's thesis is that "organizational change always begins with personal change."[3] The blame game will never lead to great and godly results.

Early in my business career, I had the opportunity to work for a CEO who did not play the blame game. When the company had recurring performance problems among the employees several levels down in the organization, this CEO took responsibility. He essentially said, "We're the leaders, and we've created the systems for training and motivating employees." Taking a page from Quinn, he was saying, "Change begins with me." You may be in a first chair role—as pastor of a church or executive director of a ministry—or a second chair staff position, or you may serve on a board or as an adviser. It doesn't matter what job you are in. Your ministry colleagues may have shortcomings, but the most important issue is your own willingness to grow as a leader. We all need to heed Quinn's advice: "The paradoxical lesson [is] that we can change the world only by changing ourselves."[4]

TWO BARRIERS TO LEADERSHIP EXCELLENCE

Robert Quinn says to would-be leaders, "The land of excellence is safely guarded from unworthy intruders. At the gates stand two fearsome sentries—risk and learning."[5] Far too often, leaders are stopped by one of these sentries. Some are unwilling to admit there is a gap between what the organization needs in its leader and their own abilities and knowledge. In doing so, they stifle the possibility of learning. Others know the gap exists, but it is daunting to step into it, so they linger in the safe harbor of "acceptable" performance rather than taking the risk that could lead to excellence.

Dino Rizzo of Healing Place Church had a severe stuttering problem as a child. As a result, he was embarrassed to ask questions, and he fell behind in school. After Rizzo worked several years to overcome his stuttering and his academic deficit, his dad told him, "You've got a lot of questions to catch up on. Get out there and ask them." This advice has shaped Rizzo's approach to leadership. He knows that he doesn't need to have the answers to every question or the ability to solve every problem on his own. He just needs to ask the right questions and to surround himself with talented people who love God and who have gifts and knowledge different from his own. Rizzo's hunger to learn and collaborative leadership approach have enabled Healing Place to have a powerful ministry presence in Baton Rouge from its inception.

Unfortunately, many ministry leaders have learned a very different style of leadership, either through training or through modeling by others. It is the style in which the first chair leader is "large and in charge," follows the adage to "never let them see you sweat," and always has the answer. It is the image often portrayed in Hollywood and the model adopted by many pastors. There is only one problem: it rarely works. Christian and secular leadership literature describes today's fast-changing environment and unanimously concludes that the solo superstar leadership model may have worked in an earlier era but is doomed to failure today. Leaders who are isolated are unable to see where they need to grow or go, are unlikely to engage in meaningful personal development, and are cut off from the valuable expertise that others offer.

In contrast, a willingness to learn from and lean on others was a recurring theme in my interviews. Judy West of The Crossing says, "We are passionate, thirsty students who are constantly learning from anything we can get our hands on. We are constant learners, but we always stop, pray, seek the Holy Spirit, and then take the parts that fit in our culture."

The leaders I spoke with have a clear understanding of their areas of weakness and are not afraid to admit this. This honest admission guides their personal development, and it also frees them to seek help from others. They do not believe in a "lone ranger" model of leadership but instead recognize the value of having many wise counselors. They are constantly learning from the outside as well. They read extensively and from a wide range of resources. They are in peer networks with others who will challenge and sharpen them. They use coaches to shore up areas of weakness. If you are not on a journey of self-understanding and personal development, the rest of this book will be of little value to you.

The willingness to take risks is an even more daunting sentry than learning. Whether you are in a secular or a spiritual organization, leadership is difficult. Success is never guaranteed, and the bigger the risk, the greater the possibility of disappointment, pain, and failure. Ronald Heifitz, author of *Leadership Without Easy Answers*, says, "People who lead frequently bear scars from their efforts to bring about adaptive change."[6] High-profile leaders are often glamorized by the media, but these portrayals rarely convey the price they pay, not to mention the many other unknown leaders who have paid an even higher price without achieving the same measure of success.

Spiritual leaders often begin their careers with an idealistic notion of what lies ahead. They are drawn to the opportunity to help people and make a difference in the world. They believe that Christian organizations should always be characterized by harmony and kindness. They forget that these organizations are made up of sinful human beings, people who are being shaped into the image of Christ but who are not yet there. As a result, they don't think that leading a spiritual enterprise should involve risk or pain. Of course, they are mistaken, and when challenges arise, these leaders are often paralyzed by uncertainty and fear.

Reggie McNeal says, "Many spiritual leaders do not lead from courage. They lead from fear. Fear drives many ministries. Fear of being disliked, fear of losing income, fear of failure, fear of conflict."[7] Scripture is clear on this point—the leaders that God uses are required to step out in courage, despite enormous uncertainty and risk. Think of Abraham, Moses, Nehemiah, Esther, Paul, and many others. Not only did these leaders take huge, Spirit-led risks, but they also walked away from comfortable lives to do so. This does not mean that risk-taking leaders are fearless. Abraham wouldn't admit that Sarah was his wife when his life was on the line, and Moses hesitated when Pharaoh balked at his demand to release the Hebrew people. Joshua needed God's frequent urging to be "strong and courageous." Some level of anxiety is natural for any risk-taking leader, but there is a huge difference between feeling fear and leading from fear.

Tim Lundy, former directional leader of Fellowship Bible Church in Little Rock, Arkansas, knows that taking risks is an essential part of spiritual leadership. One question that drives Lundy is "Are we risking enough for the Kingdom?" He explains, "The danger for any of us, when our church hits a certain size or level of success, is to stop risking because we don't have to." While at Fellowship, Lundy could have played it safe and the world would still have seen Fellowship as successful. But Lundy knew that the world was not his judge: "I'm going to stand in front of Jesus and he's going to ask me, 'What did you do with what I gave you?'" So Fellowship aggressively pursued a strategy to transform the city of Little Rock by launching more and more outward-facing ministries. The clarity of Christ's standard demands nothing less.

As you will see in later chapters, effective leaders don't take inappropriate risks. Their decisions are clearly led by God and are shaped by the counsel of godly advisers. But when the Spirit moves, they are willing to step out in faith.

Overcoming a Bigger Barrier

Risk and learning are fearsome sentries that every aspiring leader will encounter. An even bigger obstacle, however, is the leader's ego. Leaders with inflated views of themselves are less willing to admit to deficiencies and a need for learning. They may take inappropriate risks because they think that they are invincible or because they want to be seen as doing something bold and impressive. By contrast, leaders with deflated egos are swayed by the crowd. They lack confidence in their decisions and avoid risk. No one finds the right balance all the time. To offset the tendency to tilt in one direction or the other, leaders must learn to hold up the mirror of self-examination.

In Chapter One, I touched on Jim Collins's finding that "Level 5" leaders are a vital element in good-to-great corporate transitions. This discovery is remarkable given the common perception that being ego-driven is acceptable and even necessary for business success. Collins reports that his research team was "struck by how the good-to-great leaders *didn't* talk about themselves. ... They'd talk about the company and the contributions of other executives as long as we'd like but they would deflect discussions about their own contributions."[8] Collins refers to this as "the window and the mirror" and explains, "Level 5 leaders look out the window to apportion credit to factors outside themselves when things go well (and if they cannot find a specific person or event to give credit to, they credit good luck). At the same time, they look in the mirror to apportion responsibility, never blaming bad luck when things go poorly."[9] In other words, Level 5 leaders accept blame but deflect credit. They are not trying to feed their egos.

Collins created the "Level 5" terminology, but he is not the only business expert to emphasize the importance of humility. Kouzes and Posner note, "It's fun to be a leader, gratifying to have influence, and exhilarating to have scores of people cheering your every word. In many all-too-subtle ways, it's easy to be seduced by power and importance. All evil leaders have been infected with the disease of hubris."[10] So what do Kouzes and Posner recommend? Their solution sounds very Christ-like: "Perhaps the very best advice we can give all aspiring leaders is to remain humble and unassuming—to always remain open and full of wonder."[11]

The importance of humility and putting others first is a recurring biblical theme. Paul teaches "in humility consider others better than yourselves" and "look not only to your own interests but also to the interests of others." In the same passage, he instructs that our "attitude should be the same as that of Christ Jesus" who "humbled himself and became obedient to death" (Philippians 2:3–8). In the famous discourse where the disciples argue about who is the greatest, Jesus responds, "Anyone who wants to be first must be the very last, and the servant of all" (Mark 9:35).

Don't mistake humility for a lack of ambition. According to Collins, the best (Level 5) leaders "are incredibly ambitious—but *their ambition is first and foremost for the institution, not themselves.*"[12] This ambition is an important component in the success of their companies. Is the need for ambition just the way of business? In an article titled "Ambitious Like Jesus," William Willimon writes, "It's hard to imagine anybody who accomplished anything in life or in ministry without a helpful nudge from ambition."[13] When we think of great Christian leaders, it is impossible to overlook the drive—the ambition—that is central in their stories.

Willimon's title may make some Christians uncomfortable, but it raises a valid question: What should Christian ambition look like? His answer is "not to forswear all ambition but rather to pray for the grace constantly to align our ambitions with his [Christ's]." Another provocative title from a Christian leader is *Practicing Greatness* by Reggie McNeal As followers of Christ, is it acceptable to pursue and "practice greatness"? In the introductory chapter, McNeal considers the two incidents in Mark 9 and 10 when Jesus reframes the disciples' understanding of greatness:

> In neither discussion does Jesus disparage the ambition to be great. ... Rather, he takes it for granted that their motivations would push them toward achieving greatness. He just wants to point them in the right direction. He seizes the moment to contrast the prevailing notions of greatness with the genuine article and to challenge them to see greatness in spiritual terms. Jesus' idea of greatness revolves around humility and service—a far cry from our typical associations with this concept.[14]

This is the point at which we need to take our cues from Scripture and not from the secular world. In business, leaders may choose humility as a better way to get results, but when they choose the opposite, no one is surprised. The amount (or lack) of humility that a secular leader demonstrates is regarded as a personal choice or perhaps a function of personality or upbringing. As Christian leaders, humility is not optional. We may struggle with ego, but we know that we're called to be humble. We also believe in the power of God to transform the most egocentric leader into a humble servant. As McNeal says, "If the leader's heart remains in communion with God, then humility graces the leader's life. The leader maintains an absolute awareness of owing the leadership role to God."[15]

THE OVERSIZED EGO

Why is it so important for spiritual leaders to wrestle with ego? An oversized ego is unattractive to followers and prevents the leader from receiving needed advice. It can cause leaders to think they are untouchable. But the most frightening thing about ego-driven, self-reliant spiritual leaders is their lack of a deep relationship with God and the resulting ways in which their organizations may turn away from the Lord. When God is not truly first in a spiritual leader's life, the ministry turns into a tool for personal advancement or becomes limited by the leader's human vision and frailties.

This is essential for every leader to understand. There will always be a temptation to seize the reins rather than trusting and waiting on God. There will always be a temptation to create a vision or lead in a direction that stokes the fire of a leader's ego. With each step taken in this direction, leaders become more distant from God and His call on their lives. In contrast, McNeal says, "Leaders who are gripped by a call from God do well to remember that they serve the call. The call is not given to serve them. The initiative and substance of the call belong to God."[16]

In the chapters that follow, we will examine a number of practices that can improve a leader's effectiveness. But if improved effectiveness causes a leader to become more self-reliant and less dependent on God, it is all for naught. The more a leader experiences success, the more he or she must guard against this danger.

Dan Reiland is a spiritual leader who has experienced tremendous success in his career. For a number of years, he was John Maxwell's right-hand person, and he still writes a bimonthly newsletter, *The Pastor's Coach*, for Maxwell's INJOY ministry. Reiland now serves as the executive pastor of 12Stone Church, a multisite congregation that has grown explosively. When asked what keeps his ego in check, Reiland points to the "healthy accountability" among the team of senior leaders at 12Stone. He explains that in their culture, he is "willing to be checked"—challenged or corrected—by his ministry peers. If someone gets defensive or fights back when this happens, it may be a sign of an ego that is getting too big. Reiland also says, "We have phrases we use—like 'We don't *have* to, we *get* to' and 'This doesn't belong to us.'" Simple observations like these can be a powerful way to keep leaders focused on God.

The right attitude and some form of accountability are essential counterbalances to oversized egos. Greg Wallace, pastor of Woodridge Baptist in Houston, admits a strong drive to succeed, but he also remembers the words from a plaque that was on President Ronald Reagan's desk: "There is no limit to how far a man can go and what he can succeed at as long as he doesn't care who gets the credit." Other leaders reflect on dark times in ministry that give them a healthy perspective on seasons of success. And then there is Dave Ferguson, whose brother, Jon, has been with him at Chicago's Community Christian Church since they founded it together two decades ago. He laughs as he says, "It's hard to assume [that success] is due to me when my brother has been there all along. A lot of people leading large churches may not have somebody they shared a trundle bed with!" Ferguson is right. Most of us don't have a sibling by our side to keep our egos in check, but we can acknowledge the dangers of ego and put safeguards in place. No spiritual leader is immune to the pitfalls of an untended ego.

The Undersized Ego

The dangers of too much ego are obvious, but is it possible for a Christian leader to have too little ego? Perhaps *ego* is not the right word, as it has the connotation of self-reliance and self-preservation rather than dependence on God. But it is possible for a spiritual leader to lack confidence and conviction and become lost in a swirl of surrounding opinions. When this happens, the cost to the leader and the organization can be just as high as it is when a leader is ego-driven.

One of the most notable places where lack of ego becomes apparent is in the relationship between leaders and followers. You've heard that you're not a leader if no one is following you, and yet it is the followers that often make it difficult to lead. Leaders who are attempting to take bold steps will not always please their constituents. This theme runs through the Bible, through history, and through the business literature on leadership. When leaders are unsure of themselves, the dissatisfaction of the people will cause them to shrink back and avoid risk. How often do you hear of a church that wants its next pastor to be "a strong leader," but when the pastor tries to lead, the congregation is hesitant to follow? In many such cases, the frustrated pastor caves in to the pressure to not rock the boat too much. Robert Sloan, president of Houston Baptist University, finds that most Christian leaders don't like conflict. He says, "We all want to be loved. But if your greatest psychological need is to be loved and accepted, you probably can't be a great leader."

Resistance is inevitable when trying to move an organization in a new, Spirit-inspired direction, but there is an important counterbalance. Sloan completes his thought: "You have to have a sense of what God has called you to do." It is that sense of calling that drives successful spiritual leaders, even when they face opposition. Quinn calls for internally driven leadership in which "the leader and the vision are so integrated that if the vision lives, it matters not if the visionary should die, or in this case, be fired. Sacrifice of self for the good of the organization is an acceptable alternative."[17] Far too often, spiritual leaders choose to sacrifice their vision in order to avoid conflict and keep everyone happy. We will return to the challenges of organizational change in Chapter Eleven, but suffice it to say that an uncertain, insecure leader will always fall short of Quinn's standard.

Of course, staying true to a vision requires being clear about what you believe and where God is leading. I am not talking about theological convictions but rather about the ministry's direction and the means to get there. Followers are not looking for an autocrat, but they are looking for a leader with passion and vision who has the integrity to say that some things are not subject to negotiation. You may think that this is preaching to the choir, but Reggie McNeal observes, "The great temptation and debilitator for many Christian leaders is not moral failure, but compass failure."[18]

What causes this compass failure? In some cases, it is the leader's desire to please people more than God. Not that anyone would say this out loud, but actions speak louder than words. Reggie McNeal recounts the story in Mark 1 when Jesus chooses to leave Capernaum despite the demands for him to stay. McNeal says, "Many Christian leaders thrill to hear, 'Everyone is looking for you!' Living for the crowd, they die to their mission. Living only for the crowd eventually leaves them emotionally burned out and empty."[19] The voices of the crowd are often much louder than the voice of God in the leader's life, especially for those who lack confidence that God's hand is at work in their circumstances.

THE DIFFERENTIATED LEADER

The relationship between leaders and followers is a delicate balancing act, particularly in congregations where the followers are volunteers who often hold enormous power of their own. It is a subject we will explore further in Chapter Nine. Leaders may be able to momentarily withdraw from the crowd, as Jesus did in Mark 1, but they cannot be effective if they remain distant. Spiritual leaders must stay connected with the people they lead, but that closeness subjects them to the expectations and anxieties that can cause their resolve to weaken. Heifitz observes, "When serving as the repository of many conflicting aspirations, a person can lose himself in the role by failing to distinguish his inner voice from the voices that clamor for attention outside."[20] That inner voice for Christian leaders is found in a Christ-centered life that is guided by the Spirit in prayer. Without the clarity of this inner voice, a person surrenders the mantle of leadership and becomes a broker of divergent opinions trying to hold the organization together.

Edwin Friedman, who has done foundational work on this issue, emphasizes the importance of being a "well-differentiated leader." He defines this as "someone who has clarity about his or her own life goals, and, therefore, someone who is less likely to become lost in the anxious emotional processes swirling about."[21] Whether because of psychological makeup, training, life experiences, or poor role models, far too many spiritual leaders lose their way when conflict occurs. In the midst of crises, which are inevitable, they surrender to the demand for quick fixes rather than sustaining the tension that can lead to meaningful solutions. Pastors and other ministry leaders must live with the crowd but not get lost in it. The title of Friedman's book, *A Failure of Nerve*, describes one of the biggest problems in the church today. More than ever, we need the kind of well-differentiated leadership that Friedman describes.

If you stop here, you might simply decide to look in the mirror each morning and say, "Today, I will be a well-differentiated leader. I will not get caught up in the swirl." You already know that won't work. It sounds disturbingly similar to Boxer the horse in Orwell's *Animal Farm*, whose performance is never quite good enough. Because of this, Boxer repeatedly says, "I will try harder." For those who don't know the rest of the story, Boxer is eventually hauled off to the glue factory.

Friedman says that well-differentiated leaders are "self-differentiated," and that is where Christians should have a uniquely different perspective and advantage. Rather than self-differentiation, which is as an act of personal willpower, we should be "God-differentiated leaders." From the outside, there may seem to be little difference between the two. With both kinds of differentiation, leaders will appear to be clear about who they are and will not become "lost in anxious emotional processes." But internally—in the leader's source of direction and conviction—the difference is dramatic. As McNeal says, "When tempted to quit, to run away, to hide, the memory of the divine intervention beckons [spiritual leaders] to renewed determination to live up to their call."[22] The God-differentiated person faces the same obstacles as every other leader but does so with a much greater sense of purpose and never does so alone.

Because of this, the clamor of the crowd sounds different to God-differentiated leaders. Gregg Matte of Houston's First Baptist Church offers a great perspective when he says, "It's easier to please God than to please people. People are fickle. If I'm trying to please people or get my picture on the cover of a magazine, that's the liner of a birdcage tomorrow." Matte knows that it is easy to fall into this trap, so he regularly reminds himself that his responsibility is to "preach the Word and love the people." Matte's answer is striking in its simplicity and that it is not dependent on other people or factors outside of his control. His understanding of personal "success," a subject we will return to in Chapter Twelve, is rooted in God. It is the same definition Paul offers after his list of accomplishments in Philippians 3 when he says, "Whatever was to my profit I now consider loss for the sake of Christ. What is more, I consider everything a loss compared to the surpassing greatness of knowing Christ Jesus my Lord, for whose sake I have lost all things." This "God alone" mind-set is a radical departure from the accomplishment orientation found throughout our society and even in the church. It is the only thing that keeps a fragile ego from being swayed by external pressures. It is also the only thing that brings an inflated ego back to earth.

I hope you will not read another page until you have held up the mirror and reflected on yourself as a leader. Even better, invite someone to help hold the mirror for you. If it is true that "the unexamined life is not worth living," it is doubly true for leaders because of the ways their lives affect (and sometimes afflict) so many others. Only a God-differentiated person, one who leads from a quiet conviction of the soul, will be able to learn and risk in ways that propel an organization toward greatness while giving glory to God.

WHAT ARE YOU PURSUING?

- Are you on a journey of self-understanding? How is your awareness guiding your learning and development as a leader?
- What are the big challenges facing your organization? How do you personally need to change in order to meet these challenges? What keeps you from taking the first step?
- Reflect on Collins's "window and mirror" illustration of "Level 5" leadership. Does this description fit you? Or do you do the opposite, accepting credit and deflecting blame?
- How clear is your compass, both personally and in terms of organizational direction? How easily are you knocked off course?
- Do you consider yourself well differentiated? God-differentiated? What in your life gives evidence to support your answer?

PART ONE

TOOLS FOR GREAT AND GODLY LEADERSHIP

I am not a handyman. My family will laugh and tell you that's an understatement. I can put windshield wiper fluid in my car, but I should only change the wipers if the weather forecast calls for a drought. I can change a lightbulb, but if the light switch needs to be replaced, there's a good chance I will blow a fuse and plunge the whole house into darkness.

Some people were born to be fix-it types, but I was not. Beyond my natural inclinations, I have simply never learned to use tools properly. I have been around people with this expertise, and it seems to be second nature for them. They usually have a wide variety of tools and know just which one to use for every project. They can carry on a conversation while making a repair and never miss a beat. I look at the same project and the same set of tools, and I am paralyzed. I don't even know where to start.

Far too often, pastors and other spiritual leaders approach the tools of leadership in the same way that I look at a handyman's tools. They are intimidated and are unsure where to start. On top of this, many of these tools come from the marketplace, an arena that they view with some suspicion.

Ultimately, the purpose of a tool is to enable the user to complete a task that would be more difficult otherwise. I have already confessed to my ineptitude when it comes to repairs, so it should be no surprise that I don't own many tools. The only saw in our house is a simple straight-blade handsaw. Every time I need to use it, I struggle through the task, wishing I had a power saw. Too many Christian leaders are struggling to perform challenging and important ministry tasks without adequate leadership tools. Part One identifies some of these tools and explores how they might be used for more effective congregational leadership.

When archaeologists examine the artifacts from an ancient site, the tools they find tell them a great deal about the sophistication of the people who lived there and how they were influenced by outsiders. Once the residents of a particular region learned to work with metal, for example, they would never again be content with rudimentary stone tools. It would be unthinkable for them to ignore something that would advance their development so significantly. What would outside observers conclude about today's Christian organizations? Would they shake their heads and wonder why we ignored valuable leadership knowledge and resources? Great tools are available, and it's a mistake to not make the best use of them.

Let me carry the tool analogy a little further to introduce the pages that follow. Within a broad class, there are many specific tools. An uninformed person (like me) might refer generically to a "saw," but a craftsman knows that there are rip saws, bow saws, coping saws, keyhole saws, hacksaws, miter saws, table saws, circular saws, jigsaws, and more. The chapters in this section represent different categories of leadership tools, and within each chapter, you will be introduced to several specific tools. You will gain insight into the biblical and practical philosophy regarding the use of these tools. I do not, however, offer a comprehensive catalogue of every available tool or a complete theological argument. In that respect, this book will acquaint you with a variety of tools, but I don't expect anyone to become a "master craftsman" in two hundred pages.

Finally, like a good set of tools, the concepts explored in Part One are related but largely independent. That means that you should feel free to read these chapters in whatever sequence you choose or even skip ones that are not relevant for your leadership needs. If you are in a small church or organization, you may need to adjust the ways in which you use the tools, but the core concepts will still be applicable in your setting. If you are a layperson who makes daily use of leadership tools in the marketplace, you may already know a great deal about the secular application of the tools. My hope, however, is that you will gain a new understanding into the differences and complexities of using these business leadership tools in ministry settings. After all, misuse of a tool can be very costly, whether in a home remodeling project or in a leadership role in the church.

The tool analogy breaks down at one critical point. Around our house, we have dealt with my inadequacies by hiring professionals to repair leaking faucets, faulty wiring, and broken cars. At the end of the day, it costs more to do this, but it doesn't make me less of a husband and father. (In truth, I am probably a better one when I'm not frustrated by my home repair failures!) It works at home, but you can't contract out the leadership of your church. You can get advice, coaching, training, and even some direct help in targeted areas, but the leadership mantle remains on your shoulders. So roll up your sleeves and start learning about the tools of great and godly leadership.

CHAPTER THREE

IS GOD IN YOUR PLANS?

Just mention "long-range planning" around a group of church leaders, and you are sure to get a variety of reactions—deep sighs, shaking heads, uncomfortable chuckles ... and maybe a few eyes that light up. Planning is one of the most notable areas where churches can experience gridlock in the intersection of secular and spiritual leadership.

I will admit to a pro-planning bias. So when I spoke to Greg Hawkins, executive pastor of Willow Creek Community Church, he said just what I wanted and expected to hear. Willow Creek has been through several extensive strategic planning processes, each of which led to major decisions that shaped the congregation's future. Hawkins describes the balance that is essential for churches engaged in Spirit-led planning: "You want to do everything that best practices say to do. Have your facts—about the environment, about your organization's strengths and weaknesses—and do fact-based analysis. Understand your story. But you're praying through all of that and asking the central question, 'God, what do you want us to do?' So it's more a process of discernment than strategic planning." My presuppositions were confirmed: it is valid and valuable for Christian organizations to plan for the future, using practices from the corporate world as tools in the discernment of God's direction.

As I talked to a number of other pastors and leaders of successful Christian organizations, however, I heard a different story. They repeatedly said that planning with horizons greater than a year is very difficult. Jenni Catron of Cross Point Church in Nashville was as clear as anyone: "Five-year plans completely stump us. Every time we try to do one, we hit a dead end." Todd Mullins of Christ Fellowship in Palm Beach, Florida, similarly expressed, "When it comes to planning, that's where I have the biggest struggle using business principles in our church. We've never built out a five-year plan. It's not about planning as much as it is about preparing, being ready for God to move."

As I wrestled with these conflicting perspectives, I realized that everyone has a different idea of what is meant by a strategic plan or a long-range planning process. Some who said that they do not practice this kind of planning actually have very clear ideas about where God is leading their congregations. Some who feel that corporate techniques will not work in the church have misguided ideas about what corporate planning actually looks like. We need to define what planning is (and what it is not) and ask whether it is feasible for congregations to do planning. Before we do that, however, we should first ask whether Christian organizations should plan at all.

Should We Plan?

For spiritual leaders, what are the central arguments that should inform their perspectives on planning? Of course, to answer this question, we should start with Scripture. Is there evidence that God wants us to plan?

A Biblical Perspective

One of the passages often quoted to support planning is the King James Version of Proverbs 29:18: "Where there is no vision, the people perish." While leaders may love to use this verse to justify the need for a planning process, it is a weak argument. The more accurate translations say, "Where there is no revelation" (NIV) or "no prophetic vision" (ESV), "the people cast off restraint." While the verse is clear that we need God's vision or revelation in our lives, individually and collectively, it does little to justify a formal congregational planning process.

What about the passages that seem to argue against planning for the future? One of the best known is found in James: "Now listen, you who say, 'Today or tomorrow we will go to this or that city, spend a year there, carry on business and make money.' Why, you do not even know what will happen tomorrow." These verses seem to make the case against any kind of long-range planning, but the passage goes on to explain, "Instead, you ought to say, 'If it is the Lord's will, we will live and do this or that.' As it is, you boast and brag. All such boasting is evil" (James 4:13–16). The main point is to warn against a boastful attitude that assumes we control our destiny. It is an important reminder, but it does not prohibit planning. The same is true of the parable of the rich fool in Luke 12:16–21 who decides to build bigger barns to store his grain in order to "take life easy: eat, drink, and be merry." Christ does not condemn the man because he planned but because he "stores up things for himself but is not rich toward God."

Two chapters later, Jesus tells another parable with a planning theme: "Suppose one of you wants to build a tower. Will he not first sit down and estimate the cost to see if he has enough money to complete it?" (Luke 14:28). He goes on to instruct his followers about the cost of being a disciple, but he seems to acknowledge that practical, earthly planning for a future need (a building) is part of good leadership.

Another consideration is that God has assembled the body with just the right mix of gifts according to His purposes (Romans 12, 1 Corinthians 12, Ephesians 4). How are we to respond when the mix of people in our church includes experience and capabilities in the area of planning? Are we to ignore those gifts or rejoice that God has placed them in our midst? We gladly strengthen the body with the teaching or musical gifts that a person offers, and we should do the same with planning, which is one dimension of the gift of leadership.

Using the gifts that God has assembled in the body is good stewardship, and so is using our resources with an eye toward the future. We wouldn't build a new facility without thinking carefully about space needs and future uses. We wouldn't plant a church without plans for whom the church is trying to reach and why a particular location is attractive. Good stewardship requires us to allocate resources (money and people) based on where we believe God is leading us in the future. In other words, good stewardship requires planning.

Biblical narratives also are a source of insight into the questions around planning. It is clear that many of the heroes of Scripture led with some sort of plan in mind. Can you imagine Solomon telling the temple builders, "Just make it up as you go along"? This does not mean that God always gives detailed instructions to leaders or that godly leaders always get it right. Moses didn't know the Hebrew people would wander in the desert for forty years. David thought he was the one to build the temple until God told him otherwise.

Jeremiah 29:11 is another favorite verse on the subject: "'For I know the plans I have for you,' declares the Lord, 'plans to prosper you and not to harm you, plans to give you a hope and a future.'" Even though this verse is talking about God's plans, He is directing the people to settle in Babylon and "seek the peace and prosperity of the city in which they are living as exiles" (Jeremiah 29:7). In other words, God is giving broad parameters and reassurance to the people and telling them to live (and plan) accordingly.

The more you look, the less you can make an absolute biblical argument for or against planning. This tension is captured in three proverbs. Proverbs 19:21 seems to say that planning is futile: "Many are the plans in a man's heart, but it is the Lord's purpose that prevails." But Proverbs 16:3—"Commit to the Lord whatever you do, and your plans will succeed"—gives just as much approval to godly planning. And Proverbs 15:22 simply acknowledges that leadership requires some level of planning: "Plans fail for lack of counsel, but with many advisers they succeed."

Perhaps Paul gives the best and most balanced example. It is clear that Paul makes plans, some of them quite far-reaching. He tells the Romans, "There is no more place for me to work in these regions, and since I have been longing for so many years to see you, I plan to do so when I go to Spain" (Romans 15:23–24). Not only is he clear about where he intends to go, but he is also clear about leaving the areas where he has been doing ministry. Paul's plans are not limited to his personal direction. His instruction to Titus to "straighten out what was left unfinished and appoint elders in every town" (Titus 1:5) is given with an eye toward the long-term organizational needs of the church in Crete. Paul's plans are not rigid; he shows a great willingness to change when directed by God. His well-known vision of the man in Macedonia comes after the Spirit prevented him from entering Bithynia (Acts 16:7), and he had another change of plans about a visit to Corinth (2 Corinthians 1:15–17).

Paul captures the essence of Spirit-led planning. God does not prohibit us from planning for the future. If anything, He allows it and even expects us to do it as we exercise the gift of leadership. At the same time, God expects us to be listening closely for His voice and to be willing to change our plans as He directs. Robert Sloan, president of Houston Baptist University, points out, "God had purposes before the world was made, so his horizon is pretty large. I don't think you should worry about having too large a horizon." Sloan summarizes his philosophy of making Spirit-led plans as "not writing them in the sand, but not in concrete either." Plans written in sand are washed away every time the tide changes and hence give no direction to the organization. Plans written in cement leave no room for God to redirect us.

A PRAGMATIC PERSPECTIVE

The Bible should be our first resource in deciding if a practice—planning, in this case—is appropriate in a church. If Scripture does not give us a clear answer, then we can also ask the pragmatic questions of whether the practice will further God's work through our organization and bring Him glory and honor. In all my conversations with Christian leaders, I heard many more practical arguments—for and against planning—than biblical ones.

Mike Mantel, CEO and president of Living Water International, speaks clearly of the need for some type of planning in any large or complex organization. He points out that lack of planning can result in frequent directional changes that are "very costly to people's emotions and their identity. It's a kind of whiplash." In other words, unpredictability in an organization's priorities will result in poor use of its most important resource, its people. On the flip side, Mantel knows that a clear plan "can create a sense of order in people's minds."

Lack of clear direction does not just affect people—it can also lead to other wasted resources. Some leaders are more attracted to new ideas than to rolling up their sleeves to ensure the success of the existing ones, so they start a new initiative and then pull the plug after six or twelve months. The decision to cancel may be a leader's wise realization that an experiment didn't work. But if the real reason is the seduction of the next quick-fix program, as is often the case, it is poor planning and poor stewardship.

Interestingly, several of the leaders with whom I spoke acknowledge this tendency and see planning as a valuable discipline to combat it. Geoff Surratt, formerly a second chair leader at Seacoast Church, says that planning helps "filter what is a God thing and what is a shiny new toy." Greg Surratt, Geoff's older brother and Seacoast's senior pastor, says it even more pointedly when he acknowledges that planning "keeps my spontaneity from corrupting the organization." So does he like planning? "I hate every minute of [the discipline imposed by planning]," says the elder Surratt, but he recognizes "if I change horses too many times, [staff and other leaders] lose confidence in me."

What are the practical arguments against planning? The most frequently cited is the difficulty in developing plans that look more than a year into the future. These concerns often have a theological undertone, such as Gregg Matte's reference to John 3:8, which describes God's Spirit as being like the wind: "You cannot tell where it comes from or where it is going." Matte, just like Catron and Mullins, says "putting together a hard-and-fast five-year plan is hard for me as a leader to do."

Difficulty by itself should never be the reason to avoid planning, which leads to one other practical consideration. A number of the lay leaders in your congregation have probably had significant experience with planning in the marketplace. Do they wonder why you are hesitant to enter into a planning process? If your only answer is the difficulty of the task, you will lose credibility with these leaders. David Weekley, a highly successful business executive, describes the frustration he feels when Christian organizations fail to plan effectively. He believes that "people can be successful without strategic plans because they have great skills," but he is quick to add that they would be even more successful with a strategic plan. If we want to engage the capable business leaders in our congregations, our planning processes need to capture their attention and point toward the future.

What Is Planning?

When I worked for ExxonMobil, I observed a long-range planning system that was mind-boggling in its complexity. The annual process lasted several months and involved thousands of people. Experts at headquarters developed twenty-year forecasts for the price and demand for oil, worldwide economic growth, and a host of other factors. The plans that were eventually developed within each business unit were based on these predictions and the corporate priorities, and they determined the allocation of money for projects as well as the movement of people around the organization. When deciding whether to give the green light on a multiyear project to develop an oilfield or build a refinery, long planning horizons are necessary.

Several years later, I worked for a much smaller organization. We also had an annual planning process, but our horizon was not much more than a year and the process required far less time. This approach made sense because of the size of the company and the unpredictability of our market. The contrast between these two corporate examples highlights the diverse approaches to planning that are found in business. The same diversity in planning approaches is found in Christian organizations, which highlights the fact that "planning" is an imprecise concept that needs to be defined.

Defining "Planning"

At its most generic level, planning is a process to determine where an organization is going and how it will get there. It establishes future priorities for the purpose of resource allocation and communication. Notice that this description does not set a time horizon, nor does it specify how detailed the plan should be. The definition does not say how many people should be involved or how long the process should take. And it says nothing about the spiritual dimension, how discernment of God's will shapes the process and the outcomes.

All of these factors are important. The first two—the time horizon and the level of detail—point to three distinct kinds of planning:

- *Tactical* planning looks over a short time horizon (usually twelve months) and is often fairly detailed. This kind of planning is generally connected with the organization's budgeting process or the annual ministry planning cycle. At its best, it sets priorities in alignment with the vision; at its worst, it is a competition for scarce resources that is won by the parties with the most clout.

- *Visionary* planning looks over a long time horizon (five years or more) to paint an exciting, high-level picture of what the organization will look like or what it will accomplish in the future. This type of planning does not attempt to fill in a lot of details for *how* this will be done. Visionary planning is typically high on inspiration, including the prototypical fit-on-a-T-shirt vision statement, but low on answers.

- *Strategic* planning is long-range (three to five years) and detailed. It attempts to fill in some of the blanks that are missing in a visionary planning process. It can be the best of both worlds, but it is also the most difficult to do.

I am not saying that an organization needs to have three different planning processes, and I did not find any that attempted to do so. In fact, most of those in my research have a single process that may blend two or all three of these elements. Likewise, the specific labels that I am using are not as important as what they convey. They simply offer some distinctions that will be helpful as we seek to think about planning in a Christian organization.

Tactical Planning

Any successful organization does some type of tactical planning, whether independent of or in conjunction with a long-range plan, a fact that was confirmed in my interviews. Fellowship Bible Church's planning process begins in the fall with the leadership team and elder board coming together to pray and to identify the "big rocks"—the major churchwide priorities—for the coming year. Once agreement is reached at the senior level, these big rocks are the basis for priorities and new initiatives for the twelve-month planning cycle. This enables the programming staff to develop specific ministry plans, initiatives, and budget requests that reflect the new priorities as well as their ongoing programs. Tim Lundy admits that Fellowship's process is very corporate-looking, but he emphasizes that the church is quite intentional about seeking God as its leaders develop plans, and they have been willing to make

changes when God surprises them. While there are many different ways to do tactical planning, the basic steps of identifying new
initiatives and allocating resources is a common denominator.

An interesting twist on tactical planning is Patrick Lencioni's
concept of thematic goals, which is explored in his book *Silos,
Politics, and Turf Wars.*[1] Lencioni explains that a thematic goal is a
"rallying cry," a single, critical, organization-shaping initiative that
deserves the focused attention of senior leadership for six to eighteen months. His approach is short-term and includes concrete
steps, but unlike many tactical plans that only call for incremental
improvements, the thematic goal identifies and addresses a key
organizational priority. And unlike many strategic plans, the thematic goal avoids the tendency to produce too many priorities or
peer too far into an uncertain future.

Church of the Resurrection (Anglican), in Wheaton, Illinois,
uses the thematic-goal approach in its annual planning. Senior
pastor Stewart Ruch uses the summer to pray and reflect on this
overarching objective. When the formal planning process begins
in the fall, the other members of the leadership team have been
praying as well, and a central question they ask is "Are we hearing
the same thing?" Karen Miller, executive pastor, says Resurrection's
thematic goal in 2010–2011 was "Get My People Ready" because
church leaders sensed God calling them to a season of deepen-
ing in preparation for future growth. Several specific initiatives
were generated, including an increased emphasis on spiritual for-
mation (with related staff additions) and a focus on leadership
development for staff and laity. For Resurrection, this has been an
effective way to take a business process and make it God-centered.

Visionary Planning

Tactical planning can feel very businesslike and unspiritual, but
visionary plans often seem to be just the opposite. Dino Rizzo's
vision was to plant a church that would be a "healing place for a
hurting world." The original campus of Healing Place Church is
located in an affluent area of south Baton Rouge, so Rizzo says that
the church needed to be "somewhat of a Robin Hood. We wanted
to take from those who had resources and distribute to those who
did not." He continues, "We wanted to make sure that we were

here in location but our heart was in other places." This simple vision has exploded as the church now has eight campuses, an average worship attendance of seventy-two hundred people, and a far-reaching ministry to people who are hurting.

The story of a simple but profound vision that drives phenomenal growth is found in many of the high-profile churches around the country. It is Rizzo's vision of a church that is a "healing place" or Willow Creek's vision of "turning irreligious people into fully devoted followers of Christ." These are the kinds of visions that often come to mind when we think of visionary planning.

Vision is important. Business expert Peter Senge says, "Visions are exhilarating. They create the spark, the excitement that lifts an organization out of the mundane."[2] Bill Hybels echoes, "Vision is the fuel that leaders run on. It's the energy that creates action. It's the fire that ignites the passion of followers. It's the clear call that sustains focused effort year after year, decade after decade, as people offer consistent and sacrificial service to God."[3]

But there is a problem with visionary planning. Too often leaders read these words and hear stories like Rizzo's and conclude that all they need is a God-inspired vision for their organization to thrive and grow. Behind the visionary leaders and their bold visions, someone is figuring out a way to make it happen. Sometimes a single leader has the ability to see far into the future and at the same time develop short-term action plans. More often, one or more second chair leaders come alongside the visionary to work out the details. At times, translating vision into action is done through a specific planning process. At other times, it is more intuitive. But as Hybels notes, "Unless people eventually see progress toward the fulfillment of the vision they will conclude that the vision caster is just a dreamer blowing smoke, and their morale will plummet."[4]

We need leaders who are attuned to the great things that God wants to accomplish through His people and who are not afraid to declare this in inspiring ways. We also need leaders who can show the way to make this happen.

Strategic Planning

Some of the leaders that I interviewed were comfortable with a God-led strategic planning approach and found that this gave their organizations clarity and direction. Willow Creek is a prime example of this. Guided by its vision to continue to turn irreligious people into fully devoted followers of Christ, one of Willow's major planning cycles led to the decision to build a new auditorium and simultaneously launch regional campuses. The process that created this plan lasted eighteen months, much longer than a tactical planning process. Willow's plan was also much farther-reaching than a typical tactical plan yet more detailed than what is found in visionary approaches, with specific action items and goals that stretched out over five years. For example, the plans for regional campuses included steps for recruiting leaders and a core launch group, identifying locations, and establishing budgets.

Willow Creek is one of the most prominent and most advanced examples of strategic planning in a Christian organization. Perhaps that is not surprising, since senior pastor Bill Hybels has always advocated the use of business best practices and executive pastor Greg Hawkins began his career as a strategic planning consultant. But Willow is not alone. I found varying levels of strategic planning at 12Stone Church, Church of the Resurrection (Methodist), Menlo Park Presbyterian, and Oak Hills Church. Strategic planning seemed even more prevalent in other Christian organizations such as Houston Baptist University, World Vision, HOPE International, and Living Water. The leaders of these organizations are convinced that they need something more than a tactical plan if they are to realize the dreams that God has placed on their hearts. Just as I found in business, as the size and complexity of a ministry increases, so does the need for a longer planning horizon.

Interestingly, when I asked about their planning, many pastors and leaders who only described a tactical process were clearly guided by a much broader, bigger vision. In fact, my conclusion (and that of many leadership experts) is that their organizations could not have achieved such high levels of success without this broader sense of direction. Some had engaged in a visionary planning process and some had not, but all had an idea where they were going. Gregg Matte may struggle with formal five-year plans, but he "has the next couple of mountains in mind" as he leads the congregation. As evidence of this, when I interviewed Matte, the church was in the midst of a $14 million capital project to renovate and expand its sanctuary and add children's space. When pastors told me that they found it difficult to do five-year plans, they were not saying that they (and their church) lacked vision. They were saying that they had been frustrated in their efforts to do *strategic planning*.

OBSTACLES TO STRATEGIC PLANNING

Why do many spiritual leaders find strategic planning so unappealing? One reason is that they have misconceptions about corporate strategic planning. They assume that the Exxon approach is the only way—a rigorous, analytical process that results in firm, inflexible answers.

Another reason may be a bad experience with strategic planning in the past. Several years ago, Seacoast Church turned its vision of reaching people through multiple campuses into a strategic plan called Vision 2010. The plan had specific financial and numerical goals and spelled out the number of campuses to be opened each year. After about two years, Seacoast abandoned the plan. What happened? According to Geoff Surratt, "It fell apart because it was a long-range business plan without a lot of room for God in it. [It felt like] we were executing to hit the numbers in the plan rather than trying to respond to what God was doing and saying." It wasn't wrong to plan, but Seacoast needed an approach that was less rigid and more fluid.

In truth, there are many ways to do strategic planning. While it usually is anchored in factual data, it often includes the softer elements of intuition and leadership judgment. And while the corporate plan may dictate specific steps to be implemented in the first twelve months, the best businesses include ways to modify or scrap plans as necessary. In fact, Collins and Porras discovered that "visionary companies ... made some of their best moves not by detailed strategic planning, but rather by experimentation, trial and error, opportunism, and—quite literally—accident."[5]

That leads to another reason that strategic planning may seem inappropriate to many pastors. Rather than thinking of breakthroughs happening "by opportunism or accident," Christian leaders recognize the divine element. In *The Present Future*, Reggie McNeal says, "Typical approaches to the future involve prediction and planning. ... The better (and biblical) approach to the future involves prayer and preparation."[6] Gregg Matte is exactly right that the Holy Spirit is like the wind. God often shows up in the most unexpected and surprising ways, disrupting whatever plans we may have made.

If God's ways are higher than our ways and His thoughts higher than our thoughts (Isaiah 55:9), what's the point of trying to look around the corner with our planning processes? Mike Mantel of Living Water International (LWI) knows that some of the most important triggers that transformed the organization happened apart from their formal plans. At one point in its history, LWI took a group of donors on an international trip to see how their money was being used to drill clean water wells. The enthusiasm of this group led to the establishment of regular mission trips as a way to involve more people in LWI's mission and expand its ministry to the local communities it serves. Similarly, the viral growth of the Advent Conspiracy—a Christmas campaign to encourage American Christians to spend less on themselves and donate to global clean water efforts—was not in LWI's strategic plan. These were providential events orchestrated by God. And yet LWI is moving forward with its strategic planning process because Mantel and the board are convinced that this is the best way to discern God's guidance and set the organization's course for the future.

I am convinced that each congregation needs to have a clear idea of who God is calling it to be and to develop plans in line with this identity. The issue of identity is an important topic that we will return to in Chapter Ten. For identity to foster Spirit-led planning, whether short-term or long-term, whether labeled as strategic or some other name, certain elements are essential in the process.

ELEMENTS OF EFFECTIVE PLANNING

This is not a book about planning; it's a book about how secular leadership practices should or should not influence the leadership of Christian organizations. Planning is simply one of the important leadership tools to be considered. A number of resources offer further insights and guidance on planning.[7] The final section of this chapter identifies some key elements of planning that are found in many successful congregations and Christian organizations. Chapter Four explores a number of examples of how this kind of planning has shaped the direction for a variety of these entities.

BUILD ON A SPIRITUAL FOUNDATION

Naturally, if a planning process is to be Spirit-led, it must start with a spiritual foundation. As Reggie McNeal says, "God is the one with the vision for our lives and the church. It is our job to discover what He has in mind, not to invent something He can get excited about."[8] Too often, however, we are not sure how to do this, or we get caught up in the mechanics of the process and forget God. We have many tools at our disposal, and we often make the mistake of treating the spiritual dynamic as just another tool rather than the core. Jeff Wells, senior pastor of WoodsEdge Community Church in The Woodlands, Texas, expresses it this way: "Because we [the church in the West] have so much money and education, it's easy to not depend on God. We tend to ask God to lead us, then we work real hard to decide on our own, then we ask God to bless the decision we've made."

As you will see later, the selection of those who are invited to participate in the process is an important part of laying a spiritual foundation. Beyond that, the leader is responsible for setting the spiritual tone from the outset. It needs to be clearly stated that this is a discernment process in which God's guidance is being sought. That provides an opening throughout the process to ask whether a leader's personal agenda and preferences are trumping God's will. Some leaders will help lay the foundation with a Bible study. This is not simply a devotional (slightly better than a perfunctory prayer) but rather an opportunity to open Scripture and align the planning team with the heart of God. A biblical narrative that connects with the congregation can offer powerful images and lessons that shape the planning process.

Every spiritual leader needs to be aware of the factors that can squeeze God out of the planning process. For Jim Leggett of Grace Fellowship, the story of the Gibeonite deception is a vivid reminder of the risks of self-reliance. The people of Gibeon disguised themselves as people from a distant land so that they could trick Joshua and the advancing army into a peace treaty. The Israelites used their human judgment "but did not inquire of the Lord" (Joshua 9:14) and accepted an agreement that was not in God's will. Once the treaty was made, they discovered the deception, but they had to live with the consequences. This story should be a sobering reminder of the subtle dangers that all leaders face as they seek to plan for the future.

Truly relying on God is not easy. Debi Nixon says the leaders at the Church of the Resurrection (Methodist) have a phrase—"discernment by nausea"—that refers to the hard decisions that make their stomachs churn when they believe that God is leading them to do something big and risky. It is the feeling that comes when leaders make a decision based on faith rather than pure analysis. Ruth Haley Barton says, "Being this reliant on God for the actual outcome of things is a very edgy way to lead. We are much more accustomed to relying partly on God and partly on our own plans and thoughts if the issues at hand are really important."[9] A solid spiritual foundation is the only thing that can produce this kind of reliance on God, and it will also result in a unique timeline for planning.

Follow God's Timeline

The pace of Spirit-led planning feels different from corporate processes. Rather than a rigorous schedule, leaders will be willing to pause when they feel that they have not heard from God. Greg Hawkins says, "We will not prematurely declare something. We don't have any problem with people saying, 'This is taking too long.' As long as we're asking the right questions and [proceeding] diligently, we will wait on God. We will not get ahead of God. That would be disastrous." As a result, Willow Creek did not feel pressured by an artificial timeline in its eighteen-month planning process that ultimately led to the new auditorium and regional campuses.

The time element does not apply solely to the length of the process; it also applies to the way time is managed during meetings. Spiritually attuned leaders may come into a meeting with an agenda for what needs to be accomplished, but they are willing to stop to spend time in prayer or otherwise seek God's guidance. They know that investing an extra hour or two (or more) pays dramatic dividends if the result is sensing God's direction more clearly. There is great power when a leader can confidently say, "This is where God is leading us." There is even more power when the whole leadership team has this same confidence.

Several years ago, I led a planning retreat for a church that was adopting a bold new vision that involved relocation and several other major initiatives. As we neared the end of the weekend retreat, I wanted to see if we had reached a consensus on the primary conclusions. One by one, the individuals in the room voiced their affirmation and excitement about the new direction. Then one individual spoke against it. Even though I desperately wanted to move forward with an approval before leaving for the airport, I realized that this man was feeling rushed in the process. He simply needed more time to reflect and pray, and he wanted the entire group to do the same. So we stopped for prayer and agreed that the members of the planning group could reconvene the following week without me, at which time they felt a much clearer confirmation that they had correctly discerned God's direction.

The issue of timing is particularly tricky in planning because some people will be ready to move forward much sooner than others. In the business arena, the hesitation is often driven by fear and is expressed in a desire to "get more data" or "do some extra analysis." In churches, fear may still be the driver, but it may be expressed as "we just need more time to pray about this." How can you argue with prayer? Yet at some point the leader needs to move the process forward unless he or she is convinced that God is saying "wait."

Lengthy, seemingly unnecessary, delays can be particularly frustrating to the business executives on a leadership team. In their professional lives, they gather a small group, look at the facts, make a decision, and move on. Rich Stearns, president of World Vision, has a philosophy that "God can't steer a parked car. Sometimes you can be paralyzed with indecision because no one feels like they've heard God's will clearly. I'm more of the school that you have to get the car on the road and start driving before God can steer it."

I also get impatient when a decision drags out, but I know that Scripture teaches both sides of this coin. We are told both to wait on the Lord and to go about our tasks with urgency. Ultimately, I agree with Gordon-Conwell's Rodney Cooper, who asks, "Why do we have to be in a hurry?" He answers his own question: "Obviously God is not. We need to live by a compass, not a clock." The clarity of knowing the direction in which God's compass is pointing is another vital element of planning.

DRIVE TOWARD CLARITY

One area where Christian organizations should take some cues from the corporate world is in creating clarity around their planning processes. In business, the purpose of planning is to declare "this is where we are going" and then to drive the company toward that goal.

Shouldn't we do the same in the church? When controversy occurred in the early church over the disparity in how Hebrew and Greek widows were being served, the apostles developed a plan. They divided the leadership into two components, one for "prayer and the ministry of the word" and the other to "wait on tables" (Acts 6:1–4). They were clear about their purpose and devised a plan with well-defined roles, and the church thrived. Because they listened to the Spirit and put a clear plan in place, God multiplied their ministry.

Mike Mantel says that "success is not dependent on a plan, but your stewardship is." In other words, good stewardship is not possible if an organization is running helter skelter, or even driving slowly, without a clear direction. The clarity that comes from effective planning is a powerful tool for aligning people and resources. Clarity does not mean inflexibility. Tim Lundy has an interesting perspective: "By having a plan, you are actually more ready to be mobilized spontaneously by the Holy Spirit than if you are living by the seat of your pants." Without some kind of plan, it is impossible to see the implications of a shift in direction. That is one reason that the histories of many congregations show a pattern of half-baked and failed initiatives. Planning should produce clarity that will guide the organization toward a God-inspired future.

WORK WITH THE FACTS, NOT AGAINST THEM

The aversion that some Christian leaders have to corporate-style planning relates to its reliance on facts and analysis. Perhaps this is because they are not oriented toward quantitative information. Their eyes glaze over when they see a spreadsheet full of data, and they feel intimidated by laypeople who are eager to dive into the numbers. Because of this orientation, they can't imagine that the data are useful. Or perhaps they believe that once these details are introduced into the process, God leaves the room. This may be a reflection on past experiences in which a planning team thought all the answers would emerge from the analysis, apart from God. In other cases, a leader may fear that a data-driven process will shine the light on past results that reflect poorly on him or her. As long as the leader can talk in qualitative terms and not confront the facts, he or she can pretend that all is well.

Is fact-based analysis contrary to Spirit-led planning? One of Bill Hybels's axioms is "Facts are your friend."[10] He describes the importance of accurate, quantitative information in shaping Willow's plans. The Reveal survey, first done as an internal Willow Creek project, was a powerful, fact-based assessment that gave the church's leaders deep insights into the spiritual health and growth of their congregation. Without this kind of data-driven analysis, Willow's leaders would not have recognized some issues that needed to be addressed. The facts didn't just identify problems; they also pointed toward solutions and gave Willow's leaders compelling arguments to support the resulting changes.

There are two challenges in dealing with facts. The first is to get the right facts and to use them correctly. This is just as much an issue for businesses as it is for churches. Many organizations, secular and spiritual, get bogged down in a sea of data that produces little useful information. Others will work to manipulate data to paint the picture that they want, either hiding problems or advancing a particular agenda. It's the old adage that "figures don't lie, but liars figure."

The second challenge is to remember that the data are just part of the picture. In Christian organizations, we will always deal with unquantifiable factors. That is not a justification for ignoring facts, but it is a caution not to rely exclusively on them. In Alistair Hanna's consulting career, he drew heavily on facts and analysis to develop strategic plans. When Hanna founded Alpha North America, he produced a fifty-slide, fact-filled presentation, just as he had done for consulting clients. Today he still analyzes a wide range of businesslike data—number of churches using Alpha, number of training conferences, expense ratios, and so on—but he knows that the best decisions come from God speaking to him through the data and through prayer.

Foster Collaboration

The best plans are not developed in isolation. This is another area where business practices vary widely, from strategies that are developed by a small executive team to ones that involve a large number of people from throughout the organization. Christian organizations usually need to seek even broader participation and be more collaborative than businesses. Rich Stearns remembers learning this lesson in his transition from marketplace to ministry. As a corporate CEO, Stearns was not a top-down leader, but he knew that strategic decisions made by the executive team would be followed by the rest of the organization. After coming to World Vision, he realized that everyone expected to have a voice, which led him to adopt a highly participatory planning process. Before one reorganization, Stearns had one-on-one meetings with forty different managers, in addition to town hall meetings with a broader group of employees and stakeholders. Stearns and many other effective leaders know that this kind of involvement leads to a much stronger base of support when major decisions are being made.

Spiritual leaders often want to pronounce the vision and have everyone fall in line. Broad involvement is unattractive because it takes more time, opens them to more criticism, and means they have less control of the outcome. In addition, Scott Cormode of Fuller Seminary notes, pastors are trained to proclaim a message, and they bring this mind-set to planning. Cormode contends that "leadership begins with listening." When people in the organization feel their voice has been heard, their buy-in to the vision increases dramatically. When a leader listens to others, he or she will often hear God speaking as well. Discerning God's direction in community is an important part of the culture at Willow Creek. Greg Hawkins says that Willow's leadership team of senior staff and elders has confidence that God "will speak with one voice among the community of leaders." As these leaders each listen to God and to each other, a Spirit-led clarity emerges.

Listening to others is not a onetime activity. Alan "Blues" Baker is the directional leader at Menlo Park Presbyterian Church in the San Francisco Bay area, where he serves alongside senior pastor John Ortberg. Shortly after arriving, Baker initiated a planning process that involved the senior staff and elders in discerning the congregation's future direction. When the time came to put the vision in writing, Baker and Ortberg went away to craft the actual statement. This made sense to them—they had listened to key leaders, but they knew that the specific language needed to be something that resonated with the primary vision communicator (Ortberg). When they returned and announced the vision, Baker was surprised that the initial reaction from the other leaders was negative. The broader group wanted to have been involved even at this stage in the process. Baker and the other leaders worked through this setback together, but not without some heartache for Baker. In telling this story, I am not advocating vision by committee but am simply showing that effective, savvy leadership is needed to foster collaboration and build consensus.

The current strategic planning process at Living Water is an example of broad collaboration. It includes sessions at the corporate and regional levels involving dozens of different stakeholders—executives, staff, board members, and donors. Board member Rob Pettigrew participated in one of these meetings, which he likens to "digging a trench with everyone pouring their vision and thoughts into it." As the process unfolds, "you begin to see the overlap and realize that some of this is God's design." At this critical juncture in its history, Living Water believes that the right people can come together in a prayerful conversation to discern God's direction for the organization.

Don't overlook a key word: the *right* people. Spiritual discernment for an organization's future will not work if the wrong people are involved. Ruth Haley Barton observes, "One very common leadership mistake is to think that we can take a group of undiscerning individuals and expect them to show up in a leadership setting and all of a sudden become discerning! Many boards and elder groups are composed primarily of people who have been successful in business ventures but may not have had much preparation or experience in the area of spiritual discernment."[11] As I listened to leaders describe successful planning processes, I was impressed by their ability and intentionality in finding the right people, a subject we will revisit in Chapter Nine.

In addition to the right people, a collaborative process requires the right environment. Spirit-led planning occurs most effectively in the context of trust-based relationships and honest discussion. Too many planning processes are characterized by people who are carefully watching the others in the room, trying to figure out what is safe to say or how they can protect their interests. In *The Five Dysfunctions of a Team*, Patrick Lencioni says, "Teams that lack trust waste inordinate amounts of time and energy managing their behaviors and interactions within the group."[12] Without trust in the planning process, Living Waters' trench will at best be half full with people's input and at worst may get filled with the toxic input of self-serving agendas.

LIVE IN HOPEFUL EXPECTATION

A final distinction of Christian planning is that God's presence should produce hope. We should not ignore data that are negative, but we should remember that God is not constrained by the facts. We should not take indiscriminate risks, but we must not hesitate to act boldly when God calls. And when things don't turn out as expected, we should never forget that God is still with us.

Perhaps *hope* is not the right word, since its broader meaning in society does not convey the confident expectation that we should have. A unique Christian kind of hope was a common thread in my interviews. When faith and hope are at the heart of a planning process, great things can happen. It is those kinds of great things that we will be looking at in the next chapter as we consider the remarkable results that can come from effective Spirit-led planning.

WHAT ARE YOU PURSUING?

- Reflect on your past experiences with planning. What worked well? What frustrated you?
- Assess your current (or most recent) planning process. Is it more tactical, visionary, or strategic? Discuss your assessment with others in your leadership group.

- Reflect on the elements of effective planning in the second half of the chapter. Which are apparent in your planning? Which are absent?
- Within your organization, who has abilities in planning that you can leverage? What specific skills are needed to complement your strengths and weaknesses?

CHAPTER FOUR

ARE YOUR PLANS FRUITFUL?

Jesus told his followers, "Each tree is recognized by its own fruit" (Luke 6:44). We readily apply this at an individual level, but shouldn't it be true collectively as well? Our planning processes should produce fruit that gives clear evidence of God's guidance. Many of the elements of planning for Christian organizations—collaborative processes, collection and analysis of data, specific action plans, goal-oriented outcomes—may look very corporate. But as noted in the last chapter, a number of nuances distinguish Spirit-led planning from corporate practices. In this chapter, we will look at the *results* of this kind of planning.

By demonstrating some of the ways that Spirit-led planning produces different outcomes than traditional corporate models, I hope you begin to envision the possible results of your organization's plans. These outcomes include bold or unconventional moves that flow out of planning, a willingness to wait on God, surprises and redirections after plans are made, the focus to stick to a plan, and a redefinition of failure.

BOLD MOVES

One of the ways that God often works in the plans of Christian organizations is to lead them to make bold or unconventional decisions. These are the kinds of decisions that can't be fully supported by fact-based analysis but are simply explained as obedience to the Lord's voice. To be clear, leading businesses make bold moves as well. Jim Collins and Jerry Porras coined the expression "big hairy audacious goals," which they shortened to "BHAGs," to describe the way that visionary companies commit themselves to seemingly impossible challenges. Boeing's decision to build the 747 airplane, a bet-the-company commitment, is one of their examples.[1] So is Walt Disney's original decision to take a leap from animated movies into a unique theme park experience we now know as Disneyland.[2] Jim Kouzes and Barry Posner state, "Nothing new and nothing great is achieved by doing things the way you've always done them. You have to test unproven strategies. You have to break out of the norms that box you in. ... Getting extraordinary things done in organizations demands a willingness to experiment and take risks with innovative ideas."[3]

The pivotal moments for spiritual leaders and their organizations often involve this kind of risk taking. A public declaration of a God-inspired vision may seem brash to outsiders, but it is an obedient leap of faith to the leader. Rick Warren's bold announcement on Saddleback's very first Sunday is one of those moments:

> It is the dream of sharing the Good News of Jesus Christ with the hundreds of thousands of residents in south Orange County. It is the dream of welcoming 20,000 members into the fellowship of our church family—loving, learning, laughing and living in harmony together ... sending out hundreds of career missionaries and church workers around the world ... at least fifty acres of land on which will be built a regional church for south Orange County.[4]

So are we just bringing another business principle into the church when we develop bold, long-range plans? In the business world, these decisions are more about a calculated gamble based on facts and intuition, but in our churches, they should be an obedient leap of faith. After all, Collins and Porras may have come up with the acronym BHAG, but God invented the concept. When His people step out in faith, they do bold, risky things: they build arks on dry land to preserve life, they move to new territories to start a great nation and bless all humankind, they stand up to powerful kings and demand freedom for their people, and much more.

Houston Baptist University is pursuing a bold, God-inspired vision. Under the leadership of Robert Sloan, this small, relatively unknown school has declared its intention to become a leading Christian university over the next ten to twelve years:

> We seek nothing less than to guide and instruct the next generations of faithful artists, authors, actors, academics, business professionals, lawyers, musicians, doctors, teachers, scientists, and others—individuals who will understand the times we live in, and understand God's calling for their lives. We seek to produce the future leaders of the world who also live as servants in the kingdom of God. . . . We are poised to become the kind of institution that can be a leader for Christian higher education in America.[5]

The vision is supported by "ten pillars," each of which describes a key step toward the ultimate goal. These include plans to recruit on a national level, increase the time that faculty members have for research so that they can have a greater impact on society, expand the size of the student body, and add graduate-level programs.

HBU's vision and ten pillars are the result of an extensive, structured planning process that sought input from the board, faculty and staff, alumni, and students. Sloan says the Holy Spirit was active throughout the process, stirring the imagination and igniting the passions of HBU's many constituents as the vision emerged. The specific details of HBU's plan continue to be refined, but the vision is clear and unwavering.

Sometimes a leader is forced to choose between the promptings of the Spirit and the "answer" that comes from analyzing the data. The Crossing, a church in the Saint Louis area, felt led to open its first satellite campus and was carefully working on the location decision. The data clearly pointed to the fast-growing western suburbs where a number of church members already lived. As the leaders prayed about the decision, however, they sensed God directing them to Fenton, Missouri, to the south of Saint Louis, where they had far fewer members and much less favorable demographics.

It would be easy to question the promptings of the Spirit in the face of such compelling data. It would be even easier when some of the pieces don't quite fall into place, like finding the right location. As The Crossing's leaders looked for a site in Fenton, the best they found was a building that had housed a lawn mower repair center and had been vacant for eight years. Yet they proceeded with the launch, convinced that they had no choice but to follow God. The initial results have been overwhelming. Within the first few weeks, the facility was full, and before the end of the first year, the Fenton campus was averaging over a thousand in weekend worship attendance. Reflecting on this story reminds me of Paul's words to the Corinthians, "Has not God made foolish the wisdom of the world?" (1 Corinthians 1:20).

In painting these pictures of bold and unconventional plans, I have one fear: that readers will use these stories as the standard against which they should judge their own boldness. That's not the point. The only standard is what God is asking us to do. I asked Greg Hawkins to tell me about the "craziest" decision that Willow Creek has made, and he was quick to say that they have not made any. He explained that there is a difference between bold and crazy, saying, "There is nothing we've been reluctant to do for God when He has asked us to do it." But Hawkins stressed the difference between obeying God and impressing others. "If you are trying to be risky to show other people how risky you can be, that's insanity. I have no need to show anybody my ability to assume risk. I have every desire to obey my God and do whatever He asks me to do." Bill Hybels echoes this sentiment in his book *Axioms* when he says, "We take flyers. We don't bet the farm." He explains that Willow Creek's "flyers"—bold initiatives based more on holy hunches than on facts—may have seemed crazy to others, but church leaders were not "rolling the dice" in such a way that they might "lose the *kingdom* farm" that God had been building.[6]

Not all Spirit-led planning results in bold moves. Sometimes God may say "not yet." I facilitated a planning process for one congregation with the stated goal of developing a clear, compelling vision for the future. Church leaders hoped to explore options such as relocation, additional worship venues, and new mission ministries. Yet it became evident that the church was not ready for a major leap forward. After several years of growth and new initiatives, many leaders were weary, and some of the underlying processes for decision making and communication were frayed. In our planning workshops, the team recognized that the most important priorities for the coming season were mundane, nuts-and-bolts action items. The decision to pull back from any bold steps was not a "no" but a "not yet," and it ultimately set the stage for a more exciting future.

WAITING ON GOD

God often calls us to make bold moves, but not always. So as we plan, can we at least count on God to point us to the next steps that we should take? In Chapter Three, we examined how the pace or timing of a planning process can differ from in the secular arena because there are occasions when God's direction is not clear. Tim Lundy learned this lesson early in his tenure as directional leader at Fellowship Bible Church. The tradition at Fellowship is a state-of-the-church sermon on the first Sunday of each year. In this message, the pastor talks about the things that God has put on his heart and lays out key priorities for the coming year. As the date approached, the church had several major initiatives under consideration, but Lundy was unclear regarding what to say. "The only message I was getting back from God was 'wait'"—not exactly what a pastor wants to hear, especially when he is new in the role and the congregation is expecting something profound. Nevertheless, Lundy knew there was only one thing he could do. He gave the state-of-the-church message and announced that the year's theme was "Ready, Set, Wait." He explained his sense that God had something big in store, but exactly what had not become clear.

Later that year, the school next door inquired about the possibility of buying Fellowship's property. Ultimately, the church agreed to the transaction, paving the way for it to relocate and build a much larger facility that better suited its needs. Had Lundy not waited obediently, even at the risk of criticism, Fellowship might have launched other initiatives that would have precluded God's plan for relocation.

One temptation when waiting on God is to see "open doors" at every turn. When leaders are confident that God's will just needs to be discovered, they may interpret the first opportunity as a divine appointment. Grace Fellowship, a twelve-year-old church planted in one of the fast-growing suburbs west of Houston, had to wrestle with this. The church has a unique facility that was part of the Greater Southwest Equestrian Center. In 2003, Grace had just completed a building program that included worship and children's space, but its rapid growth made it clear that more land for facilities and parking would be needed soon.

During that season, the owners of the equestrian center decided to sell an additional twelve acres of undeveloped land across the street from the church's existing property. It was a pivotal moment for the congregation. Members were still paying their capital campaign commitments from the recent project. The church also had $3 million in debt and was at the borrowing limit according to its internal debt philosophy. Pastor Jim Leggett and other leaders began to wrestle with the decision. How could they pass on the land purchase opportunity when they knew it could meet future needs? How could they afford to purchase the land given their financial realities?

One afternoon, the church leaders met to discuss their options and seek God's wisdom. The room in which they were meeting had a window that looked out on the land that was for sale. During the meeting, one of the members of the team glanced across the field and said, "Look! There's a lamb. We know that Jesus is the Lamb of God. Maybe this is God's sign to buy the property."

Leggett was not convinced that God would lead the church to violate its debt philosophy, which had been developed after careful study of Scripture. He continued to pray and also polled a broader group of leaders to see how much they might give on top of their tithes and current capital commitments. When the response proved to be nowhere close to the needed amount, Grace walked away from the deal. It did not take long before the property was sold to a developer, who built apartments on the land. But that is not the end of the story. Grace Fellowship continued to grow, and a little more than three years later, another land purchase opportunity arose. This time it was for seventeen contiguous acres that included the equestrian center's plantation house and horse barn. This time the church was in a much better financial position. This time church leaders heard a clear "yes" from the Lord and moved forward with the acquisition. The plantation house became much needed office space, and the barn was converted into a wonderful worship center with plenty of parking.

WHEN GOD SURPRISES

Some bold moves grow out of spontaneous obedience to God rather than elaborate planning processes. When Chris Hodges of Church of the Highlands saw that Birmingham was the sixth most violent city in the country in murders per capita, he felt God leading him to do something about it. Can one pastor and one church—a suburban church at that—influence the murder rate in a large city? Hodges knew that this was a God-sized challenge that could only be addressed with prayer. He led the church's members to pray, but not just from the safety of their homes. Highlands partnered with the mayor's office and the chief of police and set up monthly prayer walks in some of the most crime-ridden neighborhoods of the city.

Highlands also opened the Dream Center in the downtown area, a holistic Christian ministry to address the myriad of issues associated with the cycle of poverty. Some churches ignore these needs, and others only dedicate financial resources, but Highlands made a much deeper commitment, providing leadership and volunteers to support the Dream Center. Hodges readily admits that he is "less of a strategist than an opportunist" when it comes to planning, and his commitment to respond opportunistically has made an impact. The murder rate in Birmingham has decreased by 30 percent in each of the past two years, and the mayor and police chief have publicly credited the churches in Birmingham for making the difference.

Willow Creek Community Church has a history of creating and executing comprehensive plans, but that doesn't keep the church from responding opportunistically to God. In the fall of 2011, the church broke ground on a $10 million "care center" to house its growing ministry to the poor in northwest Chicago. What is interesting is that this project was not part of Willow's strategic plan. The church's care ministries, primarily a food bank and its CARS program (receiving and repairing donated cars and then giving them to low-income single moms), had been housed at separate off-site locations. The demand for services had grown steadily, and these ministries actually had waiting lists of volunteers who wanted to get involved.

As the congregation's leaders saw this picture emerging, they felt God inviting them to join Him in even bigger ways. The proposal for an expanded, on-campus care center was taken to the church's elders, who prayed and fasted for thirty days. "God was so clear to that group of people, so quickly," says Greg Hawkins. "The evidence was clear, the movement of God was clear. Leadership said absolutely." As a result, Willow expects to add medical care, crisis pregnancy counseling, and other services and dramatically increase the number of people it assists. Willow also has a target to expand its volunteer base from seven hundred to three thousand individuals, knowing that as its members serve in these ministries, they will grow deeper in their faith.

God can surprise and redirect plans in many different ways. Grace Fellowship had intentionally and obediently put aside funds for several years for a new church plant, even as it was continuing to grow rapidly on its own. When the target of $300,000 was in hand, the search began for a pastor to lead the daughter church. The process was so effective that two outstanding candidates were identified. As the leaders wrestled with the decision of which one to call, Jim Leggett's fifteen-year-old son asked his father, "Why don't we ask both of them to come and plant two churches?" Of course, there was only one problem with this: Grace only had the funds for one plant. A few days later, one of the church's key lay leaders asked the same question. Leggett felt God speaking clearly to him through these two separate conversations, and yet it was hard to imagine how they could make the finances work, especially since they had just moved into a new worship center. But Leggett led the church to step out in faith, trusting that this was God's clear leading. Both pastors were hired, and nine months later, the church closed its fiscal year with enough surplus in its operating budget to fund the second church plant.

God's intervention is a critical element that Christian leaders must recognize in developing and executing plans. It is the reason that many of the leaders I interviewed found it difficult to develop long-range plans. Whether a congregation has a fully developed strategic plan or only a general idea of where it is going, the way it responds to surprises is a great indicator of the Holy Spirit's work in its midst.

FOCUSED ENERGY

The evidence of Spirit-led planning may be seen in a willingness to change plans; it may also be seen in a single-minded focus to see a plan through to completion and not be distracted by other "opportunities." Every ministry faces the imbalance of having more good ideas than resources to pursue and implement those ideas. It is the spiritual leader's job to discern which ideas are simply good and which ones are truly from God.

Many of the leaders with whom I spoke are visionaries. Their big dreams and boundless energy are what God has used to build great churches, to inspire others to make sacrificial commitments and join them in this endeavor. The tendency of these types of leaders is look to the next bold initiative, even before the ink is dry on the plans for the current one. So I was interested how these leaders felt about the constraints that come with making plans. Tim Lundy says, that compared to the other members of Fellowship's leadership team, "I am much more spontaneous. I like the new thing that's out there. I can't tell you how many times I've said, 'Let's do that,' and someone says, 'How does that fit in the planning process?'"

How has Lundy responded? "I've thought, 'If I hear that one more time, I'm going to puke!'" So as the directional leader, does he overrule these objections? Lundy realizes that "more times than not, [the constraints of the plan] protect me. I say that not as a person that particularly likes it but as a person who wants to see God move here and wants to be very spontaneous. I've seen the wisdom in this."

Does this mean that Fellowship follows its plans in a rigid and unwavering manner? Lundy explains, "We are open to surprises. We've had times when God stirred in our hearts in the middle of a year and we realized we needed to go in a different direction, even though that meant blowing up part of the plan. We know what the true impact will be. We need to be the first to let go of our plans when God asks us to do that." Fellowship is willing to let go, but an effective planning process has helped the church avoid doing too many different things and has kept it focused on its main priorities.

Dino Rizzo of Healing Place Church is one of the most entrepreneurial and spontaneous leaders that I interviewed. The story of this seventeen-year-old church is one of constantly adding ministries to serve the people of Baton Rouge and far beyond—significant ministry to the poor, international campuses, and a tremendous disaster response capability. Is it possible for a spontaneous leader, one who is wired to say yes, to become more focused? When I asked about this, Rizzo replied, "If we don't say no some, we won't be able to say good yeses. We're learning this as a staff. I'm learning this as a pastor." His motivation is for the church's leaders "to be faithful stewards of what God has put in our hands and make the best Kingdom investment we can." For Healing Place, that has meant reducing the number of countries in which it is involved by about half, to fifteen. It has also meant consolidating campuses, turning down some assistance and partnership requests, and ending ministries that are no longer effective.

Kevin Jenkins, president of World Vision International, has a temperament at the opposite end of the spectrum from Rizzo's. Jenkins is a lawyer and businessperson by training and was the president of Canadian Airlines earlier in his career. But Jenkins echoes the same theme as Rizzo when it comes to focus. He says that "strategy is identity," and that means that World Vision must be crystal clear about "who we are and who God is calling us to be." Jenkins says, "People have a hard time with the question 'What should we stop doing?' because everything you're doing is good." For Jenkins, however, it is not a question of whether something is good. He wants the organization to answer "Is this what we're called to be doing?" The clarity that comes from asking and answering this question can even lead his organization to walk away from funding offers that are not consistent with its identity. World Vision's focus does not have the same financially driven edge that would be found in business. If that were the case, it would operate in far fewer countries. Nevertheless, Jenkins is mindful of the danger of spreading out too thin by chasing good ideas.

The best leaders in the business world know the importance of focus. Jim Collins points to the way that many leaders seem obsessed with adding more to their plates, a habit that is rarely successful. According to Collins, the best leaders "made as much use of 'stop doing' lists as 'to do' lists. They displayed a remarkable discipline to unplug all sorts of extraneous junk."[7]

Is this another leadership principle from the marketplace that we need to scrutinize? According to Andy Stanley, this principle is actually much older than Jim Collins and much more biblical. In *Visioneering*, Stanley follows the story of Nehemiah and his God-inspired vision to rebuild the walls of Jerusalem. When his opponents summon him to a meeting in a renewed effort to stop the project, Nehemiah responds, "I am doing a great work and I cannot come down. Why should the work stop while I leave it and come down to you?" (Nehemiah 6:3).

Stanley explains, "Nehemiah knew what he was about was a God thing. It was an important thing. He was doing a *great* work. He didn't have time for a meeting. He would not allow himself to be distracted from his *great* work. He would stay focused. . . . He would be relentless about this thing God had called him to do." And then Stanley gives his readers a pointed application: "Every day of your life, every day of my life, opportunities come along that have the potential to distract us from the main things that God has called us to do."[8] The best leaders and organizations are clear about the great work that God has placed before them. This gives them resolve to say no to other work, and it empowers them to say yes if and when God truly leads them in a new direction.

REDEFINING FAILURE

When corporate executives evaluate a new initiative, they will consider the "facts" and recommendations and then make a decision whether to proceed. Of course, facts are not always accurate, and the people implementing the plan are not infallible, so business plans may fail. When this happens, good leaders ask "why?" In some cases, the "why" question may lead to the dismissal of an individual who did a poor job in planning or leading the effort. In many cases, the company chalks it up as a lesson learned and moves on, expecting to do better in the future. Peter Senge says, "Failure is an opportunity for learning. . . . Failures are not about our unworthiness or powerlessness."[9] Business experts know that creating an environment that encourages risk taking and accepts the occasional but inevitable failure is important for a company's long-term success.

As spiritual leaders, our faith should give us a huge advantage compared to our marketplace counterparts when a plan "fails." We have the benefit of knowing that our true worth is not defined by the success or failure of a plan. The fact that we are children of God and that nothing can separate us from His love is far greater than anything we might accomplish on earth. This assurance should also help us avoid the human tendency to blame others rather than learning from setbacks.

In dealing with failure, however, we also face two troubling issues. The first is that our work has eternal significance. Rich Stearns of World Vision was formerly CEO of Lennox, which produces and sells fine china. When times were tough at Lennox, he would sometimes say, "Relax, it's only dishes. If we sell a few less, the world won't end." Now that he is leading World Vision, failing to meet a goal matters much more to Stearns. "It really is a life-or-death thing. If we lower overhead by two percent, that might mean a thousand lives could be saved. There's a lot at stake because of the nature of the ministry we have." Whether you are in a global compassion ministry or a local church, whether you are in a first or second chair role, your work matters, and the consequences of failure will feel significant.

A second issue is a spiritual crisis that can arise out of failure. If we have poured our prayers and our hearts into a plan that we believe will advance the Kingdom, only to see it fail or fall short, it can leave us feeling defeated and can shake us on a deep spiritual level. If the plan has been birthed out of a season of seeking the Lord, then how should we interpret its lack of success? If we're not careful, we can allow this failure to undermine our faith. It is inevitable that we will fall short at times, but we can lean on God's grace to keep from being crushed.

Greg Hawkins has a great perspective on this issue: "God never said, 'Do this because it will work.' He says, 'Do it because you want to obey me.' " When plans don't work, Hawkins reviews them to understand what he can learn and what he can do differently in the future. He also asks, "By whose standard did it fail?" Perhaps God is using a different standard for success than we are. At the end of the day, Hawkins knows he can let go of the outcome if the process has been authentic and spiritual.

A pronouncement of failure may be premature in some instances, as Cross Point Church discovered with two of its new campuses. In one case, the campus was launched with high expectations and a correspondingly large budget. After a few months, attendance and giving were below target, and the campus was running a much larger deficit than expected. Was this a failure? Did Cross Point need to pull the plug on the campus? Executive director Jenni Catron explains that the leadership team took a hard look at the numbers but also recognized the many positive spiritual signs and ultimately decided that the campus should continue its ministry. Catron worked with the campus pastor to streamline the cost structure, and within a few months, it was operating in the black while continuing to reach people with the gospel.

Another Cross Point campus was scheduled to launch at the beginning of 2010 but ran into a number of roadblocks in site acquisition and preparation. When it became clear that it would not be possible to open in January, the optimal time for a launch, the church's leaders wondered what to do. They were convinced that God still wanted them to proceed, so they made plans to open in the middle of May, just before the normal summer slump. Two weeks before the campus was scheduled to open, Nashville experienced its worst flooding in a century, and the new site was in the middle of the area that was hit the hardest. The Bellvue campus, which had not even held its first worship service, became a hub for flood relief and immediately established a presence in its community by being the hands and feet of Christ to people in need of help. Fortunately, Cross Point didn't apply the "failure" label too quickly in either case.

When a plan does fail, leaders must choose what message to communicate to the organization. Dave Ferguson, lead pastor of Community Christian Church and one of the innovators of the multisite movement, reflected on how his church processed the closing of a campus. In a churchwide leadership meeting, the staff members from the closed campus were brought on stage. Ferguson then told the entire audience, "We all agree that this [new campus] is something we were supposed to do. [These campus leaders] had the courage to do it, and we were behind them. We don't know exactly why it didn't work, but the most important thing is that God is calling all of us to take risks and be faithful. Every one of these people who is standing in front of you right now was faithful to the mission, and I want you to express your appreciation to them." In private, Ferguson and his team did what good leaders do: they "conducted an autopsy" to understand what factors had caused the campus to "fail" so that they could learn and avoid making the same mistakes in the future. This story illustrates the balance of having faith in God despite setbacks and at the same time striving to do one's best with the abilities and resources that God has given.

It's one thing if the purported failure is actually just a delay or if it only affects one part of the overall ministry, but how should a pastor respond when the entire plan is derailed? That's the question that Greg Wallace had to answer. Sand Creek Mission was a small, struggling, four-year-old church in Houston when Wallace came as its bivocational pastor in 1992. Under his leadership, the church grew steadily, built its first facilities, and changed its name to Woodridge Baptist Church. Wallace left his corporate job in 1999 to become the church's full-time pastor, and the congregation continued to grow. By 2007, average weekly worship attendance was eleven hundred in four worship services on a campus that was rapidly approaching its capacity.

Wallace and the church's leaders felt that God was leading them to relocate, so they obtained the congregation's approval and bought a fifty-one-acre site. Then the obstacles started to mount. A longtime, very popular youth minister left to plant a church. A megachurch in the city launched a campus in the community where Woodridge was located. And the crowning blow came when they discovered that the new land had deed restrictions, undisclosed by the seller, that would require a lengthy legal process before the church could build. The wave of excitement and momentum rapidly slipped away.

Over the next few months, the congregation's leaders concluded that God was telling them "no," or at least "not now." So they shifted gears and dealt with the space problems on their existing campus by building a new sanctuary and converting the old sanctuary into youth space. Sounds like a great story of taking lemons and making lemonade, right? During that same period, however, the church lost two hundred fifty members and another key staff member left. Once in the new space, the church experimented with changing its worship style in an effort to reach younger adults, but this was not successful.

Wallace, a former corporate executive, says, "The last three or four years are the first time in my adult life that I haven't been highly successful." This is the kind of story that can send any leader into a deep tailspin, so how did Wallace respond? "Studying more, reading more, praying more," while at the same time asking the hard questions of what needed to change and rolling up his sleeves to rebuild the congregation. He conveys a deep faith that God is still in control, an optimism that Woodridge has regained its momentum in recent months, and a belief that God still intends for the congregation to grow and eventually to relocate. He is a picture of a leader who is driven to succeed but whose faith isn't dependent on success as defined by society.

Ultimately, the way Christian leaders handle failure is closely related to how they handle success. They may say, "Give God the credit" when things are going well, but is that what they truly feel deep in their souls? In reality, too many leaders want the credit for themselves and feel their efforts are responsible for the success of the endeavor. If that is true, then the failure of other programs must also rest on their shoulders. Whether we are dealing with success or failure, pursuing God-inspired plans or reacting to God-directed detours, we would all do well to remember that God is in charge.

WHAT ARE YOU PURSUING?

- How would you answer the question in the chapter title: Are your plans fruitful?
- As you read the stories in this chapter, is there one kind of fruit that is found most often in your organization's plans? One that is missing?
- Have there been times when the Spirit has prompted you to act boldly? To wait? To detour? How have you responded?
- Reflect on a time when a plan "failed." What might you have done differently? How did you handle the setback?

CHAPTER FIVE

WHO IS ON THE BUS?

Grace versus stewardship. When I asked Christian leaders about their practices related to human resource (HR) management, this tension was mentioned over and over. An exciting plan for the future is important, but the way people are managed affects their willingness to follow just as much as a compelling vision. Jim Kouzes and Barry Posner declare, "Leadership is a relationship between those who aspire to lead and those who choose to follow. It's the quality of this relationship that matters most when we're engaged in getting extraordinary things done."[1] Yet when it comes to finding and managing people to achieve the best results, and dealing with those who fall short, Christian leaders often struggle.

Jim Collins's *Good to Great* research found that great companies had a "first who, then what" philosophy. He says the great companies "*first* got the right people on the bus (and the wrong people off the bus) and *then* figured out where to drive it."[2] In other words, having the right people is more important than having the right strategy. When I did a Google search on the phrase "right people on the bus," the result was over two million hits. Collins's catchphrase is widely known, in the business world and the nonprofit arena, by people who have read his book and by people who have never heard of him. Being widely known, however, does not mean that leaders have figured out how to apply this principle.

Leaders of churches and Christian organizations, in particular, struggle with the harsh edge they hear in Collins's findings. They are in favor of getting the right people on the bus, but they wonder if getting the wrong people off the bus is a Christ-like response. Randy Frazee, senior minister of Oak Hills Church in San Antonio, Texas, says, "The concept of getting 'the right people on the bus' [aligns with] Romans 12, that you need to use your gifts according to your measure of faith." He continues, "The language of on-off the bus is an appropriate analogy, but the church, in addition to being an organization, should function as a family. In other words, every member of the body is equally valued." Frazee's use of the family metaphor highlights the challenge we all face.

Houston Baptist University's Robert Sloan has been around Christian leaders—in academia, denominational bodies, and local churches—for his entire career and has observed their struggles in this area. He notes, "Christian leaders have a very difficult time with personnel decisions. There's a pretty soft view among Christian leaders as to what constitutes redemption or grace or love or forgiveness because our thinking is so muddled on those issues. Christian leaders have a hard time making personnel decisions and dealing forthrightly with personnel problems."

If you are leading in a setting that is not multistaff, you may think that this chapter does not apply to you. It is true that certain aspects of HR relate only to employees and that the illustrations on the following pages refer to paid staff, but an organization with only one paid position has volunteers who are functioning as staff in many respects. Whether a person is paid or unpaid, leaders must face the challenges of selection, motivation, management, and at times separation. As leaders, we will all wrestle at times with grace and stewardship.

GRACE VERSUS STEWARDSHIP: DO WE HAVE TO CHOOSE?

I don't know how many times I have heard the leader of a Christian organization say, "We err on the side of grace when it comes to making tough personnel decisions." In other words, when people are not meeting performance expectations, these leaders will give them extra chances to improve, change their duties, or even lower the requirements of their jobs. But I have also heard a number of leaders explain their philosophy by saying, "It's a stewardship issue. We've been entrusted with precious resources, and it's my responsibility as a leader to use these resources effectively." In essence, they are saying it is bad stewardship to pay people who are not doing the jobs they were hired to do. Both arguments have deep biblical roots. So must we choose between grace and stewardship?

IT'S ALL ABOUT GRACE

In describing Seacoast Church's practices, Geoff Surratt says, "We are much more grace-filled than you would see in a business. It's hard to get fired here." Who can argue with grace? After all, it's at the core of our faith. Not only does salvation come by God's grace, but the gifts we have received and the ways in which we are called to serve are solely through His grace. In Ephesians 3 and 4, Paul refers to his own ministry and to the offices of the church as being gifts of grace. If our theology is right and our relationship with God is deep, we should constantly pinch ourselves in amazement at all the manifestations of God's grace in our lives, including the leadership roles with which we have been entrusted. As Willow Creek's Greg Hawkins says, "God in His sovereignty is showing me all the ways that things turn out well in spite of me. I shouldn't be doing what I'm doing."

God's grace is the foundation on which other biblical teachings about relationships are built. The Bible is full of verses and stories that talk about love for one another, forgiveness, reconciliation, and the like. The capstone verse on relationships that many of us learned as children is Ephesians 4:32: "Be kind and compassionate to one another, forgiving each other, just as in Christ God forgave you."

Our deep sense of gratitude for God's grace and the clear biblical teaching on relationships should permeate every aspect of our lives. So what does this mean about the way that Christian managers should treat employees? It means that our HR practices should reflect grace, second chances, forgiveness, and love. But does it mean that we cannot hold people accountable for poor performance? Perhaps this is exactly the kind of "muddled thinking" that Robert Sloan described.

The Call to Good Stewardship

What is "success" to you? When I asked Mitch Peairson, executive pastor of Grace Fellowship, he answered with the question he asks himself: "How are we doing in stewarding what has been entrusted to us—the staff, the volunteers, the finances, the facilities?" It is a question that weighs on most leaders. On a personal level, every believer is called to be a good steward of the gifts and resources entrusted to him or her by God. For individuals in positions of leadership, being good stewards also means making wise use of the collective resources of the organization.

The parable of the talents in Matthew 25 is the classic passage on being good stewards. As leaders, none of us wants to be like the servant who was rebuked by the master because he hid his one talent in the ground and failed to earn any return. And while we might not tolerate a deadbeat employee, many of us find staff members falling far short of the "double your investment" productivity demonstrated by the other two servants in the parable.

When we think of stewardship as it relates to staff, we immediately think of the cost of salary and benefits. But compensation alone is not the extent of the stewardship issue. An underperforming employee requires more management attention, which leaves less time available to develop lay leaders, launch new initiatives, or attend to a host of other priorities. Performance problems tend to spill over into the broader organization. Other staff members may lose motivation because a colleague is "getting away with" consistent shortfalls, or volunteers may get frustrated when they work with someone who doesn't care about excellence. If the poor performer eventually leaves (voluntarily or otherwise), there is the additional cost of turnover. Some business experts estimate that the cost of employee turnover—to find, hire, and train a replacement—is equal to one-and-a-half times the person's annual salary. It is clear that managing staff well is a big stewardship issue.

Practicing Grace *and* Stewardship

We do not have to choose between grace and stewardship. The arguments up to this point are not full representations of either. Let's start with a more complete picture of grace. No one will argue that parents are to love their children deeply and unconditionally. But we would never say that unconditional love means giving them anything and everything they want. Nor does it mean an absence of correction. My love for my children is to abound in grace, but this will be expressed in encouragement, forgiveness, boundaries, and discipline.

To think that grace in employer-employee relationships means accepting poor performance is the same as thinking that "unconditional love" means never disciplining my child. In *Courageous Leadership*, Bill Hybels explains, "Extending grace does not mean closing our eyes to the truth in order to 'be nice' or to avoid uncomfortable conversations or tough decisions. Grace does not mean that we should carry a staff person who isn't performing adequately."[3]

Some people may think that "getting the wrong people off the bus" sounds ruthless and lacking in grace. But Jim Collins makes an important distinction between rigorous and ruthless practices. He explains, "To let people languish in uncertainty for months or years, stealing precious time in their lives that they could use to move on to something else, when in the end they aren't going to make it anyway—*that* would be ruthless. To deal with it right up front and let people get on with their lives—that is *rigorous*."[4] For Collins, a rigorous process is fair and consistent, and it is in the best interests of the company and the employee. I suspect that spiritual leaders will always struggle with how to handle performance problems, but they should do so with a complete understanding of grace.

What about stewardship? When we define it narrowly, we focus on the financial impact of poor performance. This is obviously a large and important consideration, but it is not the only one. As leaders, we also have a stewardship responsibility for the people that we are called to shepherd. If we focus too much on the financial side of the equation, we can overlook the even more important human factor. Geoff Surratt comments, "We can either make our decisions based on money and dishonor people, or we can make our decisions based on people and not squeeze the dollar quite as tight." Stewardship is much more than a financial responsibility for Christian leaders.

It is possible to practice grace and stewardship simultaneously. Dave Ferguson of Community Christian Church says, "On a scale of 1 to 10, God created everybody to be a 10. If [certain people] are not a 10, they're in the wrong spot or we've not given them the tools they need." When true grace and stewardship are combined, leaders do not say, "It's OK to be a 5." Instead they say, "Your job is not in jeopardy because you're a 5 today, but we are committed to helping you become a 10, and you need to have the same commitment."

Grace versus stewardship is the most pronounced tension related to managing staff, but it is not the only one. Grace versus truth is another tension that Christian leaders wrestle with. Some leaders are hesitant to confront poor performance. In the worst cases, a leader may redo the work of a subordinate rather than letting the person know of the problem. This and other kinds of conflict-avoiding behavior are done in the name of being "kind and compassionate." When we do this, however, we ignore the additional teachings in Ephesians 4 to "speak the truth in love" and "put off falsehood and speak truthfully." Leaders need to balance grace and truth, not ignore one or the other.

One other tension that Christian leaders may experience is redemption versus realism. Because we believe in God's redemptive and transforming power, we should never label another human being as a "lost cause." In employment situations, "next time will be different" and "give him another chance" are phrases that convey the redemption mind-set. I am quick to affirm God's ability to change anyone, but we must also be realistic. If a person has shown no aptitude for a job or has shown little progress after multiple chances, it is unlikely that he or she will succeed. The same is true with hiring decisions. Greg Holder of The Crossing says, "We're big believers in God's healing and restoring." The Crossing has hired people who were deeply wounded in prior ministry settings, believing things would be different in a healthier environment. Holder has been disappointed when some of these individuals were unable to function effectively, which leads him to say, "We need to be very realistic about someone's chance to succeed."

Pastor *and* Manager

The tension of grace versus stewardship directly affects the role of the leader in a Christian organization. Rich Stearns, who had been the CEO of two large corporations, says one of his biggest realizations after becoming president of World Vision was that the staff was looking for "a spiritual leader." Stearns explains, "The president was the person who was going to inspire them, cast a Christian vision for the work that we do together, and expound on the spiritual principles that undergird our ministry." For Stearns, it was "a very new and somewhat uncomfortable realization that I couldn't just be a smart business guy, that my legitimacy would also have to include spiritual legitimacy." Other leaders experience the opposite challenge. They are comfortable with the spiritual dimension, but they feel ill-prepared for the managerial expertise that their organization needs.

There is nothing inherently wrong with an expectation that Christian leaders should be pastor and manager, but few people are adept at both roles. As Stearns explains, "The Christian culture gets confusing. You'll have devotions and pray with someone in the morning. In the afternoon, you might have to terminate them or put them on probation or give them a tough performance review." In the business arena, no one expects the boss to be pastoral. I once heard a human resource manager advise pastors against becoming too involved in the lives of their employees. In essence, she said that they should deal with performance issues in a detached manner because you can't be pastor and manager at the same time. The audience disagreed strongly. The best Christian leaders are always striving to do both, no matter how difficult that may be.

"We're Not a Business"

When a Christian leader is talking about a personnel matter and says, "The church is not a business," what does this mean? Specifically, what does this leader think "business" does that is contrary to the way human resources should be managed within a Christian organization? Beyond the obvious spiritual difference, this statement usually refers to an underlying belief that businesses are heartless, rigid, or overquantified. Are these perceptions accurate? In truth, when it comes to personnel practices, the gap between great businesses and great Christian organizations is narrower than you might think.

Heartless?

We have all known people who were chewed up and spit out by large corporations. Perhaps they received an unfair performance appraisal that led to their termination or reassignment into a dreary job. Or they may have survived a "downsizing" only to find that they were expected to do the work of three people with no regard for their personal life. Maybe they had an abusive boss or a miserable job with no opportunity to escape. Or perhaps the corporate culture encouraged cutthroat competition between employees who wanted to advance.

Many people think this is "just the way business operates"—employees are cogs in a big machine whose sole purpose is to make money. In this view, ruthless competition is a form of survival of the fittest so that the best employees can be identified and promoted, and the firing of poor performers is necessary and justified. Some companies do operate this way, but is this what the "best practices" from business suggest?

The advice from leading business thinkers sounds surprisingly biblical and is a striking departure from the heartless image. Consider these examples:

- Jim Collins acknowledges that great companies are demanding places to work, but he reveals something you may not expect: "The good-to-great leaders, however, would not rush to judgment. Often, they invested substantial effort in determining whether they had someone in the wrong seat before concluding that they had the wrong person on the bus entirely."[5]
- Patrick Lencioni says that anonymity is one of the "three signs of a miserable job." He counsels, "All human beings need to be understood and appreciated for their unique qualities by someone in a position of authority."[6]
- Kouzes and Posner break the stereotype of the domineering leader by stating, "A leader-constituent relationship that's characterized by fear and distrust will never, ever produce anything of lasting value. A relationship characterized by mutual respect and confidence will overcome the greatest adversities and leave a legacy of significance."[7]

- Kouzes and Posner also note, "Managerial myth says leaders shouldn't get too close to their constituents, that they can't be friends with people at work. Well, set this myth aside. . . . People are just more willing to follow someone they like and trust."[8]

Some businesses may have environments and practices that are harsh for employees, but the great ones have a culture with many Christian attributes.

RIGID?

Are corporate HR practices always governed by unbending rules—rules for how to hire, promote, evaluate, discipline, compensate, do a job, and so on? There is some degree of truth in this perception, especially in large businesses with thousands of employees. Some of the rules are dictated by governmental regulations, and others are created for the sake of efficiency or fairness. For example, if a company hires dozens of people each year for a certain type of position, it makes sense to have standards—rules—for how to evaluate and compensate these candidates rather than treating each as a unique case.

Some companies go far beyond efficiency in their rule orientation. They create structures and processes that are designed to maintain control over staff. Collins found that "most companies build their bureaucratic rules to manage the small percentage of wrong people on the bus."[9] The best companies, however, find the right balance of rules and freedom to allow their people to thrive. They know that tight control is not necessary if the right people and a clear vision are in place.

The perception of rigid rules is more a function of size than whether an entity is a business or a church. In practice, a church is more like a small, family-owned business than a corporation. In a small business, each person may have a different job, but everyone wears more than one hat and pitches in to make the company successful. Many of the policies and processes that are found in corporations don't exist in family businesses, or they are less formal. So if a key lay leader says, "This is what we do in my (large) company," don't reject the suggestion outright. Instead, try to understand how it might be adjusted to work in your situation.

OVERQUANTIFIED?

The critics who reject corporate HR practices believe that businesses rely too much on quantitative measures. Numbers are everywhere in business—a required score on an assessment tool to qualify for a job, a quota for the number of sales calls made, a ranking system that determines promotions and raises. Even the best businesses have scorecards for evaluating success at the corporate and individual levels.

Many Christian leaders are inherently skeptical of this quantitative approach, an issue that we will explore in more depth in Chapter Six. They believe that you cannot assign a number to some of the most important factors related to staff performance. Business expert Patrick Lencioni knows that measurement is important for motivating people, but he observes, "In many cases, trying to overquantify measurables by assigning strictly numerical metrics makes them irrelevant because the metric is artificial. The most effective and appropriate measurements are often behavioral in nature."[10] Once again, we see that the gap between secular and sacred organizations may not be quite as wide as we had thought.

RECOGNIZING THE REAL GAPS

Even though many best practices for HR may be transferrable from business to church, leaders must never lose sight of one important dynamic. Personnel issues are always messier in a church than in business because of the ways that people are connected. In the marketplace, there is a clear distinction and relatively little connection between the three major constituent groups: customers, employees, and shareholders. Even when a connection exists, the relationships are typically superficial. As a result, the effects of personnel changes—when an employee is fired or moved to a new assignment—are limited.

In congregations, the employee (organist, youth pastor, receptionist) often has deep relationships with certain members and key lay leaders. This makes all personnel decisions much more complicated. If an employee is disciplined or terminated, an inaccurate version of the story may be circulated, causing divisions or other tensions. Church leaders may feel pressured to hire a member who is a "nice person," irrespective of his or her qualifications for the job. Of course, church staff will also frequently go far beyond the call of duty because they love their church.

The relational webs will always be a distinguishing characteristic for Christian organizations, but this should not be an excuse for sloppy HR practices. Al Lopus, president of Best Christian Workplaces Institute, says, "Christian organizations should set the standard as the best, most effective places to work in the world." In the institute's surveys, however, many Christian organizations fall far short of being the "best places to work." Lopus explains that the biggest frustration among employees in Christian organizations is a lack of effective management. This includes the processes for attracting, directing, motivating, and developing staff. Lopus sees a "dramatic reluctance" by Christian organizations to adapt best practices from businesses because the leaders "see processes and procedures and policies as anti-Christian."

Just as God is displeased if a church operates exactly like a business, He must be displeased if we are poor managers of the valuable resource we have in our employees. Don't let the differences between church and business become handcuffs that hinder you from accomplishing what God wants you to do for and through the people you manage.

Practices That Keep the Bus Rolling

If you stop and think, it is amazing that the personnel practices in most Christian organizations are so sloppy. After all, most of these entities spend half or more of their budget on salaries and benefits. In addition to this financial cost, our "business" is people, and our success depends on people doing their jobs with passion and excellence. Our organizations should be known as outstanding places to work, but most Christian organizations place little emphasis on human resource infrastructure and practices.

In contrast, the best businesses invest heavily in their HR practices. You may think, "Of course, but they can afford to do so." Keep in mind that these same companies are focused on profit—they spend money only if they see a benefit. They invest because they know that a bad hiring decision has repercussions that extend far beyond the immediate employee. They know that low morale or uncertainty about evaluation criteria will drag down organizational effectiveness.

We will never get every hiring decision right or know exactly what every person needs for his or her development, but Christian organizations can do far better simply by giving more attention to their HR practices. The biggest leaps forward can come from creating clarity around roles and expectations, investing on the front end of the employment process, and adopting a coaching mind-set. And of course, Christian organizations can learn a lot about how their secular counterparts respond when someone truly is "the wrong person on the bus." In the remainder of this chapter, each of these topics will be examined further. A number of additional tips for HR practices are presented in Appendix B.

CREATE CLARITY

Why is it that organizations that depend on clear external communication often do such a poor job internally? The proclamation of biblical truths is a central element in churches. Delivering a compelling vision is a vital part of setting direction and enlisting support (financial and volunteer) in Christian organizations. Yet clarity is often lacking in the day-to-day management of staff.

The Gallup organization conducted extensive research to discover best practices in managing people, and the results were published in *First, Break All the Rules*. Authors Marcus Buckingham and Curt Coffman identify the most powerful questions that correlate with employee satisfaction. At the top of the list is a simple question, "Do I know what is expected of me at work?"[11] When answered in the affirmative, this is one of just a handful of factors that separate great managers from those who are average. It seems like a basic question, doesn't it? But stop and ask yourself how the people who work for you would answer.

Across the breadth of Christian organizations, you will find many employees who say, "I don't really know what is expected of me in my job." Clarity is often lacking from the very beginning of the hiring process, when the duties and expectations of the job are not well defined. When priorities shift, as they often do in small organizations, staff members and volunteers may not understand how or why their responsibilities have changed. The criteria against which they will be assessed are often vague because measurable objectives and evaluation processes are missing.

Dino Rizzo says that Healing Place Church is currently on the ground floor but has a new focus on the development of formal HR practices. With so many ministry opportunities, why has the church decided to make this a priority? Rizzo says, "It helps the staff have more clarity. What's good for that person is good for us. It's about creating life-giving tracks for people to work in."

As I wrote this section on clarity, I had my own church in mind. In the previous year, we had a transition in senior pastors, added staff, and developed a new vision. Even though these changes were greeted enthusiastically, we repeatedly heard one cry from the staff: "We need clarity." Our leadership team was tempted to say, "It's clear enough," but we realized that a lack of clarity kept the staff from doing their jobs well. They needed us to define "dotted line" reporting relationships, priorities and expectations for their jobs, and authority for decision making. Simply by listening to them and making strides toward clarity, we saw morale and productivity improve.

Most of this chapter is written from the perspective of the pastor, executive pastor, or other organizational leader who directly manages people, but let me say a word to lay leaders and board members. The first chair leader in your organization does not have a "boss," at least not like other employees. One of the greatest gifts you can give this leader is clarity—about the expectations for the role, standards for evaluation, what is working well, and what concerns you have. One of the needless tragedies in Christian organizations is when leaders lose their jobs and never see it coming. The issue of lay and staff leaders getting on the same page is the focus of Chapter Nine, but you can start now by creating clarity.

INVEST ON THE FRONT END

Any church leader with more than a couple of years of experience can tell at least one horror story that began with a hiring mistake. It is not easy to find and hire good people at any level in an organization, from senior leadership to administrative and custodial positions. Because hiring well takes so much time and effort, churches often cut corners in the process. But no matter how much you invest on the front end to get someone on board, it pales in comparison to the time and cost associated with a bad hiring decision.

By contrast, good hiring decisions can propel the organization forward. The same church leaders who tell horror stories of past mistakes can testify to the incredible lift that one well-placed person can provide to the organization. Buckingham and Coffman note, "Casting for talent is one of the unwritten secrets to the success of great managers."[12] We will never have a 100 percent success rate at bringing people onto our staffs, but we should all ask, "How can I make the best possible hiring decisions?"

To start, senior leaders must recognize that the process of finding the right people and getting them on board is one of the most important things they will do. If they have that mind-set, they will personally invest in the process and will expect the same of others. As the leaders at Christ Fellowship evaluate candidates, they ask, "If this is not the best person in the world for this job, why should we settle for less?" Churches that invest in the front end cast a wide net looking for great people, evaluate them thoroughly, and help them understand their role over the first few months. Some churches require detailed written applications or present a covenant to prospective staff members as part of this process. In contrast, many Christian organizations look at only one or two candidates or make their decisions after a one-hour interview. That is not enough time for employer or employee to make a well-informed decision.

Todd Mullins at Christ Fellowship emphasizes a high level of competence in hiring decisions, but he is quick to recognize that competence alone is not enough. Bill Hybels's "three C's"—"character, chemistry, and competence"[13]—are used at Christ Fellowship and in many other churches as a basis for evaluating potential staff. Hybels brings an important counterbalance to the business mind-set that says that the stuff on a person's résumé—educational background, experience, accomplishments—is all that matters. Peter Greer of HOPE International says, "We put a lot of credence in 'get the right people on the bus and get them in the right seats,' but for us the most importance piece isn't technical competence; it's attitude and humility and someone who's sold out for the cause of Christ." Jim Mellado of the Willow Creek Association has seen how important this is. He reflects, "When we've measured and overvalued the expertise and experience and undermeasured and undervalued the need for significant spiritual maturity, we've paid every time." Someone may be a star performer in terms of ministry competence, but if he or she does not display Christian character, it will leave a trail of damaged relationships that will hurt the organization every time.

This leads to the dynamic that is most different for Christian leaders compared to their counterparts in business: spiritual discernment in the hiring process. When I interviewed Jeff Wells, WoodsEdge Community Church was searching for a person to fill a senior-level position. Regarding this search, he said, "I'm doing almost everything that corporate America would do; I'm just trying to do it with a lot of prayer and a lot of dependence on God." Someone may look ideal on paper and in interviews, but if something in your spirit is squelching your enthusiasm about bringing the candidate onto your staff, put on the brakes. After all, the person you hire for any position is more than an employee; he or she will become a co-laborer in ministry and an integral part of your faith community.

A prayerful process could even cause you to leave a role vacant despite what seems to be an urgent need. When The Crossing launched its Fenton, Missouri, campus (described in Chapter Four), the church had not found the right person for the campus pastor role. A year later, the campus had grown to a thousand in worship attendance and was still looking for this leader. Church leaders knew it was better to leave the position open and wait on God rather than to rush and fill it with the wrong person.

Alternatively, you may feel a strong leading from God to move forward with a person who does not fit your ideal profile. As Randy Frazee points out, "God will sometimes pick the least likely candidate by which to bring about a victory so as to point to the glory and power of God, not the natural abilities of the person." We should have a clear idea of what we're looking for in the ideal candidate, but we shouldn't be slaves to this profile if God leads in a different direction.

Hiring processes should be thorough and prayerful, but they will never be perfect. As Jim Collins says, "There is no perfect interviewing technique, no ideal hiring method; even the best executives make hiring mistakes." That is why Collins notes, "In the social sectors, where getting the wrong people off the bus can be more difficult than in a business, early assessment mechanisms turn out to be more important than hiring mechanisms."[14] Those early assessment mechanisms are part of the coaching mind-set.

ADOPT A COACHING MIND-SET

Every once in a while, a new staff person hits the ground running with just the right set of skills, an uncanny intuition that enables him or her to make all the right decisions, and an immediate connection with the people that builds powerful relationships. But only every once in a while—probably less than 5 percent of the time. So why do Christian organizations operate as if this will happen 95 percent of the time? Sports teams have coaches for a good reason. Someone needs to get the most out of the players and decide who should be in the game so that the team can succeed. Why do we not invest the time to coach staff members for success?

The best managers in the corporate world know that this is important. Remember that "I know what is expected of me at work" is the most important response to the questions on Buckingham and Coffman's list. Employees who are able to say this are more likely to be engaged in their jobs. Three other questions in the top six are "Do I have the opportunity to do what I do best every day?" "In the last seven days, have I received recognition or praise for good work?" and "Is there someone at work who encourages my development?"[15] Good managers are actively involved in positioning their staff for success. They do it by creating an environment in which clarity, a positive spirit, and personal growth are the norm. As Kouzes and Posner found, "Leaders get their best from others not by building fires under people but by building the fire within them."[16]

The need for effective management is arguably even greater in Christian organizations than in businesses. Praise for good work, along with caring for staff (another issue on Buckingham and Coffman's list), is a threshold requirement in ministry settings. Staff members expect the church to be different from the marketplace, and if they don't feel appreciated or cared for, their morale will plummet. This is another place where Christian leaders are expected to be pastoral. But coaching doesn't stop there. Job responsibilities and the criteria for success are often poorly defined in Christian organizations. When formal clarity is lacking, the supervisor's role as coach becomes even more important.

At this point, you may think that coaching simply means periodically having warm and fuzzy conversations with staff members, but it is much more intentional and sometimes confrontational. Buckingham and Coffman say, "Regardless of what the employee wants, the manager's responsibility is to steer the employee toward roles where the employee has the greatest chance of success."[17] This is equivalent to Collins's instruction to get people into the right seats on the bus.

I heard this practice from a number of pastors, including Dan Reiland of 12Stone Church, who had just completed a major personnel shuffle that included moving three interns into permanent positions. After the two-year internship, church leaders knew they wanted to keep all three on board. As Reiland explains, "It's a developmental process in which we watch them rise into their gifting, and if and when a position opens up, we move them into it." Moving staff to new roles has happened a number of times at 12Stone, but Reiland also recounts a yearlong development conversation that helped one pastor clarify his calling and move to a different church.

What does a coaching mind-set imply with respect to holding employees accountable? Sports coaches expect the very best performance from their athletes, and the same is true in the workplace. Kouzes and Posner note, "Successful leaders have high expectations of themselves and of their constituents. These expectations are powerful because they are the frames into which people fit reality. As human beings we tend to live up to—or down to—our leaders' expectations."[18]

Of course, that means that we need to be clear about those expectations and communicate them to the people we manage. A number of organizations—secular and Christian—have formal goal-setting processes that facilitate this communication. At 12Stone Church, each ministry leader has a ministry action plan (MAP) that includes core responsibilities for the job, new territory goals that relate to the church's main priorities, and personal growth goals. Staff members develop their own goals, with input from their supervisor, which becomes a tool for development and evaluation.

The developmental perspective is an important aspect of coaching. Debi Nixon says that the Church of the Resurrection has "a culture of coaching." She explains that when performance concerns arise, the goal is to have "the right conversation" with the particular staff member. To obtain meaningful feedback, Resurrection uses a 360-degree survey in which a variety of people who work with the staff member submit anonymous feedback. Nixon concludes that even when people are put on probation due to performance issues, coaching means "providing them all the resources they need, whether that's counseling or additional training or education."

The coaching culture at Resurrection reflects another finding from Buckingham and Coffman: "Great managers excel at 'holding up the mirror.' They excel at giving performance feedback." The authors clarify, "Don't confuse this with the once-a-year performance appraisal chore, with its labyrinthine form filling and remedial focus. ...The feedback given by great managers is quite different."[19] It is real-time feedback that looks forward and focuses on the employee's success. Formal evaluation processes (something many Christian organizations lack) still have their place, but they will be the final and anticlimactic step when a coaching mind-set is in place.

Of course, some people defy development. Dan Reiland goes to great lengths to find a place for staff members who are miscast, but he is quick to say, "We refuse to pay for a bad attitude." Todd Mullins at Christ Fellowship tells of one staff member who was destroying relationships because of the way he interacted with other people. A guiding principle for Christ Fellowship is that "how we do what we do is just as important as what we do." After trying for several months to address the issue, the staff member had not made any progress and was let go. That leads to the final place where churches can learn a great deal from the world of business: what to do when someone needs to leave.

Getting Someone off the Bus

Don't be naive—up-front investment and proactive coaching will greatly increase your success rate with employees, but there will be times when someone needs to leave despite your best efforts. I am not talking about the blatant failures that lead to termination for moral or other reasons. As painful as these may be, they are much easier than the situations where someone must be released for performance or financial reasons or because a position is no longer needed. These conversations are deeply troubling and are often handled poorly.

Despite the reputation of being hard-nosed, managers in the marketplace also struggle with terminations. Buckingham and Coffman report, "During Gallup's interviews, many managers, both great and average, confessed that they were physically sick before each conversation of this kind. No matter how you approach it, no matter how accomplished you are as a manager, removing someone from his role is never easy."[20] In the best businesses, termination is the final step in a transparent process in which the employee has been given clear feedback and ample opportunities to succeed. The same should be true in the church. Greg Brenneman, a former corporate CEO, has had plenty of these hard conversations: "It sounds cold, but it's really not. It's being honest with [the person] and with God. Churches have a hard time with that. What I found in business is once you're honest and you have the conversation, it's a relief. The person knows it deep down."

Because terminations seem so difficult, many Christian leaders try to ignore the problem. They engage in wishful thinking, hoping that the person's performance will improve or that he or she will voluntarily leave for another job. Even though I often heard phrases such as "we're slow to fire," the leaders I interviewed understood the difference between giving someone a second chance and being unwilling to address performance problems or lack of fit. The conversations about these issues are difficult, but they are necessary. Buckingham and Coffman observe the crippling effect when these conversations are avoided: "In the long run, like wrapping pristine bandages around an infected wound, it is deadly for the company."[21]

The best managers, according to Buckingham and Coffman, practice "tough love" when employees fall short. "It [tough love] is a mind-set that forces great managers to confront poor performance early and directly. ... Because great managers use excellence as their frame of reference when assessing performance, *tough* love simply implies that they do not compromise on this standard."[22] The authors go on to explain:

> The most effective managers do genuinely care about each of their people. But they imbue "care" with a distinct meaning. In their minds, to "care" means to *set the person up for success*. They truly want each person to find roles where he has a chance to excel, and they know that this is possible only in roles that play to his talents. By this definition, if the person is struggling, it is actively uncaring to allow him to keep playing a part that doesn't fit. By this definition, firing the person is a caring act. This definition explains not only why great managers move fast to confront poor performance, but also why they are adept at keeping the relationship intact while doing so. All in all, the tough love mind-set enables a great manager to keep two contradictory thoughts in mind at the same time—the need to maintain high performance standards and the need to care—and still function effectively.[23]

Practicing tough love can be especially hard in small organizations if finding the right seat on the bus becomes like a game of musical chairs. You may have several talented staff members but not have the right seats for all of them. One may be struggling in her current role, but you know she would excel in a different one. Unfortunately, her ideal seat is already occupied or cannot be funded. The temptation in these cases is to accommodate the staff person and reshape her role, but a miscast staff member rarely thrives, and the organizational cost is always high.

Our compassion for others and the complex web of relationships makes a termination difficult, but our core beliefs and our practices should also make it easier than in non-Christian environments. How can that be? It starts with a belief that God has given each person certain gifts and that God has a plan for each person's life. Employees know when the job closely matches their gifts and passions. They know when they are excelling and when they are falling short. If a person is in a role that doesn't match his abilities, it is poor leadership to leave him in that position because he will never perform at his best. If the right role doesn't exist within our organization, we can trust that God has good things in store for him somewhere else.

Beyond this, Christian organizations have an opportunity (and an obligation) to handle terminations with a level of care that is uncommon in the marketplace. Even in corporate layoffs, Greg Brenneman says, "You want to be thoughtful and caring and treat people with dignity and respect." Christian leaders can be both boss and pastor to employees who lose their jobs. They should provide generous assistance so that the employee has time to look for another position. When Willow Creek was forced to reduce staff after a financial downturn, it made a sizable investment in severance pay and career counseling for those who were affected. When asked why the church spent so much in a time of financial stress, Bill Hybels responded that it was important to show "the dignity of employment at our church and how we care about our people," and concluded by simply saying, "It was the right thing to do."[24] What is the result when terminations are handled well? One clear image comes from Jim Mellado of the Willow Creek Association, who says, "I can worship with people that I fired. I can hug them. I can be in community with them."

One of the most vivid stories that demonstrate this practice comes from Willow Creek's executive pastor, Greg Hawkins. In the midst of a recession in 2002, Hawkins was at the center of a process that led to thirty people losing their jobs. During this turbulent season, he struggled with how to behave in the conversations with those who were being laid off. One option was to stay detached—"It's just a business decision; it's not personal"—but that did not seem right. For Hawkins, the core question was "Am I going to let my heart be engaged in my conversations with each of these people?" Ultimately, he says, "I chose to do it with my heart fully exposed, with a spirit that I'm going to enter as a human being in these conversations, being compassionate and kind, while being firm and clear about what we're doing. I'm going to let it hurt me." In doing so, he was able to pastor those who lost their jobs. The result? One former staff member that Hawkins personally laid off asked him to perform her wedding several years later.

To close this chapter, listen to one more biblical-sounding thought from a business expert. At the end of *The Three Signs of a Miserable Job*, Patrick Lencioni says, "I have come to the realization that all managers can—and really should—view their work as a ministry. A service to others. By helping people find fulfillment in their work, and helping them succeed in whatever they're doing, a manager can have a profound impact on the emotional, financial, physical, and spiritual health of workers and their families."[25]

The bar is set even higher for any Christian leader who manages people, and rightly so. We should be able to worship with someone we fired or be asked to perform a wedding for a former employee. We should be great coaches who care about the personal well-being and professional development of our staffs. Businesses should look to us as the benchmark for hiring and motivating people. We should be known for our grace *and* our stewardship.

What Are You Pursuing?

- Do you lean more toward grace or stewardship? How can you do both well?
- Does your staff have the clarity they need to do their jobs well? Don't trust your own answer; ask them!
- Do you have clarity about your own role? Ask your boss or board to explain what is expected of you.
- Does your staff know they are appreciated? Do they know you will support them in their personal struggles?
- If your goal was to find the best person in the world for a particular position, how would that change your hiring practices?

- Think like a coach. Put together a game plan for one key employee or volunteer, and discuss it with the person. Then reflect on what you learned from this experience.
- In your heart, who in your organization doesn't belong on the bus? What are you doing about it?
- Of all the ideas in this chapter, what is one specific practice you need to focus on? Talk to a trusted friend about your intentions.

CHAPTER SIX

DO YOU MEASURE
WHAT MATTERS?

"Measurement has been a troublesome thing for the church for two thousand years, since the church was launched at Pentecost." That is how Jim Mellado of the Willow Creek Association responded when I asked about the challenge of measuring congregational success. He continued, "It's incredibly hard to measure transformation in a heart, and that's what we're all after." Regardless of how you might state the ultimate goal of your ministry, I doubt that you will argue with Mellado's assertion that it is difficult to measure the things that truly matter.

The church is not the only place where measurement is a challenge. When I began work on this book, oil was still gushing into the Gulf of Mexico from a drilling accident at the Macondo site. It was being described as the worst environmental disaster in history because of the widespread effect on the Gulf and its shoreline. As I write this chapter, the oil has stopped flowing and the most intense cleanup work is complete, but the incident is far from over. Several storylines are currently in the news: investigations to determine the cause and assign blame for the blowout, debates over the restrictions to impose on future offshore drilling, and assessments of the economic impact of the spill.

How does this relate to the topic of measurement? Actually, measurement is an important subplot in this story. In the weeks after the blowout occurred, two measures received a lot of attention: the number of days that it took to cap the well and the amount of oil that had escaped into the environment. The first was easy to quantify but of little value to anyone except the media. The second, the amount of oil, was much more difficult to measure. Various scientific models to estimate this number produced a wide range of answers that were hotly debated.

Once the well was capped, the debate on the amount of oil that had leaked into the environment continued, and it caused me to wonder: Does it matter? Apart from sensational headlines, how does the quantity of oil from Macondo make any difference for the future? In the aftermath of the oil spill, what matters the most going forward? It matters if beaches are clean so that families can enjoy vacations on the Gulf. We need to know if it is safe to eat fish and shellfish from various parts of the Gulf. If there are steps that we can take to protect the environment or accelerate the recovery, that matters. The official government estimate is that 4.9 million barrels leaked into the Gulf, but apart from the size of the fines that are assessed, this measure has no impact on the most important issues for the Gulf Coast.

The measurement challenges facing the church, and Christian organizations in general, have many parallels to the Gulf oil spill. The things that matter the most—transformed lives, ministry effectiveness, spiritual growth—are the hardest to measure. So we settle for metrics that are easier to obtain but much less meaningful. We may develop strategies in light of these inadequate measures and fail to achieve what we really want. In essence, we focus on quantifying barrels of oil rather than environmental impact. Reggie McNeal observes, "I am convinced that the reason for much burnout, lack of commitment, and low performance in our churches among staff and members is directly related to the failure to declare the clear results we are after. We don't know when we are winning."[1] People are motivated by a meaningful scorecard and the chance to be on a winning team.

So far, I probably haven't told you anything new. McNeal is one of many voices that point out the inadequacies of the metrics used by the church. The problem is that the critics far outnumber the people with constructive solutions. If you are looking for *the* answer, skip this chapter, because I don't believe in a one-size-fits-all approach. However, I do believe that what you measure matters a great deal. And I believe that learning from business experts and other Christian leaders can stimulate our thinking to find better metrics that will lead our organizations to greater Kingdom impact.

Getting Clear on Definitions

At the heart of the measurement challenge in Christian organizations is a lack of clarity around the desired results. Getting clear about direction and priorities, as described in Chapters Three and Four, will help, but even then many Christian organizations struggle because they confuse inputs and outputs. Outputs are simply the results produced by an organization or a process. Inputs are what the process starts with or what it uses along the way. For example, a bicycle-manufacturing plant starts with steel for the frame and rubber for the tires as key inputs. It uses labor, machinery, electricity, and paint as further inputs in the process. Can you imagine the plant manager boasting, "We set a record for the amount of steel we used this month"? Of course not. The accomplishment that truly matters is for the plant to produce a record number of bicycles and to do so within its budget. This doesn't mean that the plant manager ignores the usage of steel. If steel consumption increases more than bicycle production, something is wrong in the process, and the plant may lose money. Monitoring steel consumption (or labor hours or any other input) is important, but merely as a tool to achieve the ultimate output goal.

If only measurement in Christian organizations were this simple. The bicycle manufacturing plant can clearly describe its desired outputs and can accurately measure them. It understands how its inputs relate to the outputs. Heat and machinery consistently forms a slab of steel into a bicycle frame, but the processes for "forming" disciples are much less predictable. In churches and other Christian organizations, the outputs are not as clearly defined or as easily measured as the number of bicycles produced.

Because the desired results (transformed lives, healthy congregations) are extremely difficult to measure, some people just measure inputs. They assume that getting the inputs right will accomplish the goal. Of course, every experienced leader knows that things are not that simple. The relationship between inputs and outputs is much more tenuous in spiritual matters than in manufacturing. Putting more money (an input) into the youth ministry doesn't automatically lead to teens with a deeper commitment to Christ. Holding an event at which a sports celebrity is the speaker may generate a large audience, but it is not guaranteed to raise the spiritual temperature of the congregation. Loaning money to a seamstress in a developing country may not build a successful business that lifts her family out of poverty.

Another option is to find a surrogate measure that corresponds to the main goal, but choosing a relevant surrogate is not easy. In *Reveal*, Greg Hawkins and Cally Parkinson note, "When it comes to numbers, we as leaders start to actually believe that attendance is the only thing we need to look at. It becomes a simple equation: *increased attendance = people growing*. We're not poor leaders when we think like this; it's just that we don't have any other practical way to measure heart change."[2]

Hawkins and Parkinson point to the inadequacy of simplistic measures like attendance, but Reggie McNeal takes the argument a step further, stating that the typical metrics in the church can lead to the wrong behavior. In arguing for a shift to missional thinking, McNeal says, "The old church scorecard of how many, how often, how much—all bottom-line measures that are calculated in terms of church activity—is counterproductive to participating in the missional renaissance. The old scorecard keeps us church-absorbed. As long as we use it, we will continue to be inward-focused, program-driven, and church-based in our thinking and leadership."[3]

One other challenge is that we may not even agree on whether something is an input or an output. Consider a church that emphasizes the importance of every person being equipped for ministry. Is the number of people who take an "equipping class" the right output to measure? Or is this simply an input? If the class is designed and taught well, participation should produce the desired result of equipped members, but simply counting people in the program seems like an inadequate metric. It again raises the question "Are we measuring what matters?" In this example, you can make a strong argument that *doing* ministry, not just being equipped for ministry, is what really matters.

Other Measurement Challenges

Clearly defining the results to be measured is a major issue for Christian organizations. Unfortunately, it is not the only challenge. Most spiritual leaders encounter several other barriers to creating useful metrics.

Measurement Seems Unspiritual

When you think of the secular applications for measurement, it is easy to conclude that they have no place in the church. In education, pressure around state-mandated exams pushes some teachers to "teach to the test," training their students in techniques to make a passing grade rather than focusing on broader educational objectives. In business, measurement is part of a mechanical process. When key indicators are off, managers are expected to pull the right levers to "fix" the problem.

If you bring that mind-set into the church, it seems cold and unspiritual. As a result, some leaders contend that all measurement efforts are inappropriate and should be discarded. In essence, they say that you can't measure what matters. That frustrates a leader like Rich Stearns, who says, "I think a lot of churches are very poorly managed because they don't feel that excellence and accountability fit well in a Christian environment."

It is true that numbers don't tell the whole story. Greg Holder of The Crossing points out that broad congregational measures do not adequately show how individual people are growing in their faith. He says, "Our metrics aren't the only way that we define whether God is doing something effective here. You have to celebrate the smaller stories. Otherwise this stuff blurs into meaningless numbers." Leaders at The Crossing pay attention to the numbers, but they also listen for stories of life change and celebrate them in corporate gatherings. Measurement can be unspiritual, but the best leadership is informed by facts, not practiced in a vacuum.

Measures Can Be Misleading

Sometimes metrics don't tell the whole story, and sometimes the story they seem to tell is inaccurate. Greg Surratt of Seacoast

Church says, "If you stay around long enough, you'll have several seasons that you go through as a church. You'll go through growing seasons, and that's what everyone wants to stay in. You'll go through harvesting seasons; you'll go through pruning seasons. We do look at metrics. But you also have to put that up against, 'What season are we in right now?' Sometimes you don't worry about the numbers when you're in a pruning season." Wise leaders pay attention to the metrics and discern whether a downward trend indicates a problem to be addressed or a pruning that will ultimately strengthen the congregation. They know that even if the numbers don't meet their expectations, God can still be at work in powerful ways.

On the other side, a pattern of growth is not always satisfactory. Todd Mullins describes Christ Fellowship's decision to completely revamp its discipleship process: "The big numbers were strong. We had a lot of people in life groups and taking classes, but it didn't seem to have the life it needed." Despite "positive numbers," Christ Fellowship's leaders knew that the old model was producing participation, not the spiritual growth God desired. One of the themes of this chapter is the need for spiritual leaders to use godly discernment as they apply worldly measurement tools.

Not Everyone Wants Accountability

Poorly designed or unspiritual metrics do not serve the church's mission. Sometimes, however, the critics of measurement are looking for an excuse to not address poor performance. David Weekley notes that measurement often isn't a priority because ministry is relational and "some people might get their feelings hurt." Without the concrete evidence that comes from measurement, a leader can let an underperforming staff member or volunteer slide and not risk a broken relationship.

Sometimes it is the leader himself who wants to avoid accountability. Andy Doyle, bishop of the Episcopal Diocese of Texas, offers an interesting perspective: "In the church, we rest on Augustine's total depravity so much that we let ourselves off the hook of accountability to our Lord." Rich Stearns observes that a segment within the Christian culture seems to say, "We're good people doing good things, and that ought to be good enough." In other words, as long as our intentions are good and the work that we're doing is worthy, we should not be held accountable for actual results. And Dave Peterson of Houston's Memorial Drive Presbyterian Church honestly admits, "I'm like a lot of people—I hate metrics in the sense that they can be starkly unbending. They can exaggerate all your insecurities."

Even though accountability causes discomfort, these same leaders emphasize the need for measurement. Stearns bluntly states the "good enough" mind-set "is really an excuse for mediocrity." Doyle comments, "I believe that individuals, though they have a tendency toward depravity, are ultimately responsible for the mission they've been given. We can't let ourselves off the hook for our lack of engagement in the world." Peterson finally told himself, "Dave, get over it. The church is in a difficult time. But the church doesn't understand it's in a difficult time because it doesn't know the truth about itself." So if you find yourself or a colleague making excuses to avoid measurement altogether, take a step back and ask, "Are we afraid of discovering something we don't want to know?"

Needed Skills and Tools May Be Lacking

If you put me at the bottom of a cliff and say, "Climb to the top," I am likely to give up quickly if I lack the skills and equipment for the task. Many Christian leaders feel the same way when they are challenged to measure what matters. They may readily agree that typical measures are inadequate and that quantitative measures must be balanced with spiritual discernment, but they have no idea what to do next. Neither their training nor their temperament has prepared them for this challenge.

On top of that, church databases and other information systems are often not designed to provide the needed information. If a leader said, "I think it would be helpful to track X," there is a very good chance that the current system cannot produce the answer. Standard church databases are generally designed to measure the simple, standard metrics like attendance and giving, and it is difficult to adapt them for other metrics. Creating a new scorecard requires not only a different set of skills but also often calls for data that are not currently being captured to be analyzed in a system that does not currently exist.

Because of the gap in skills and tools, spiritual leaders may need to lean on others to devise measurement systems. When you look for outside wisdom on this question, you may get more than you bargained for. Many experts will tell you what "the answer" is and what needs to be measured. The problem is that the answers are all different!

In *Natural Church Development*, Christian Schwartz reports, "To my knowledge, our research provides the first worldwide scientifically verifiable answer to the question, 'What church growth principles are true, regardless of culture and theological persuasion?'"[4] He subsequently lists the eight characteristics and offers a survey to measure them. Thom Rainer and Eric Geiger, authors of *Simple Church*, report, "In our extensive research of more than four hundred evangelical churches, we discovered the simple church revolution." They explain that "simple churches are growing and vibrant,"[5] and they also offer a survey-based tool for assessing the simplicity of a church. The Vital Congregations Research Project for the United Methodist Church has its own list of characteristics that are found in dynamic churches.[6]

Each of these resources offers a "solution" that will lead to a healthy congregation. Each is survey-based and can be deployed in any congregation. The message is "Use our measurement tool, apply the recommendations, and you will see dramatic improvements." While there is some commonality, each expert's solution has a different thrust, which again raises the question "What should you really measure?"

The measurement challenge can seem insurmountable. Some people are motivated by challenges; others shut down when facing such a daunting task. We need to ask ourselves, "Is this challenge impossible or merely difficult?" If the former, we should give up. But I believe it is the latter—a difficult but not impossible task. That leads to one more question: Is it worth the time and effort to measure what truly matters?

Does Measurement Matter?

You can find plenty of people who critique the metrics that are used in a typical Christian organization, but you won't find many who say that measurement doesn't matter at all. Reggie McNeal comments, "A universal maxim of human behavior—in families, at school, at work, wherever—is that what gets rewarded gets done."[7] When the spotlight of measurement is pointed at an activity or an outcome, people pay attention. It is drilled into us from an early age with report cards in elementary school and scoreboards for children's sports. Accomplish the measured goal or exceed the target, and you'll receive praise. Fall short of the mark, and you'll face the disappointment of others (or worse).

We have seen some of the arguments against measurement in ministry settings, but the people I spoke with see great value in the right assessment tools. Dave Peterson notes that "metrics are becoming increasingly important to me as a way to gauge effectiveness and also as a way to introduce opportunities." Kevin Jenkins of World Vision International believes that "timely truth-telling" based on the right metrics allows leaders to "use the fact that we're followers of Christ as an inspiration to excellence, not as an excuse for mediocrity."

Measurement may be a great tool to identify problems and opportunities or motivate people, but does it really matter to God? This is not just a question of whether God cares about how and what we measure. It is a question of whether "success," particularly measurable success, is something that concerns the Creator. Chris Hodges of Church of the Highlands has a response for people who resist measurement: "I'm just saying they haven't read the New Testament. They need to see how much of an accountant Jesus is because he was counting a lot. You measure what matters."

Hodges makes a good point. A number of Jesus' parables—the mustard seed, the sower, the great banquet, the talents—have quantitative or growth-oriented messages. This continues in the book of Acts, where there are several references to the numerical growth of the church and where the church experiences explosive geographic expansion. In the epistles, Paul focuses more on the doctrinal and behavioral issues facing the church, but he clearly expects believers to continue to spread the gospel (Ephesians 3:10, Philippians 1:18, Colossians 1:6, 1 Thessalonians 1:8). His writing comes out of a conviction that if God's children are being transformed individually, the church cannot help but grow in health and in numbers.

God cares deeply about the spiritual growth of people and about the health of His church, and healthy churches should produce tangible fruit over the long haul. Appropriate metrics are a way to assess the church's fruitfulness and to identify the changes that need to be made to lead toward greater health and growth. But if I stop there, I have not presented a complete and balanced perspective. Even with a well-designed measurement system, the hard data will not tell the full story. Greg Holder expresses this well: "If God is doing something here and we are yielding to him and following him, I don't think that you'll see unhealthy numbers. But that's not the 'be all and end all.' I just don't see any annual reports in the New Testament." Beyond that, Holder accurately notes that some assessment "is going to be squishy. Was Jeremiah faithful? I don't know how anybody looking at [Jeremiah's] 'numbers' is going to celebrate in the short-term."

A few months after my interview with Greg Holder, I happened upon the web site of Elevation Church in Matthews, North Carolina. What caught my eye was the button on the site to download the church's 2009 annual report. I couldn't resist and clicked on the link. The document had the look and feel of a company's annual report, complete with professional-quality pictures, vignettes of life change, and lots of statistics. Elevation's approach is a bit too corporate for my taste, but the stark last page caught my attention. The page was blank except for this statement: "We are all about the numbers. Because every number, every statistic, represents a life that was changed, a life filled with hope and purpose, a story of redemption and grace. People far from God filled with life in Christ."[8]

So how are we to think about measurement? Think of it as a tool to give a strong indication of health or effectiveness, but not one to be used apart from godly wisdom. Todd Mullins says, "Healthy things grow. If we don't see growth taking place, we must ask ourselves, 'Why not?' In a ministry as large as ours, which spreads across all these different campuses and teams, if we don't have measurement tools in place, areas that are unhealthy could go unnoticed for years."

Dave Peterson is an experienced pastor who has only recently discovered metrics that go beyond the standard attendance and giving data. He explains, "I'm like a kid with a new toy. I'm discovering that these metrics have great potential." One story of discovering this potential is the church's new emphasis on young adults. A fresh look at church data revealed three hundred young, single adults who had been relatively invisible as a group. This awareness led to new funding for ministry and identification of potential leaders. Peterson concludes that metrics "paint the real picture of who we are. I'm convinced that until the church wakes up to the reality of its situation, it's not going to be motivated to change."

In truth, no set of metrics will paint the full picture of a congregation, but if the measurement system offers a more complete and accurate look and helps leaders make decisions, it will have served a powerful purpose. Greg Hawkins, a strong proponent of measurement, explains, "You have to be clear about what your ultimate outcome is. If you don't have any ways to measure that, then you are using intuition and rules of thumb, and you are prone to ego, biases, and group think." He challenges other leaders, "How are you going to sleep well at night if you don't have some thoughtful way of understanding how your resources are working to produce life change and movement toward Christ? If there is something available, that with rigorous thinking and application of the mind God gave you can make you a little better, you have to pursue that. Otherwise it becomes like malpractice."

LESSONS LEARNED FROM OUTSIDE THE CHURCH

None of us wants to be accused of pastoral malpractice. Even if you think Hawkins overstates the point, you still want to be an effective leader, and if better metrics will help you do so, they are well worth pursuing. So what can we learn about measurement from other arenas? Does the business world, which works from a quantifiable bottom line that is starkly different from that of the church, have much to offer? The answer is a resounding yes.

One key lesson from business is the importance of moving beyond broad financial measures. Profitability is the ultimate scorecard for a business, but leaders will not be successful if they focus solely on this outcome. They must understand what drives profitability, which leads them to a broader set of measures, many of which are not purely economic.

Robert Kaplan and David Norton propose the use of a "balanced scorecard": "Think of the balanced scorecard as the dials and indicators in an airplane cockpit. For the complex task of navigating and flying an airplane, pilots need detailed information about many aspects of the flight. They need information on fuel, air speed, altitude, bearing, destination, and other indicators that summarize the current and predicted environment. Reliance on one instrument can be fatal."[9]

So what do businesses measure with their balanced scorecard? Kaplan and Norton explain that it depends on the company's vision and strategy. The key indicators of success for one company will be quite different than for another. For 3M, a company built on innovation, the percentage of sales from new products is a key measure. For auto companies, the length of time from concept to full-scale production of a new model is critical to success. For a hotel chain, high customer satisfaction leads to a great reputation, which leads to repeat visits and word-of-mouth advertising. Successful businesses are clear about their strategy and about the key factors that will enable them to achieve their goals, and that determines what they measure.

You may also be surprised to learn that businesses don't try to quantify everything, at least not in the way that you might think. Even though Patrick Lencioni advocates clear feedback when he says that "immeasurement" is one of "three signs of a miserable job," he cautions against overquantifying. Lencioni says the "appropriate measure ... might simply call for an informal survey of customers, or even merely an observation of behavior that indicates satisfaction."[10] In other words, don't limit your measurement to a set of purely objective numbers. Stepping beyond rigid quantification opens up a variety of ways to think about measurement.

As I was doing my research for this chapter, a headline caught my attention: "Oil Spill Report Card: Scientists Give Gulf a D." The article, written in the aftermath of the Macondo spill, reported, "On a scale of 0 to 100, the overall average grade for the oiled Gulf was 65—down from 71 before the spill."[11] I immediately wondered how anyone could come up with a grade for an ecosystem as complex as the Gulf of Mexico. The body of the article explained a number of factors that scientists took into account in arriving at this conclusion. Not all the scientists agreed on the factors or on the overall assessment, but what interested me was that anyone would even attempt to boil it down to a single value. I don't know if 65 is accurate, but I am sure of two things. First, just the effort to calculate the grade forced the experts to discuss what is most important. Second, creating a report card, even if it is flawed, creates an opportunity to track progress and to direct cleanup efforts. Regardless of accuracy, this grade is a much more helpful metric than the number of barrels of oil that leaked from the Macondo well.

This leads to an important observation from Jim Collins. *Good to Great* is based on comparing the long-term financial returns between companies, but his monograph for the social sectors addresses the need for a different standard: "In the social sectors, the critical question is...'How effectively do we deliver on our mission and make a distinctive impact, relative to our resources?'"[12] Collins goes on to explain, "What matters is not finding the perfect indicator, but settling upon a *consistent and intelligent* method of assessing your output results, and then tracking your trajectory with rigor."[13] We will never find a perfect indicator for spiritual growth or congregational health, but we can strive for a "consistent and intelligent" set of metrics.

MEASUREMENT THAT WORKS

By now, I hope you are convinced that measurement matters. But that doesn't tell you what to measure. In the remainder of this chapter, you will hear perspectives and specific examples from other Christian leaders. Some additional ideas are presented in Appendix C. Before we start, though, I need to offer an important caution: don't copy what others are doing. None of these leaders would say that they have found the perfect tool for measurement. Furthermore, each set of metrics is designed around a unique organization and its vision. One of the key lessons of this chapter is that measurement must be connected to vision. Since your vision is unique, the things you measure should also have a unique flavor. Another lesson is that it is better to measure something imperfectly than to get stuck trying to design the perfect measurement tool.

I hope the stories that follow will give you ideas to improve what you're measuring and avoid getting stuck.

WORKING WITH THE BASICS

When Chris Hodges described the key metrics at Church of the Highlands, my initial thought was, "This isn't rocket science." And that is precisely the point. When asked how Highlands defines success, Hodges responded, "The measure of success is the Great Commission." He translates this into four goals: "Win people to the Lord, pastor them, disciple and train them, and deploy them."

Highlands has designed its measurement system around these four areas. The church tracks the number of new visitors, total attendance, and the number of professions of faith as key indicators for winning people to the Lord. In using these three standards, Highlands recognizes that the ultimate goal, salvation, is the work of the Holy Spirit and that the number of new visitors is an important input and a sign of the church's evangelistic climate. That seems simple, but how do you measure the next area, ensuring that people are pastored? Hodges defines this as "helping them through their issues." The church's strategy is for this to be done in small groups, so the key metric is the percentage of people in the church who participate in small groups. For discipleship and training, Highlands has developed a "growth track process" and tallies the number of people who complete this process annually. The final element, deployment, is what Hodges calls the "ultimate touchdown." Highlands refers to all the volunteers in all its ministries as the "Dream Team," and it keeps track of the total number on this team and the number who are added each year.

Now that you've read through this list of metrics, what is your reaction? Not rocket science, right? But what impresses me is how clearly Hodges defines the church's goals and how closely the metrics correlate with them. It is obvious that these are important to him and to the church. Hodges not only told me what the church measures but also gave me targets and recent results for each area. This is in contrast to many Christian leaders, who talk about what their organization is trying to accomplish but fail to connect the vision with specific goals or a way to evaluate progress. Highlands is a great example of a church that has decided what matters and has created a basic measurement system to tell if it is moving in the right direction.

Drilling Down

Simple, high-level metrics are great for communicating overall success and inspiring an organization, but they may not point leaders to specific problems or opportunities for improvement. To be most useful, a measurement system needs to be designed to allow the leaders to "drill down"—to gain more detailed insight into what is happening so they can take appropriate action. Beneath Church of the Highlands' top-level metrics is another layer of data that look at specific campuses, ministries, and initiatives. Hodges says that two or three ministry areas always seem to need attention, but once leadership focuses on them, the results improve. Metrics that only inform are useless; they need to lead to decisions and action.

Consider the widely publicized statistic that a high percentage of teens who are active in youth groups walk away from the church (and from God) once they go off to college. Most churches can tell you average youth attendance for the year, but they can't tell you what percentage of their former youth are active in church (any church) one year after graduation. Even if they could answer this question, what would they do with the information? If they want to reverse the trend, they need to know if the teens disconnect after graduation or while still in high school. It would be important to know the depth of their spiritual life in high school. And it would be relevant to know if these young adults had simply joined a campus parachurch ministry instead of a church or if they were truly questioning their faith and turning from God. The answer to these and other questions should guide any programming changes. Without the ability to drill down and obtain more information, the leader's chosen course of action is just a best guess.

Alistair Hanna, who leads Alpha Latin America, knows the value of drilling down. Alpha is an international, nondenominational program that introduces the basic tenets of Christianity to skeptical people. At the top level, Alpha International has goals for the total number of people who complete the Alpha course and the number of churches teaching it. But these numbers can be overwhelming. Alpha can set an inspiring goal for the number of participants, worldwide or in Latin America, but what can one man who lives in New York City do to reach this goal? Hanna says, "The key is to know what your levers are and to know how to pull them." He continues, "For me, the lever we have is to train people how to run Alpha. We have to find a way to run as many training programs as effectively as we can in as many cities as we can." If Hanna can develop positive relationships with church leaders in a city or region so that they will enthusiastically host a training course, he knows that he can expect a good turnout. That in turn translates into his ultimate goals for Alpha courses offered in Latin America and total participants.

When a leader is able to drill down, the insights he or she obtains can shape future initiatives for the organization. That is why Dave Peterson feels like "a kid with a new toy" as he has gathered a richer set of data on his congregation. But the ability to drill down has a negative side as well. In an age in which we are able to capture more and more information, it is possible to drill down only to create mountains of meaningless reports. Kevin Jenkins of World Vision International (WVI) describes the dangers of going overboard with measurement. At one point, WVI had a big grid of metrics that field workers had to fill out. They spent so much time reporting results that it cut into their primary job of helping children. Consequently, WVI streamlined its metrics and reporting. Leaders must guard against the data dump syndrome that can result from the ability to drill down.

Beyond this, leaders sometimes get lost in the trees when they drill down. Jenkins says that "sustainable transformation" is a top goal for WVI. Even as the number of children that receive food, education, and health care is increasing, the "sustainable transformation" goal forces WVI leaders to ask a bigger question: "Are we successful if we give a child a great childhood but at age thirty he's in a Jakarta slum?" Don't misunderstand me—leaders of large organizations need to be able to drill down. Jenkins is able to identify countries or ministry areas that are underperforming, and that allows him to focus attention on them. He can find places with great results and highlight their best practices for others to use. But in the end, he must never lose sight of the ultimate goal. The fact that millions of children are being lifted out of extreme poverty through World Vision sponsorship makes it a very good organization. The fact that WVI's leaders have set sustainable transformation as their standard and are seeking to measure progress toward this goal helps make WVI a great organization.

Beyond the Easy Data

World Vision's goal of sustainable transformation points to another lesson from effective organizations: their goals often require them to look beyond the easy-to-measure things. Community Christian Church's purpose is built around three C's: celebrate, connect, and contribute (serve). At the top level, the metrics and goals are fairly typical: increase worship (celebration) attendance by 15 percent, see 75 percent of the people connected in small groups, and have 50 percent of the congregation serving (contributing) in a ministry. Lead pastor Dave Ferguson realizes that this last metric is inadequate because it doesn't help "mobilize everyone in our church for missional engagement." He explains that one business owner "started one of his business centers in partnership with one of our New Thing [church planting ministry] churches in the Philippines." This man is intentionally combining his vocation with ministry, but in Community Christian's database "he would show up as a '2C Christ follower' because he's not doing anything in our specific church programming." Ferguson plans to change the church's stated goal to "100 percent contributing (serving) in the mission of Jesus." This will be much harder to measure, but Ferguson is willing to make the effort in order to track the church's progress toward its true calling.

When it comes to measurement, many Christian leaders wonder, "Are all the important goals quantifiable?" Some say no and create systems that blend hard and soft indicators of success. Dan Reiland says 12Stone Church's strategic plan has a number of metrics to track progress, but he also notes, "We're far more storytellers than we are numerical at the larger level. God just seems to add the numbers if we don't worry about them too much. We lead with story and we lead with heart." For example, 12Stone has internal goals for baptisms and small group involvement, but these are not publicized to the congregation. Instead, church leaders regularly tell the faith stories of people who are being baptized or whose lives were changed in a small group. Reiland recognizes that these are much more powerful than charts showing percentage growth.

Similarly, Tim Lundy, formerly of Fellowship Bible Church, regularly asked, "Was there buzz around that?" when evaluating an event or a program. "Buzz" should translate into numerical results (growth in a program, people taking a next step), but this simple question is a way to start a real-time discussion of whether something is working. Effective leaders include anecdotal information in their assessments, but they recognize the potential for bias that comes with this and seek to create robust metrics.

Surveys can be a powerful tool to bridge the gap between the standard metrics and those that are purely anecdotal. A well-designed survey tool can quantify things that are subjective or personal. David Weekley, a no-nonsense businessperson, is leery of the bias that comes from reporting only stories. He has seen tremendous value in using "customer impact surveys" in his business and in the Christian ministries that he works with. A simple web-based survey can provide valuable feedback on whether a program or initiative is having the desired impact. Weekley acknowledges the difficulty in developing accurate surveys, but that doesn't cause him to give up. Instead, he says, "We find out what works and what doesn't work. It's an iterative process, and you end up someplace better than you would have been."

Geoff Surratt has first-hand experience with surveys. Seacoast Church's database captures some key measures—giving, attendance, baptisms, and volunteers. But when it comes to gathering other information, Surratt explains, "We've tried every system we can for measurement, and honestly we've found that the most accurate measure is to survey everyone that comes on a weekend once a quarter and ask them five or six very simple questions." One survey designed around Seacoast's key metrics asked about frequency of worship attendance, participation in a small group, use of a spiritual growth plan, serving in a ministry, and praying for nonbelieving friends.

One of the most powerful current survey tools for churches is Reveal from the Willow Creek Association. Reveal grew out of an internal effort at Willow Creek Community Church to answer the basic question "Where are we as a church?" Greg Hawkins and

Cally Parkinson knew they needed a different approach because "when it comes to spiritual growth, we need to be able to measure the unseen."[14] The survey approach that eventually emerged, through their efforts with Eric Arnson, is designed to "find evidence of spiritual growth in people, and then figure out what types of activities or circumstances triggered spiritual growth."[15] No survey is perfect, but Reveal is one of the most sophisticated tools available. It is built on proven research and analytical techniques from business, and it draws on the insights from more than twelve hundred congregations and the 280,000 people that have taken the survey.

Ultimately, the results from a survey are like any other metric. They give leaders information that helps them answer questions such as "How are we doing?" "What are we doing right?" and "What do we need to do differently?" Reveal is a great example of creating a measurement tool that starts with the Spirit's leadership and the organization's vision and then leverages the best that business has to offer.

To close this chapter, I want to share one of the most interesting metrics that I heard in my interviews. Remember the importance of measuring things that are connected to your vision and Jim Collins's admonition to choose "a *consistent and intelligent* method of assessing your output results." Oak Hills Church's strategic plan (described further in Chapter Eleven) is built around "four environments in which we accomplish our mission," according to senior minister Randy Frazee. In each environment, the church has developed one or more specific initiatives related to the overarching goals of belonging, growing, and serving. For the "family environment," Frazee says, "we are putting in place initiatives to get the family back to the dinner table. We believe that getting families back to the table in a healthy and spiritually vibrant way is the single greatest mechanism that we can choose to return the family to a place of belonging." The planning team developed this approach after studying biblical and secular resources, including research from Columbia University that found that families who eat five meals per week together avoid many of the serious problems that often beset teenagers. Oak Hills will teach on this and even provide training on how to make family mealtime more meaningful. They will use surveys to determine how many of their families eat at least five meals together per week and if these families experience a sense of "transformational belonging."

I don't expect anyone reading this chapter to create a church-wide survey to determine how many families eat meals together regularly. But I hope you have a greater awareness of the value that can come from effective measures. The right metrics highlight and support the vision. They define what constitutes a "win" and get everyone on the same page. They create accountability at all levels of the organization. And in doing so, they will help your organization become what God intends for it to be.

WHAT ARE YOU PURSUING?

- What is your attitude toward the use of metrics? What has shaped your attitude?
- What are you currently measuring? How closely do these metrics relate to your vision?
- Do you communicate results to other leaders? To the organization as a whole? Is this communication effective?
- What is one thing you would like to know but currently don't have a metric for? Why is this important? How might you create an "intelligent and consistent" way to measure it?
- Sit down with leaders from other churches or Christian organizations and businesses and find out how they approach measurement.

CHAPTER SEVEN

HOW WILL YOU FINANCE THE DREAM?

When I began my research for this project, I asked several friends to help me connect with interesting Christian leaders for interviews. Their success meant that over half of the interviewees were people that I did not previously know. So on a hot Wednesday morning in August, I was scheduled to talk to two pastors that I had never met. It was an ironic and providential twist, as our discussions about finances showed me two very different perspectives and gave me plenty to think about.

The first conversation was with Todd Mullins of Christ Fellowship. As he gave me a brief history of the church and some of the huge financial faith steps taken over the years, Mullins said, "In the early days of the church, there was not a whole lot of financial planning." One decision that defied common sense was when the leaders of the small congregation felt God leading them to move out of their temporary space and buy their first property, an old, rundown horse farm. Even though the congregation had fewer then one hundred people at the time and still fit comfortably in a school cafeteria, they knew God was calling them to something much bigger. So when the banks balked at the church's loan request, many members made deep commitments, including second mortgages on their homes, to complete the purchase.

At a later point in Christ Fellowship's history, the church was in the midst of a building campaign when the leaders felt God calling them to start a local children's home. It was a major financial commitment, especially since the capital campaign had not yet met its goal, and some influential members expressed great reservations. Ultimately, Christ Fellowship pressed ahead because of the conviction that God was in this opportunity. Place of Hope, the ministry the church started, recently celebrated its tenth anniversary and has expanded to include a number of other services, thanks to the bold faith steps taken by Christ Fellowship and its leaders.

An hour later, I spoke with Chris Hodges. Church of the Highlands, where Hodges serves as senior pastor, has grown to more than fourteen thousand in worship attendance in its first ten years. The church operates on a frugal budget and a conservative financial philosophy. Highlands met in a high school auditorium for its first six-and-a-half years, even as attendance grew to five thousand worshipers. When the church was ready to build its first permanent facility, it had $16 million in the bank. This enabled Highlands to buy 128 acres of prime land with cash and complete the construction with only a small amount of debt. The bylaws of Church of the Highlands state that the current year's budget cannot exceed 90 percent of the prior year's receipts. That might make sense for a struggling church, but at Highlands this means operating on a 2010 budget of $16 million while expecting receipts of approximately $24 million.

The difference is striking when you compare the financial philosophies of Christ Fellowship and Church of the Highlands. But as I reflect on my two conversations, some of the similarities are also striking. Both of these pastors are following deeply held convictions about how they should manage the church's finances. In both cases, this has made a deep impression on the culture of the congregation. In both churches, many people are becoming followers of Christ and there is ample evidence of God's blessing. And in both cases, what they are doing flies in the face of conventional financial wisdom.

That may be more obvious with Mullins and Christ Fellowship, where trust in God's provision defies any kind of spreadsheet analysis. No financial adviser would recommend that individuals should take out second mortgages to start a church or that a major, unplanned initiative should be added on top of a capital campaign. But what about Hodges? Actually, many business experts would question the "opportunity cost" of staying in temporary facilities for so long while holding on to such a large amount of money.

Business logic says, "Invest for the future. You can grow faster by being less conservative." I can use my business skills to critique Mullins and Hodges, but after that Wednesday in August, I was ready to take off my business hat for a while.

Of course, it is virtually impossible to talk about financial matters in the church without employing some business knowledge. So what can we learn from business and from other Christian leaders in this area? This chapter is not intended to turn anyone into an accountant or a chief financial officer or a lead fundraiser; there are plenty of other experts to do that. My hope is that you will gain new insights into ways to raise and manage the resources your organization needs to pursue its God-given dreams.

Philosophy Drives Practice

The contrast between Mullins and Hodges highlights the wide philosophical variations that exist within Christian organizations when it comes to money. In business, you will also find a range of philosophies, but the world of corporate finance tends to establish narrower boundaries. The business arena also has a well-developed language that enables executives to get on the same page when discussing financial decisions. For example, when considering a new venture, business leaders will talk about how much money they will earn on an investment or the risk-reward trade-off. In churches, when leaders try to make financial decisions, it often seems like they are talking in completely different languages. One talks about stepping out in faith while another sees the church taking a foolish risk. One advocates a sensible reserve policy and the other says it is God's money that should be put to work for Kingdom purposes. One sees the budget as an instrument for control while the other thinks of it as just a guideline for spending. Underneath these specific issues are theological differences that complicate the financial conversations in Christian organizations, particularly around the questions of risk and reserves.

Risk or Faith

At the heart of the Christ Fellowship story is a belief that God has called the congregation to step out in faith multiple times, despite great uncertainty and risk. When Todd Mullins's father, Tom Mullins, led the early core group to buy the horse farm that became the church's first property, it was a faith-filled decision. Outsiders would look at this as a very risky, even crazy decision. When the bank refused to loan money for the property purchase, it was basically saying, "The numbers don't add up. It's too risky." To the Mullins family and the other leaders of Christ Fellowship, it was not a risky decision because it was what God led them to do.

Their faith was rewarded when the church flourished, and a culture of taking Spirit-led leaps was established. The decision to start Place of Hope while the church was in the middle of a capital campaign is another example. Yet another chapter in the Christ Fellowship story is the church's Royal Palm campus, which launched with a group of people meeting in a school cafeteria and quickly grew to seventeen hundred in attendance. As the leadership team looked around for a larger, long-term facility, two options became available. A nearby Christian school with a large auditorium was interested in becoming Royal Palm's home and offered to do so for a nominal rent. The other option was the purchase of a former retail store. Christ Fellowship chose the latter, spending $18 million for the purchase and renovations at the same time that the church's original campus was doing a major (150,000-square-foot) expansion. This decision positioned the Royal Palm campus to reach its community more effectively, and it has paid off with weekly worship having now grown to six thousand.

From a strict financial perspective, none of these decisions made sense, but Christ Fellowship's leaders don't approach decisions this way. In describing their culture, Todd Mullins says, "Our elders don't vote on anything; our elders pray and fast. If there's not a oneness of the Spirit of God that the Lord is moving on some big initiative like this, then we just push the pause button and wait until there's clarity." It's not that they ignore the facts. Mullins explains, "We allow the business planning and financial perspective to guide the prayers but not to determine the outcome. The Spirit of God trumps man's logic and man's planning." This was made explicit in one of the church's earlier decisions when the senior Mullins led the elders in their second major purchase by saying, "We're not going to talk about it and weigh out the pros and cons. We're just going to talk to the Lord about it." Todd Mullins looks back over Christ Fellowship's history and sees a pattern in which "we prepare ourselves to step out in faith by stepping out in faith," with each step being bigger than the previous one.

Does the Christ Fellowship story mean that every church should take big risks with the assurance that God will reward it? Can we conclude that Christian organizations that don't take big financial risks have little faith? After listening to Chris Hodges and others, I hardly think it is this simple. Greg Surratt has seen God work in powerful ways in Seacoast Church's history, but the church has a relatively conservative financial approach. When I asked him about this, his response was, "I don't want the bank to have to operate on our faith." There is plenty of evidence of faith-filled obedience to God in the Seacoast story, just as there is at Christ Fellowship, but Seacoast's underlying financial philosophy is quite different.

Not every story of risk and faith turns out like that of Christ Fellowship. Jeff Wells planted WoodsEdge Community Church in 1995 in the middle of a large suburban community near Houston. The congregation made the typical progression from a school to a permanent facility but eventually began to feel constrained even in that space. Because the church did not have options to expand at its existing site, WoodsEdge purchased a much larger parcel of land just outside the community and built a new facility. Construction of the new building exceeded the budget, and at the same time the economy experienced a downturn, leaving the church with much more debt than anticipated. WoodsEdge was forced to cut its operating budget, including layoffs and salary reductions, and renegotiate its loan terms with the bank. In reflecting on this experience Wells says, "My attitude used to be, 'We can't take enough risk. God's going to take care of it.'" He has never lost faith in God, but his attitude toward financial risk has changed. Wells actually delivered a repentance sermon in September 2009, explaining the church's financial position and asking forgiveness for allowing it to become overextended.

WoodsEdge experienced a temporary setback. The church is still a vibrant fellowship in which people are coming to faith and growing spiritually, and it is well on the way to financial recovery. Other Christian leaders have taken huge faith steps only to see their organizations crumble completely when they have gone out on a limb. Simply stated, the financial dynamics of faith and risk are complicated for Christian leaders. I have the deepest respect for Todd Mullins, Chris Hodges, Greg Surratt, and Jeff Wells. Each is a person of great faith who genuinely and earnestly seeks to follow God in the financial leadership of his congregation. Each has developed a different philosophy toward debt and risk in his journey. Their stories demonstrate that your own Spirit-led convictions are far more important than anyone else's model.

RESERVES THAT PAY DIVIDENDS

Closely related to the issue of risk is the organization's use of financial reserves (or lack thereof). If a church has a conservative budget or creates a significant reserve fund, does that mean it is not operating in faith? Does this mean the church is hoarding money that should be used for immediate ministry purposes?

Let's go back to Church of the Highlands and Chris Hodges. Is it good stewardship to have a budget that is only two-thirds of projected receipts? It depends on what the church plans to do with the excess. In the case of Church of the Highlands, I came away from my conversation inspired by the leadership's faith-filled approach to finances. Generosity is a core value that Highlands lives out. The church gives away much of the excess that is created as a result of its conservative budgeting approach. It has made substantial financial gifts to strategic missions and to church planting. The Dream Center in Birmingham, started by Highlands and described in Chapter Four, was funded from these reserves.

Highlands' philosophy goes deeper than just the opportunity to generously support other ministries. Hodges has found that many business-minded people are drawn to the transparent and conservative approach at Highlands. It also makes him a better pastor. He explains, "When pastors get into [financial] pressure, they pressure people." Hodges wants to be the kind of pastor who loves and leads people, not who pressures them, and he believes this will result in more financial and spiritual fruit at Highlands.

I was surprised at how often the concept of reserves or financial margin came up in my conversations. Dan Reiland of 12Stone Church describes financial margin as "a spiritual discipline that has profound ramifications." Like Highlands, 12Stone's conservative budgeting approach provides seed money that the church uses to fund new, unbudgeted initiatives that God brings its way. One year, some of 12Stone's margin was used in conjunction with a ministry partner to produce a short film, *The Candy Shop*, which was used in a national awareness campaign against child sex trafficking. Brent Messick explains that the budget process at the Church of the Resurrection (Methodist) is divided into the main operating budget and "Box 2" for special initiatives. The latter has included a wide range of onetime needs and new program ideas, such as improving signage and launching a ministry for parents of toddlers. Church leaders can review the Box 2 proposals and decide which ones to fund in light of the church's financial picture and its strategy. Even at Christ Fellowship, Todd Mullins says, "For us to walk in those God-given opportunities, there has to be margin." So church leaders are building margin into their budget "for the purpose of being ready and prepared" to act when God leads.

Financial margin can be a strategic way to fund new initiatives, but another legitimate use is to create a reserve account as a "rainy-day fund." Some people might argue that this kind of preparation for a downturn lacks faith, but I contend that it is good stewardship. Virtually every ministry will experience a season of financial stress. It may be caused by a general economic downturn, the loss of a major donor, or a huge unforeseen expense. The question is not whether this will happen but how the ministry will handle it. Organizations that operate without any reserve can be completely derailed by a relatively minor financial interruption. A church with an aging facility may suddenly face a major repair bill. If it lacks reserves and is unable to raise the funds, it will be forced to cut programming or staff costs. Members may become disgruntled and leave, causing further financial shortfalls and more cuts. This can quickly become a downward spiral that could have been avoided if the church had built a reserve account in better years.

A year before the economic recession that began in 2008, leaders at The Crossing decided to "do life differently" and not enter a building campaign, even though the church had four worship services that were at capacity. Greg Holder explains, "We went into that crisis with a significant amount of money in our savings account. We didn't sit on that money. We kept a wise amount in reserve, but we did go ahead and launch our first multisite with a significant investment." The Crossing's approach demonstrates the wisdom and value of putting some funds aside so that future ministry can continue, even in the face of a downturn, and using the rest for Spirit-led purposes. The choice was relatively easy because the church had previously established a clear financial philosophy and had the right tools to use once the decision was made.

FINDING THE RIGHT TOOLS

The financial philosophy of a Christian organization should be guided primarily by biblical principles and God's Spirit and secondly by business "wisdom." But once a philosophy is in place, business has many useful tools to offer. That is the consistent story from my interviews. Successful organizations get key leaders (pastoral and lay) on the same page philosophically, and then they rely on the expertise of business-minded people to create or refine the necessary tools. Even simple tools for forecasting and understanding receipts or managing expenses can help many Christian organizations grow in their effectiveness.

TOOLS FOR THE "TOP LINE"

The first question to ask is how well you understand your organization's receipts. I am not asking, "Do you know last year's total contributions?" I am asking, *"Do you understand how you got there?"* The answer is important, because if you don't understand what led to last year's financial results, it will be very difficult to determine if you are on track this year or to plan for next year or to develop new strategies to grow the top line.

One of the simplest aspects of understanding receipts is to know the seasonal giving patterns. Every nonprofit organization must come to grips with December 31. Because of tax laws for charitable contributions, end-of-year bonuses, and Christmas giving traditions, ministries can expect a large portion of their contributions to come in the last two weeks of the year. Yet many ministries use a straight-line method to forecast receipts. If their fiscal year ends in December, that means that they go through the entire year saying that they are behind budget. In reality, they may or may not be behind compared to historical giving patterns. Without accurate information, they may curtail spending unnecessarily or may continue spending and end the year in a deficit. Brent Messick says Church of the Resurrection uses a monthly cash flow projection to inform decisions. Similarly, Greg Holder never wants to communicate that "we feel all warm and fuzzy about this, so trust us." His church has a model for "predicting how we see our revenue, as best we can tell, with God's help." These and other leaders are using the tools of business, while not ignoring God, to manage their church's finances.

The best financial models, in business and in ministry, allow leaders to do more than make seasonal adjustments in their forecasts. One of the metrics that Seacoast Church tracks is per capita giving. (This is calculated as the total receipts divided by average worship attendance, expressed in dollars per person per year.) If per capita giving is going down, this may be a sign of dissatisfaction in the congregation. It may also be due to a poor economy or an influx of new believers who have not grasped the principle of tithing.

This kind of analysis enables leaders to understand receipts at a deeper level so that they can adjust their strategies. Churches that thoroughly analyze giving will be interested in trends from core members, new members, and lost contributors and the impact of onetime gifts. The final section of Appendix C presents additional ways to assess contribution patterns.

Businesses routinely seek this type of information, not about "contributors" but about buying patterns with customers, sales of different product lines, revenue per store, and the like. As they ask and answer these questions, successful companies adjust their plans in order to achieve their financial goals. Even though the church is not a business, it is difficult to be a good steward without using these kinds of tools. When a wise spiritual leader sees a pattern that new members are not giving or that support from core members has decreased, he or she will make adjustments to address the problem. Similarly, this more robust understanding may help a leader identify and build on things that are working well.

Business tools offer insights, but they can't answer one important question: How is God going to move in the hearts of people to spur their giving? My church learned that first-hand in 2010. Right after moving into the senior pastor role, Roger Patterson felt God leading him to pray for receipts far above our $4.2 million budget. He also felt clearly led *not* to appeal to the church and to tell only the staff and a handful of leaders. So he began praying that we would close the year with receipts of $4.35 million. Coming through a year of pastoral transition and in an economy in which many churches were cutting budgets, he believed that this was something only God could do. Our financial models (actually, my financial model) indicated that we would finish the year below the desired amount, but we did nothing out of the ordinary in December to communicate our financial goals. Yet when we closed the books, we had exceeded the $4.35 million target by $2,000. Even though the models gave us confidence regarding our budget, nothing prepared us for the ways God moved in the hearts of a broad base of new and longtime members.

Tools for the "Bottom Line"

As a leader in a Christian organization, what happens inside you when the word *budget* is mentioned? The frequent response is a tightening of the collar and sweaty palms. Budgets, and the related processes for managing expenses, should be helpful tools but they often fall short. In the best cases, financial tools reflect the organization's vision and enable ministry leaders to pursue that vision more effectively.

In businesses, budgets are the fundamental way that resources are allocated to accomplish the stated priorities. If a company plans to launch a new product, funds will be allocated for product development, marketing, sales personnel, and other related costs. In fact, the budgeting process helps clarify the organization's true priorities. An idea is not a priority until it is supported financially. If a company says that new product research is vital to future success but fails to set aside adequate money for this research, the research is not truly important. The intense budget-setting debates that often occur at senior management levels can be a healthy process to clarify the real priorities for the coming year.

Corporate financial management systems also allow leaders to monitor and manage progress once the budget is set. If a research manager is given $500,000 to develop a new product, it is a red flag if half the money has been spent in the first three months of the year. This doesn't necessarily mean that the research manager is doing a bad job, but the financial system should help the manager plan expenses and should alert the leadership if spending is off track. Perhaps a large piece of equipment was needed to begin the research and total spending will still fall within budget. Perhaps the initial experiments failed and the company needs to decide whether to continue with the research at a higher cost than anticipated. Effective financial systems provide timely information to facilitate conversations about reaching organizational goals.

The best financial systems in business are consistent with the overall culture of the organization. Two different companies with the same goal to develop a new product might approach the finances quite differently. One asks the research manager how much is needed, approves the $500,000 request without any detailed explanation, and simply expects the manager to deliver by the end of the year. Another company may ask for a breakdown of what is included in the $500,000 and then monitor spending against this. Neither approach is right or wrong; the approach should flow out of the company's philosophy about financial management and about empowerment and responsibility for its managers.

As you think about your own budgeting and financial management systems, be aware of some of the common mistakes that occur in Christian organizations. Overcontrol is a frequent problem in older and small churches, as well as in organizations that have had financial scandals or other problems in their history. In these cases, the systems are often designed to micromanage every expenditure. This may mean a rigorous purchase order system or some other approval step before money is spent. Another scenario is a finance committee that conducts in-depth monthly reviews and asks for justification for every dollar that was spent. Not only is this approach demoralizing, but it is also inflexible; if a new, Spirit-led ministry idea comes up in the middle of a fiscal year, the people who control the money will tend to answer, "It's not in the budget," rather than search for a way to provide the needed financial support.

At the other end of the spectrum are financial practices that provide little control because the process of budgeting and accounting is too sloppy to provide meaningful information. This may happen when an organization outgrows its financial system or when it is using categories and processes that were created years earlier. Spending may exceed the budget before anyone is aware, or expenses may be charged to whatever account "sounds closest" or "has the most room." For example, a church may decide to host a block party for community outreach. If this event was not budgeted, the costs may be placed in an underspent category, such as facility maintenance. That may cause problems if a major repair need arises later in the year or if leaders want to use prior-year spending records to develop the budgets for future years.

Even if the accounting system is solid, the budgeting process may not support the ministry's goals. The best budgets are driven by vision and start with a clean slate, but the more typical approach is to make a few small tweaks to the categories and numbers from the prior year. Leaders often default to this approach because it takes less effort and keeps the peace. If you are conflict-averse, you may have recoiled when I noted earlier that intense debates often occur over the allocation of funds in businesses. But this kind of debate can actually help clarify the organization's true priorities and propel it forward. As Patrick Lencioni explains, "When a group of intelligent people come together to talk about issues that matter, it is both natural and productive for disagreement to occur. ... Avoiding the issues that merit debate and disagreement ... guarantees that the issue won't be resolved."[1] If you want to make the best use of the resources God has provided, you must be willing to engage in conversations that may become frank and contentious. When this is done in an environment of trust and respect and in light of a clear vision, these conversations can be highly productive.

It is impossible to talk about budgets and financial management without touching on the biggest expense category for most ministries: personnel. How does the cost for salaries and benefits fit into this discussion? Any financial system should make it easy to add up the payroll (and benefits) for all employees so that the annual cost can be forecast. The more difficult task is making sure the personnel resources are aligned with the vision. Too often a church's leaders will talk about pursuing new priorities, but the only thing that changes is the reallocation of a few programming dollars. If the organizational structure and the specific staff duties do not match the stated goals, little progress will be made.

One business concept that can be powerful in ministry settings is the zero-based budget. In this approach, the leaders begin with a blank sheet of paper and ask, "If we started over, what staff positions would we have? How would we be structured? What programs would we fund?" It is hard not to think about the current realities (a favorite program or a staff member who is a good friend) in this kind of exercise, but when leaders take an honest look at these questions, they often realize that their blank-page answers are far different from their current reality. For example, an emphasis on ministry to young adults might cause a church to eliminate a position for men's or women's or senior adult ministry in order to create a position for ministry to college students or single adults. This does not mean that staff must be fired overnight or ministries canceled immediately, but it should lead to strategic conversations about the long-term changes that need to be made.

Even though Christian organizations face many challenges in their use of financial management tools, some find great power in them. Christ Fellowship has shifted to a six-month (rather than twelve-month) budget cycle to bring ministry and spending plans more into line with the Spirit's leading. At Alpha, Ali Hanna developed a metric for the net cost per new Christian who comes through the program. Some colleagues objected to this metric as being unspiritual, but it gave Hanna a way to measure the organization's stewardship effectiveness and to compare various options for resource allocation.

Similarly, having a good handle on overhead costs helped Rich Stearns at World Vision drive toward a more efficient use of resources. When the depth of the 2008 recession became apparent, World Vision laid off fifty people and froze salaries for the rest of the staff. The organization's financial management system helped identify where costs could be cut without crippling the ministry. Layoffs can be demoralizing to the people who remain, but Stearns explained to employees and other constituents, "We take the hit before the children that we serve take the hit." World Vision didn't just attack expenses; a comprehensive database enabled the organization to shore up receipts by making eighty-three thousand calls to thank donors for their support in the midst of difficult times. A weekly cash report helped the management team update projected receipts and make real-time spending decisions. The financial systems and the vision all worked together to help World Vision through a difficult season and to come out even stronger in the end.

One reason that financial systems in Christian organizations are underdeveloped is that leaders often have little aptitude in this area. Most pastors don't have M.B.A.'s and extensive business backgrounds like Rich Stearns. When I asked Christian leaders what most drains them, one of the common responses was dealing with finances. But not dealing effectively with financial matters can create a huge barrier between ministry leaders and some of their key constituents, the businesspeople who serve on their boards and who provide financial support. This delicate dance is a final area to consider for financing the dream.

THE DONOR DILEMMA

We can't talk about finances without touching on the changing perspectives of donors and the organization's interaction with them. Just like every other aspect of the religious landscape, this one is changing rapidly. Some people still give to churches or Christian organizations out of habit or a sense of obligation, and some give because they personally like the leader. The growing trend, however, is for financial support to come from people who believe in the vision, see a clear connection between vision and execution, and have confidence in the financial integrity of the system. This is especially true for people who have significant wealth. Today's donors have more giving options than ever before, and these options are easier to access and are being marketed in increasingly sophisticated ways. At the same time, donors are aware of financial scandals in Christian organizations, whether through the well-publicized greed of a national personality or embezzlement by a local church bookkeeper. Whereas people once believed their money was in good hands when given to a ministry, they no longer extend this trust in carte blanche fashion.

The starting point is for your financial system to establish credibility in the eyes of the members and donors. Credibility can be created through the availability and transparency of financial information, openness to questions and forthright answers to them, and a respected team of laypeople who oversee the finances. Chris Hodges emphasizes the importance of financial integrity: "We have a fully disclosed cash flow statement every year. Everybody can see it, from salaries to stamps, just as a point of accountability." Greg Holder recognizes the importance of surrounding himself with "men and women who understand best practices and actually speak the language of business." When someone has questions about a financial matter at the church, Holder is able to direct the person to these lay leaders who can give clear answers. Credibility is the ground floor for engaging and keeping donors.

Holder's comment points to the next level: actively seeking wise outside counsel on major financial decisions. Laypeople do not need to approve every expenditure or otherwise enmesh themselves in day-to-day operations, but there is usually great financial wisdom in the body that should not go untapped. Terry Looper is a highly successful businessman, a committed Christian, and a generous donor to his church and to other causes. He is the kind of person that is often asked to serve on the board of nonprofit organizations, as he did in the early years of Houston Christian High School (HCHS). When the school was under construction, a number of factors created significant financial pressure for the fledgling organization. Pledges from donors and a bank loan covered construction of the main building, but HCHS lacked funding for a gym and athletic fields.

As the board evaluated this situation, a business owner (who was also the parent of a student) offered to loan the school the additional $8 million it needed for the sports facilities. Looper was deeply concerned that HCHS would not be able to afford the payments for this loan on top of the operating budget and the primary note to the bank. Because of his aversion to this level of debt, Looper was prepared to resign from the board. But he also offered a solution: What if the second loan were interest-free and had no timeline for repayment? In essence, Looper proposed that the school not begin payments on the $8 million until after the primary loan had been repaid. Board members doubted that the business owner would agree to this, but they authorized Looper to make the request. When Looper's proposal was accepted, the school was able to take the loan, build its athletic facilities, and avoid becoming overburdened with debt.

Looper's story shows the benefits that wise advisers can bring if they are allowed to become involved in key financial decisions. Jan Davis describes a pivotal moment when she was executive pastor at Christ United Methodist Church in Plano, Texas. The church designed a new sanctuary and other expansions and was preparing for a capital campaign. But a soft economy caused church members to question the project, and their senior pastor began to have second thoughts about the church's ability to raise the $10 million needed. Even the campaign consultant expressed doubts about reaching this goal. Davis felt a strong spiritual conviction that the project should move forward, but the decision was not hers to make. So she encouraged other leaders to seek God's guidance on this matter and to remember the congregation's spiritual history. Several influential business executives on the building committee felt God's nudge to move forward, and this swayed the senior pastor and the rest of the committee. The church proceeded with its building campaign and ultimately reached its goal.

Do the business leaders and financially savvy people in your organization always have the right answers? Sometimes pastors are tempted to assume a direct correlation between a person's wealth and his or her spiritual maturity. When you read this statement in black and white, it is obviously wrong. People who are successful at handling major decisions in the marketplace may have a great perspective on financial matters, but that does not mean that they have the same depth of insight into spiritual decisions involving money.

Because wealth is not necessarily a reflection of spiritual maturity, Christian leaders should not over-rely on the advice of wealthy donors. They should, however, realize that people with significant resources have a fundamentally different way of thinking about financial gifts. The nonprofit world has steadily shifted toward active, rather than passive, philanthropy. This means that people with significant wealth are not content simply to write a check to an organization based on personal affinity or the worthiness of the cause. Active philanthropists dig deep to understand how effectively the organization is being run. They want to know what kind of "return" will be generated by their investment. They are not looking for a financial return, but they want to know that their investment will have the greatest possible impact. Greg Brenneman, a former corporate CEO, explains that the mind-set of most "surplus givers" is, "I have lots of ministries I can give money to. Tell me how you steward this money." He continues, "It's a big red flag for a surplus giver if [an organization's plan] is not close to being aligned with its strategy or vision."

Some wealthy donors are interested in having a seat on the board as a way to ensure a positive impact for their contributions. Some want to avoid serving on the board, especially if they sense that the governing body gets tangled up in what they consider petty issues. They may prefer to serve in some other kind of advisory role. Either way, spiritual leaders may be intimidated by the hard questions asked by successful businesspeople, but the only way to benefit from their wisdom and generosity is to understand that they look at the world through a different lens. In the best cases, the relationship between spiritual and business-minded leaders can be a powerful partnership, which is the focus of Chapter Nine.

Major donors are also sensitive to an organization's reliance on their gifts. They want to know that the organization won't collapse if their giving stops. They ask questions like "What percentage of the budget does my gift represent?" "Can we use my gift for special onetime needs?" and "Can we create a matching opportunity to stretch the value of my gift?" Because of these concerns, people with significant wealth often direct only a small portion of their giving to their local church.

Ultimately, financial resources are a vital tool for moving your church or Christian organization toward God's vision. But "tool" is an inadequate description. Your use of the tool of finances is a powerful sign that everyone can see. In difficult financial times or when faced with major financial decisions, a leader's true colors will show. The Crossing is one of the founding churches of the Advent Conspiracy, a widespread initiative to encourage Christians to "worship fully, spend less, give more, and love all." Each year during The Crossing's Christmas Eve services, the offering plates are passed and every dollar that is collected is given to the Advent Conspiracy. At the end of 2009, with the country having spent more than a year in a recession, the leaders of The Crossing had a decision to make: Would they hold on to a portion of the Christmas

Eve offering to supplement the church's operating budget? Giving for the year was flat, and the church wanted to avoid a shortfall that could lead to layoffs. Greg Holder says that the board discussed the matter, but "there wasn't a lot of indigestion in that meeting." They decided to again give away every dollar of the Christmas offering.

In deciding to stick to their principles and trust God, The Crossing's leaders sent an important signal to the congregation. It was a signal of seeking wise financial counsel and ultimately deciding to live by principles and by faith. Every organization needs funds to operate, but in the end, the money belongs to God, and the financial management systems are just another tool to achieve His mission.

WHAT ARE YOU PURSUING?

- What is your philosophy about finances? Do other leaders know and share your philosophy? If not, what steps can you take to develop a common framework?
- What are the past stories related to finances that shape your beliefs and those of other key leaders?
- How well do you understand the "top line" of your organization? What are three things you would like to know about giving patterns?
- What adjectives describe your budgeting and financial practices?
- How much money do you have in reserve? Do you have specific policies or guidelines for setting aside a reserve fund and for spending from it?
- Who might be able to give you a better understanding of a donor's perspective? Pick three people who are (or could be) significant contributors. Ask them to read the last section of this chapter, and then discuss it with them.

CHAPTER EIGHT

ARE "ALL SYSTEMS GO"?

All the leadership tools in the world will not produce the desired results without systems that support meaningful, consistent progress. As soon as I mentioned "systems," some of you reached for the top right corner of the page to turn to the next chapter. The topic of systems is boring or confusing to many people. I even thought about skipping this chapter, but I decided that the risk of neglecting this important subject outweighed the risk of frustrating my audience. For those who are not convinced, an analogy may help you grasp the hidden power of systems.

Houston, where I live, is the fourth largest metropolitan area in the United States. The city sits at an elevation of forty-three feet above sea level, a height that doesn't change by more than a few feet over the fifty miles from eastern to western suburbs. Houston has not always been a major city, and in fact you could argue that it didn't have the ingredients to become one.

A number of factors contributed to Houston's rapid growth in the second half of the twentieth century, but one factor that may be overlooked is bayous. With its flat topography, the Houston area had large, swampy landmasses that were best suited for rice farming (or alligator hunting). The natural bayous that existed were sufficient to gradually drain the lowlands toward Galveston Bay and the Gulf of Mexico, but when they were enlarged and deepened, developers were able to reclaim land for residential subdivisions, retail centers, office space, and transportation infrastructure. That helped Houston attract businesses and become a major city.

The development of healthy systems in a business or a congregation is akin to Houston's bayous. A swamp may not prohibit people from living in an area, but it will change the way they live. Being surrounded by swamps results in a slower pace of life and a smaller population. When you think of the long-term development of a low-lying city, bayous are never the objective. They are simply a means to achieve the goal of urban development.

It is the same way with systems in organizations. If you are content for your ministry to remain relatively small, formal systems are not particularly important. If God is calling your organization to something far beyond where it currently is, then you will need to invest in the right systems to reach your full potential. Without that investment, the growth will either not occur at all or not withstand the storms that eventually come. Systems should never be the primary focus of the organization; they should be treated as a means for achieving God's vision.

UNDERSTANDING SYSTEMS

What are systems? They are the routine sets of steps or activities that an organization uses to accomplish a desired result. Organizations create systems to improve efficiency and reliability. For example, most congregations have a system to connect with first-time visitors, invite them back, and move them toward membership. The system for doing this may include several steps, such as registration in the worship service, a welcome call from a pastor, an invitation to join a Bible study or small group, and participation in a new members class. Two churches may have similar objectives (for example, connecting with visitors), but the way they design their systems will vary considerably. These variations grow out of different philosophies, organizational needs, and size. If a church has two or three new visitors each week, it may have an informal system in which the pastor makes personal calls to welcome each one. If the number of new visitors is two or three dozen, a more formal system for tracking people and assigning calls is needed. Regardless of size or philosophy, the complete absence of a system will yield meager results.

Many spiritual leaders have trouble developing effective systems because they overlook the web of connections within their organizations. Norman Shawchuck and Roger Heuser refer to this tendency as "organizational myopia." They explain, "Leaders who experience organizational myopia lose the ability to view the congregation as a whole entity. They fail to understand the interrelation of all the discrete structures and processes that comprise the church. They are unable to foresee the results one action or decision will have on all the other attitudes and operations going on. With the complexities and demands of everyday activities, it is very easy to lose sight of the big picture."[1] Leading complex organizations requires overcoming this myopia and establishing the systems that will connect vision to action.

Going back to the system for reaching visitors, the pastor may decide to "improve" the system by personally calling each new visitor and making in-home visits whenever possible. Sounds like a simple change, right? But consider the potential domino effects. The time spent on these contacts has to come from somewhere. It may mean less time spent on staff management or on sermon preparation or with family, but someone is going to feel the shift and may not like it. In addition, the visitors may now feel a much closer personal connection with the pastor and may expect more contact in the future, further increasing demands on the pastor's time. The fact that these visitors are more likely to come back and join the church may eventually create the need for more space. As new members, their connection with the pastor may open the way for them to serve in key leadership roles. This could bring new energy and ideas (a good thing) or resentment by the old guard who are being displaced (a bad thing). What seems like a simple idea to improve a basic system turns out to be quite complicated. In truth, the words *simple* and *system* don't go together.

There are many types of systems in congregations and other Christian organizations. Each of the topics from earlier chapters in Part One—planning, personnel, measurement, and finance—will have multiple related systems. For example, the broad category of human resources includes systems for hiring, evaluating performance, and assigning work. There are also systems for communication, scheduling, managing ministries, and making decisions. Other systems are designed to assimilate members, disciple them, and deploy them into ministry. Some systems may be formal and well documented, but lack of formality does not imply the absence of a system. The question is not whether you have systems but whether you need to invest to improve them.

A Reluctant Investment

Many leaders are hesitant to invest in better systems. If you ask why, they might acknowledge the need but say they are too busy with other mission-critical initiatives or with the day-to-day requirements of the organization. No doubt they are busy, but this statement also says that they are not convinced that the benefits justify the effort and investment.

The Bridgespan Group is a consulting firm that works exclusively with nonprofit organizations. In its work with more than two hundred of these entities, Bridgespan has found that "many nonprofits appear to be strongly led, but undermanaged. Why is this so?... The environment in which they operate often reinforces visionary leadership at the expense of management disciplines." Creating effective systems is a core management discipline, and it is one that is often put off by visionaries who want to focus on the next exciting opportunity. But as Bridgespan discovered, the organizational cost is high when systems are underdeveloped.[2]

On the flip side, a well-managed organization with well-designed systems will be more efficient. It can get more done with fewer financial resources and less time invested by employees and volunteers. It is amazing how much waste and frustration can be eliminated when the right systems are in place. Well-designed systems also make organizations more effective. An "effective" congregation has a clear sense of its mission, and the people and processes are aligned to accomplish this. Staff and laity understand their roles in light of the mission, funds are spent on the right priorities, and decisions are made by the right people at the right time for the right reason.

This is not simply a pragmatic argument. Once again, we are confronted with the biblical command to be good stewards, and managing our organizations to maximize their effectiveness is good stewardship. That is why Villanova University established the Center for the Study of Church Management. Director Charles Zech is fond of saying, "All churches need managerial help." He further explains, "We have a stewardship responsibility to use our resources effectively to carry out God's work on earth." When the right systems are in place, morale soars because employees are clear about their roles and feel they are making important contributions toward a God-ordained vision. The same is true for volunteers. In addition, donors are more likely to give generously to an organization that is well run. Investing wisely in systems has far-reaching benefits.

When Ken Williams came to WoodsEdge Community Church as executive pastor, the church did not have an adequate system in place for budgeting or financial management. In essence, spending decisions were based on whether the church had money in the bank rather than from a predefined set of priorities. Williams notes, "No one could plan, and no one knew what [one] could spend money on." So he instituted a budgeting process to plan the church's expenditures over a year and to align these with its stated priorities. It wasn't easy to impose this new discipline. "Nobody liked it when we were putting the budget together," Williams explains. "[People] said, 'This is like corporate America. Why do we have to do this?' They felt like they were going to be controlled. But once we went through it for a year, the staunchest antagonists became the staunchest protagonists. They wanted it." Rather than having to get approval every time they wanted to spend money, the staff could plan farther in advance, which helped them create better programs.

The right systems are valuable, but indiscriminate use of business models is not the answer. Before becoming Cross Point Church's executive director, Jenni Catron worked for a large Christian music company. Having plenty of experience with sophisticated systems, her role at Cross Point was to use her management expertise "to put feet to a vision." When she tried to implement corporate-style systems, she came to a screeching halt because the size and culture of the church were so different from her large-company background. This was particularly true when Catron tried to initiate a comprehensive staff development process. Her first attempt, using a complex multipage form, confused the staff. Rather than giving up, Catron modified the form into a simple one-page document that fit Cross Point's needs. This enabled her to have fruitful conversations with each staff member about their dreams and about ways they could improve.

Catron's story illustrates some of the obstacles to bringing systems into Christian organizations. Business approaches must be adapted, not adopted, because the environments are usually quite different. Even when adjustments are made to reflect the specific organization, the people who will be using the system may rebel. In some cases, their rebellion is innocent and comes from a lack of understanding. In other cases, their resistance is a response to the new and unwanted constraints that are being imposed.

The need for better systems has been heightened as 12Stone Church has added new campuses. Dan Reiland and the staff have talked openly about their reluctance to become more structured. Even though they don't like it, they know it is part of the price to be paid for growth. Senior pastor Kevin Myers offers a great analogy to the staff: "We love the trip, but we hate the airport. We hate the tickets and baggage and lines and security. But we sure want to get on the airplane and go for that ride!" The challenge, as Reiland explains, is to create needed policies "without letting it suffocate us. We work hard to keep the systems subordinated to the Spirit. We don't serve the policies; the policies serve us."

This fear of lost flexibility is a significant factor that keeps many pastors from investing in needed systems. Small organizations often lack formal processes, thus giving the first chair leader wide latitude in making decisions. For example, a new church may have an elder board whose members are handpicked by the pastor. As the church grows, a respected leader may suggest that the church formalize the process for selecting elders. Even though this is a common practice in many Christian organizations, the pastor may get anxious because he or she perceives that the new elders will be less likely to agree with his or her proposals.

These concerns must be recognized, but they should not prevent the implementation of healthy systems in a church or Christian organization. But what are "healthy systems"? They are the ones that facilitate ministry without strangling it—and finding this balance is no small feat. As Ken Williams says, "Every hour spent on structure and process is an hour not spent on ministry." When that hour invested in systems multiplies the hours available for ministry, it's a great investment. But business-minded leaders should remember that the church rarely needs the same level of sophistication that is found in business, and to impose this may stifle the work that God wants to do.

SYSTEMS IN ACTION

In all likelihood, the place where you serve (as the leader, a staff member, or a volunteer) has a number of systems in place. It is just as likely, however, that those systems are not meeting your current needs. The reason is that changes in the organization or the external environment often happen faster than the investment in systems. It is the same thing that occurs in a growing city when the construction of new subdivisions happens faster than the expansion of transportation infrastructure. New homes quickly lead to clogged highways. Systems can help or hinder dynamic organizations in a variety of ways, as will become apparent in the remainder of this chapter.

GROWING BEYOND THE START-UP PHASE

In business, start-up companies that survive the early years must next face the hurdle of multiplication. This occurs when the company becomes large enough that a leadership team is needed rather than a solo leader, and the founder and entrepreneur can no longer make all the decisions. When the success of the business outpaces the development of systems, problems start to pop up everywhere. As Jim Collins observes, "What was once great fun becomes an unwieldy ball of disorganized stuff."[3]

The same is true for a young church. It starts as a close-knit group of friends doing life together and sharing the gospel with others, and it grows to a community that no longer fits in someone's living room and can't make decisions by group consensus. When staff members are hired or facilities are needed or programs are created, the church needs to establish more formal systems. The need may not be pressing for a while, but at some point the lack of systems will hurt the growing body. It may happen when two leaders schedule major events at the same time or when members feel left out of an important decision. It may take years before the need becomes acute, but size inevitably requires more structure.

Living Water International (LWI) is a young, fast-growing organization that has been successful with relatively simple systems for all its history. CEO Mike Mantel recognizes that "the pace of growth sustained over a long time has stressed our systems and people. The challenge is to shore up our structure—caring for people in the field, inventory management and accounting, security procedures, human resource systems, insurance. We have people with tremendous capacity, but we need to intentionally build some underpinnings so we can sustain that pace." Mantel knows that this won't be easy and that some people may see this investment in systems as taking resources away from "real" ministry, but he knows that it is an essential step for LWI's long-term success.

Moving to the Next Level

If the challenge for a young organization is to create brand-new processes, the challenge at the next level is to revise (or even dismantle) processes that have become obsolete. Whether due to growth, a change in vision, or outside factors, out-of-date systems are not just an inconvenience; they can become a major impediment to future ministry effectiveness.

The Staff-Parish Relations Committee (SPRC) in a typical United Methodist Church is a group of laypeople with oversight responsibility for the congregation's paid staff. In the Methodist denomination, clergy are appointed by the bishop, so one of the SPRC's functions is to conduct an annual review of the pastor and submit this feedback to the bishop. The SPRC, as implied by its name, is also an intermediary between church members and staff when problems arise. This entire system was created in a day when the typical Methodist church had one clergyperson and no more than one or two other staff. But what happens if the church has grown and now has a dozen or more employees? Should an SPRC "supervise" the people who report to the pastor or associate pastor? Should they be involved in evaluating the performance of an administrative assistant?

The obvious answer is that the role of the SPRC needs to change as the church grows. The reality is that once a process is created (for example, oversight of all staff in a Methodist church), it can be very difficult to change. You may be thinking, "I'm glad

I'm not Methodist," but if your church has existed for more than a few years, you have systems that need to change to facilitate the ministry that you are currently called to do.

WHEN THE TAIL WAGS THE DOG

The SPRC example is mild compared to other cases. Some systems squeeze the life out of the organization. In one phase of my business career, I was managing a start-up environmental company. One of our most promising markets was a series of government-owned facilities that had massive cleanup needs. I still remember meeting with the manager at a particular site to explain how our technology could solve one of its problems. He seemed interested, but then he explained that he would need to obtain permission from fifty-nine other people before our company could do a small demonstration project. Needless to say, we did not get the contract because of a system that worked against the organization's needs.

This happens far too often in churches and is particularly prevalent in older, struggling congregations. Systems are designed for control, as if "control" will keep the ship from sinking. Whether it is a financial policy that requires lay approval for any expenditure over $100 or a committee that must review every use of the building, systems designed for tight control can become the proverbial tail that wags the dog.

"UNLEASHED" SYSTEMS

It is a challenge to keep systems updated and in sync with the organization's size and vision, but consider the value of a well-designed system as seen at Fellowship Bible Church in Little Rock. Fellowship's identity is built on being a "church of irresistible influence." The church encourages members to use their gifts in some sort of outward-facing ministry and defines success in terms of its impact in the community. Tim Lundy says, "I've never been in a place where I've seen more ministries spring up by laypeople." To support this, Fellowship has created the Unleashed Department to serve as a wise sounding board for new ministry ideas.

The concept, according to Lundy, is "to get the right people as your checkpoints and to let people [with entrepreneurial ministry ideas] go through a defined process." Lundy sees a number of benefits from this system: "In some cases, we've been great in empowering [entrepreneurs]. The church can help leaders before they jump out there and do more harm than good." Lundy knows that Fellowship doesn't always get it right when screening ideas and that some people believe the church has too much red tape. Ultimately, the process gives Lundy freedom to encourage entrepreneurial leaders and then point them to a next step where the hard questions will be asked. As he explains, "Some of us are wired more as gas [pedals], some as brakes. You need to have both in the car. The guys that are brakes say no a lot. They keep you safe. But if all you have is brakes, you're never going anywhere. If all you have is gas, you run off a lot of roads." This is the picture of vision and systems coming together to maximize Kingdom impact. The system to screen and launch new ministries is working in support of Fellowship's desire to be a church of irresistible influence.

Entangled Systems

One of the most touching moments in my research was my interview with Bishop Janice Huie. As the head of the Texas Annual Conference of the United Methodist Church, she provides leadership to more than seven hundred congregations and their clergy. When I asked about personnel practices, Huie paused for a second, and the look on her face told me that I had touched on a sensitive topic. She began by saying, "I've stayed awake at night more over this issue than any other."

Why is this such a vexing issue for her? As described earlier in this chapter, bishops in the denomination have oversight responsibility for all clergy, including their appointment to specific congregations. But the denomination also has a long-standing practice of "guaranteed appointments," meaning that clergy will not be fired unless they are guilty of moral failure or other serious misconduct. Poor performance can lead to a reassignment, but it almost never leads to the dismissal of a clergyperson. Bishop Huie articulates her dilemma clearly: "It's not right to put a pastor who's less than effective in a congregation. On the other hand, the church has not historically provided alternatives."

No alternatives? Is she being defeatist? Unwilling to make the hard leadership decisions? Before you rush to judgment, consider the multiple systems that are at work. The Texas Conference has only recently defined what it means to be an "effective pastor," and even this definition is somewhat vague. Without a clear standard based on well-defined and meaningful criteria, an adequate evaluation of a pastor's performance is virtually impossible. Does declining attendance always indicate a leadership deficiency? Or could the decline be a function of other issues in the congregation or community? Each congregation's SPRC submits an annual evaluation of its pastor to the bishop, but these reports are very subjective. A positive assessment may simply be due to a tendency to "be nice"; a negative one may be nothing more than a person with an ax to grind.

When she looks at Scripture, Bishop Huie sees passages that teach compassion and others that call for effective congregational leadership, and she feels conflicted. As a leader, she can communicate the rationale and the need for change. At the same time, she is sympathetic to the cry from many clergy, "This is not fair! The rules have changed in the middle of the game." In the past, she acknowledges, "no one held them accountable, no one asked if their church grew or declined. People weren't looking at [performance data] at that point, and now we are."

Bishop Huie has no control over the seminaries that prepare clergy to be pastors. The conference has increased its emphasis on leadership development and has established a small fund for sabbaticals, pastoral care, and career transitions, but in a time of constrained funding, these are costly options. A final process that handcuffs Methodist bishops is a polity that gives the clergy considerable influence over major policy changes. Bishop Huie concludes, "If I didn't think this is the way God was leading me as a bishop, I wouldn't have the stomach to do it." Even with her conviction, the shift toward clergy effectiveness and accountability is slow and painful.

This story illustrates the importance and complexity of systems. Everything truly is connected to everything else, which makes it impossible to change just one thing. A system that facilitated ministry in the past can become an impediment to changes that are needed in the present. The challenge facing the Texas Annual Conference goes beyond systems to deeper issues of team building, culture, and change management, subjects we will explore in Part Two. Nevertheless, as Bishop Huie is experiencing, the systems related to planning, personnel, finance, and measurement and the ways they intermesh are critical for success. The individual tools of leadership are important, but a leader must never lose sight of the fact that everything is connected in complex ways. Effective systems are the only way to keep the organization coordinated and moving in the right direction.

WHAT ARE YOU PURSUING?

- Do you suffer from "organizational myopia"? If so, what can you do to correct it?
- Reflect on a disappointment that your organization has experienced. Spend time identifying how different systems may have caused (or contributed to) the problem. It is best to do this in a brainstorming session with a small group.
- What is one area where lack of systems or poor systems are holding you back? What steps can you take to address this problem?
- If systems and processes are not your strength, the person who may be able to help the most is also a person who frequently frustrates you. Sit down and ask this person for ideas on how your systems might be improved and how these improvements would benefit the organization.

PART TWO

BEYOND THE TOOLS

As I confessed the beginning of Part One, I am not a handyman. But let's imagine for a moment that I am a multiskilled, highly talented craftsman who has a shed filled with every imaginable tool and the resources to buy whatever supplies I need. (Believe me, that takes a lot of imagination!) If that were true, I could build a simple house for my family to live in. I could make furniture for the house. I could use my skills to earn enough income to provide for my family's needs.

But if I were asked to build something much larger—an office building or a hospital or a church—I would be lost. My imaginary skills and tools would certainly be needed for this kind of project, but they wouldn't be enough. Large, complex building projects require more than the skills of a master craftsman. They require an architect to envision the entire structure and translate this into a design. They require a construction manager who can break the design into separate steps and assign them to different people according to their expertise.

Effective leadership in the church requires the tools described in Part One, but it also requires skills and understanding beyond these tools. A pastor who becomes more proficient in the use of the tools will see a huge leap in his or her leadership. If a congregation is reasonably healthy and not too large, these core skills may be enough to take the organization to the next level. But "reasonably healthy" and "not too large" are big qualifiers. Some of you are leading large organizations, and many of you may sense that there is something deeper that is holding you back. That is why you need more than tools.

In large construction projects, a team of people—architects, construction managers, various trades—bring their expertise together to build something much greater than any could have done individually. That's where the comparison with the church is partly right and partly wrong. The complex, multidimensional task of leadership calls for a team, not just one individual. It is not reasonable or feasible for a pastor or the executive director of a ministry or a university president to be an expert in every facet of leadership. But someone is still the lead leader, even in a healthy, collaborative, team-oriented organization. Beyond a general understanding of the leadership tools from Part One, that leader needs to have a firm grasp on the issues described in Part Two.

Like Part One, this part does not provide a comprehensive list of everything a leader needs to know. Instead, it focuses on four "beyond the tools" topics that are vital to effective leadership: the importance of creating and maintaining a unified team, the foundational power of culture, the complex dynamics of change, and the critical need for soul care. Failure in any of these areas can completely undermine all the hard work that a leader has done with the tools of leadership. In each of these areas, there is much to learn for the journey to greatness and godliness.

CHAPTER NINE

IS EVERYONE ON THE SAME PAGE?

The opening pages of Part Two described the importance of having a team of leaders with a variety of gifts and perspectives. So consider this scenario: You are introduced to a highly successful businessman who is also a dedicated Christian. He is very serious about using his gifts—his knowledge, his experience, and his wealth—to further God's Kingdom. In fact, he regularly meets with a small group of like-minded Christian businessmen who challenge one another in this regard. His commitment is to give away half of his time and half of his annual income to Christian ministries and other nonprofits, with the latter commitment resulting in five- and six-figure contributions to selected causes. The organizations that have been the beneficiaries of his time have taken huge steps forward in organizational effectiveness. Would you want him on your team as a board member or in some other key advisory role?

Before you say yes and ask for his contact information, think about what you would do if this person was interested in helping your ministry. Even better, think about how you actually do treat others like him who are already connected with your ministry.

Who is this man? Does he wear a blue suit with a red cape and a big *S* on the front? The particular man, in this case, is David Weekley, president of David Weekley Homes. But the reality is that there are plenty of others like Weekley. Many men and women who are highly successful in business are also committed Christians, seeking to use what God has given them for greater purposes. The deeper reality is that their offer to help, with financial resources or talent, is not always received with open arms. Pastors and other spiritual leaders may do more to push these individual away than to invite them in.

Creating a unified leadership team with a great mix of gifts should be a high priority for every leader. As God gives bigger challenges and opportunities to a ministry, the importance of this diversity increases. And the more diverse the leadership team, the more difficult it is to remain unified.

I have intentionally not defined the term *leaders* in this context. If you are in a multistaff church, then the staff (or senior staff, if it is a very large church) is a leadership team. Even small fractures within this group will spread throughout the congregation, often with crippling effects. The staff has the advantage of spending time together on a regular basis, and that can help promote mutual understanding and appreciation. An even bigger challenge is getting the members of the key lay leadership teams on the same page. They need to work well with each other and must establish a strong partnership with the pastor and other senior staff members.

The discussion in this chapter is applicable for any group of leaders who want to work together effectively for their enterprise to thrive. It is particularly aimed at the interface between a spiritual leader who heads the ministry and the key volunteers who fill primary leadership roles. This is the interface where great and godly leaders need to collaborate but often collide. When they are truly on the same page, the church becomes the powerful body that God intends it to be and against which the gates of hell will not prevail (Matthew 16:18).

WE NEED EACH OTHER

If you sit in the first chair role in your organization, you need to ask yourself, "Do I truly believe that I need others to share in the leadership of this enterprise? Do I think the involvement of people with different experiences, gifts, and perspectives will help us make better leadership decisions? Or do I merely tolerate their input because I have no other choice?" If you think you can do it all on your own, this chapter may not be for you.

If you are a key leader who is not in a first chair role—board member, vice-president, executive pastor, close adviser—you need to ask yourself different questions: "Do I have confidence that the senior leader is God's person for this role, despite whatever differences there are in our abilities and outlooks? Or do I find myself thinking that I could do a better job if I were in charge?" I cannot force you to respect your lead leader, but I can promise that you will always struggle if respect is lacking. As you continue reading, I hope you will focus on the personal changes you need to make rather than the shortcomings of someone else on your team.

TEAMWORK: JUST GOOD SENSE

We need each other. To accomplish God's mission, Christian organizations desperately need to leverage the combined talents of a diverse leadership team. I don't know of anyone who will publicly disagree with this statement, but people's actions often indicate otherwise. Leadership is messy, and deep down, many of us would rather not have to make room for the opinions and personalities of other people. We are easily lured by the image of the all-powerful leader who makes unilateral decisions.

The problem with this image is that it rarely works. One pastor has practiced this "command-and-control" style throughout his long tenure, and the church has gone from nondescript to megachurch. He has advised other up-and-coming leaders to follow his example: "Take charge. Show them you're the boss." Unfortunately, many of these leaders have taken his advice to heart and have caused deep conflict in their own churches. The strong, solo leader model is attractive because it seems like it will be more efficient, and it certainly feeds the ego of leaders. It may occasionally work, but far more often it leads to disappointing or disastrous results.

The broader wisdom on organization leadership does not support the solo model. Kouzes and Posner explain, "Exemplary leaders know that 'you can't do it alone,' and they act accordingly."[1] Ron Heifitz says, "Even if the weight of carrying people's hopes and pains may fall mainly, for a time, on one person's shoulders, leadership cannot be exercised alone. The lone-warrior model of leadership is heroic suicide."[2] These and many other experts have found that turbulent times require a multidisciplinary leadership approach that is possible only through true collaboration. They know that two heads are better than one. They point to a model in which a group of leaders comes together in a high-trust environment to wrestle with the organization's strategic issues. In this setting, each leader contributes from his or her unique expertise and perspective to shape a better answer.

One of the best resources on this subject is *The Wisdom of Teams* by Jon Katzenbach and Douglas Smith. Their very specific definition is that a team is "a small number of people with complementary skills who are committed to a common purpose, performance goals, and approach for which they hold themselves mutually accountable."[3] Katzenbach and Smith contend that we often use the word *team* for a group that does not fit this definition. They use the term *working groups* to distinguish nonteams from true teams. Katzenbach and Smith recognize that creating true teams is hard work and acknowledge that some situations call only for working groups. They conclude, "When specific performance challenges require the real-time contributions of people with different skills and experiences, choosing a team approach promises significant performance potential and offers important benefits over a working group."[4] Far too often, leaders in Christian organizations run from anything that hints at the common goals and mutual accountability that Katzenbach and Smith describe. Far too often, Christian organizations need true teams but their leaders operate in working groups.

Some leaders do not embrace a collaborative approach because they are not convinced it will lead to a better result. Like a group project in school, they think they will end up doing the work anyway or that the participation of others will actually hurt the final product. Even if you think you know the "right" answer and don't need input (which is rarely the case), involving key leaders deeply in the decision-making process has another important benefit. In *The Fifth Discipline*, Peter Senge describes the "different attitudes toward a vision" that can exist in an organization. He says that we often settle for *compliance* when we should be striving for *commitment*. Senge explains, "There *is* a world of difference between compliance and commitment. The committed person brings an energy, passion, and excitement that cannot be generated if you are only compliant. ... A group of people truly committed to a common vision is an awesome force. They can accomplish the seemingly impossible."[5]

Commitment happens most readily when people feel that their voices have been heard and reflected in the decision-making process. The leadership experts point to the huge potential that can be released when an organization taps into the gifts and energy of the people who are already there. The same potential exists in churches, and the same failure to reach this potential occurs far too often.

TEAMWORK: GOD'S SENSE AS WELL

Does the Bible teach something different about teams than what is found in secular best practices? We may think of Moses or some other biblical leader as the prototypical example of the solo leader. Indeed, there are times when someone receives a special anointing and message from God, and these directions are not subject to a committee decision. God told Moses to lead the people out of Egypt. He told Joshua to cross the Jordan and gave specific instructions on how to capture Jericho. But don't lose sight of the fact that Moses still had Aaron, Hur, Miriam, Jethro, and Joshua as key "second chairs." Keep in mind that Caleb served alongside Joshua throughout the conquest of the Promised Land. And don't think that this model—"God has spoken to me, so follow"—is the only image in Scripture.

Romans 12 and 1 Corinthians 12 are well-known passages that emphasize the importance of each part of the body and how the different parts need to work together. Paul, who was certainly a strong leader, was sent out on his first missionary journey with Barnabas as his partner and only after the elders in the church in Antioch had collectively felt this to be God's will. Rodney Cooper of Gordon-Conwell Theological Seminary says, "It has to be affirmed on various levels for you to actually be a leader. God never calls individuals to just be leaders. He calls them to communities." We need each other, not just as a pragmatic matter, but because it is the biblical model.

In my interviews, this was a common refrain. Christ Fellowship is a church with a culture of Spirit-led decisions. In some congregations with this kind of culture, that means God speaks to the pastor, who then tells the rest of the leadership, "This is what God said." Todd Mullins does not shrink back from leading boldly and from telling the elders what God has put on his heart, but as noted in Chapter Seven, he also believes that God will lead them to a collective, unified decision. A key verse for Mullins is Proverbs 1:5: "Let the wise listen and add to their learning." For Mullins, these are words to live by as he interacts with the elders at Christ Fellowship.

Greg Holder was a counselor before becoming pastor of The Crossing. In a congregation with many successful marketplace leaders, he knows that their leadership and business experience far exceeds his own. Holder recognizes the value of surrounding himself with "men and women who understand best practices and who actually speak the language of business." By listening to their wisdom, he is able to grow as a leader. And by letting them into the inner circles of leadership, he is able to establish greater credibility with other leaders in the congregation.

Before going any further, let me offer an important clarification. Many of the examples in this chapter focus on the gap between business-minded leaders and pastors. However, the gap between leaders can take many forms. It can occur between a seminary-trained pastor and the mostly blue-collar members of a congregation. It can occur when a young pastor with new ideas tries to lead a rural congregation with a long history. It can occur when the passionate leader of a nonprofit organization is forced to answer pragmatic questions from a down-to-earth advisory team that doesn't see how to make the money work. It can happen in any organization where the leadership team brings widely divergent backgrounds and perspectives to the table—something that is usually the case in Christian organizations.

WHY GOOD AND GODLY SENSE IS REJECTED

So why don't pastors embrace these leaders and create a more collaborative environment? One of the biggest reasons is that spiritual leaders are not sure how to relate to businesspeople and are even intimidated by powerful, hard-charging executives. Michael Lindsay, president of Gordon College and a sociologist by training, has done extensive research in the area of leadership. In *Faith in the Halls of Power*, Lindsay examines the faith practices of high-level leaders in business, politics, media, and academia. He found vibrant faith practices to be common in his interviews with 360 evangelical leaders in these fields, but one finding should be troubling for any pastor. Lindsay reports that "the general trend among leaders I interviewed is an overall distance from local church life" and that they "felt more comfortable in the parachurch's corporate environment, where decision making was quick and centralized compared to the deliberative, democratic process that typified many church boards."[6] In other words, the local church is often not benefiting from the talents of highly capable Christian leaders.

Lindsay, who is a committed Christian and active church member, wanted to understand why these business leaders often distanced themselves from local congregations, so he explored this in his interviews. He says, "Dozens of evangelical business leaders spoke of ongoing tensions with their ministers, and nearly all attributed them to personal insecurity on the part of the pastors or a general inability to lead congregations that included recognized business leaders."[7] When the business leader in the room is accustomed to making multimillion-dollar decisions and directing an entity that has hundreds of employees, his or her leadership abilities may overshadow those of the senior pastor. For many pastors, it can be threatening to bring this kind of high-level leader into the inner circles of decision making.

Even when pastors or ministry leaders invite high-level businesspeople onto a leadership team, the spiritual leaders may not know how to work with the newcomers. Terry Looper, who is the president of his own successful energy company, has left the boards of ministries when they have been unwilling to heed outside advice. Looper is not insistent on getting his own way, but he does want to feel that his time is being well spent and that his voice matters. His decision to leave a board is not a power play but rather a personal move to avoid becoming cynical. If a ministry repeatedly sees business-minded people leaving its board, this should cause its leaders to pause and ask why.

When Menlo Park Presbyterian Church made the decision to create the position of "directional pastor," senior pastor John Ortberg was specifically looking for someone who "leads recreationally." In saying this, he meant a second chair person with strong leadership gifts and experience who would complement Ortberg's own ability to "communicate recreationally." Menlo Park Presbyterian is a diverse congregation that includes people who have been very successful in the marketplace, and Ortberg recognized that these other leaders would respond well to someone who was like them. So the church called Alan "Blues" Baker to this role, a man who had risen to the rank of rear admiral in the Navy and who received theological degrees from Fuller and Gordon-Conwell seminaries.

If you are a pastor who is long on theological training and short on leadership training, you don't have to follow the Menlo Park example and hire an experienced second chair leader. Memorial Drive Presbyterian Church is another congregation with many accomplished members, and Dave Peterson knew that he needed to connect with them in order to lead effectively. Peterson is an intelligent, articulate, experienced pastor, so I was surprised by his candid admission that he had to push himself to get out and meet with these marketplace leaders. Peterson explains, "The world of business is mysterious to me. We almost speak foreign languages. I confess to being quite intimidated [by business leaders]. I go into a meeting with a level of anxiety, and I come out with a level of appreciation."

The result is that Peterson has grown in his own leadership and in his respect for these corporate leaders: "They have a way of cutting through a lot of stuff that sidetracks me. They have a capacity of discernment that identifies core questions and issues." By acknowledging his fears and working through them, Peterson has become a better pastor and the church has benefited from its pastor's growth and from the expertise of a group of leaders who might have otherwise stayed distant. We need each other, and we all need to take concrete steps toward collaboration and teamwork.

THE FIRST STEPS

The distance between spiritual and business leaders can be huge, but you can begin to close the gap. It starts with recruiting the *right* leaders and establishing a viable structure in which collaborative leadership can occur. This sounds simple and obvious, but too many ministries stumble in these basic steps.

Recruiting the Right Leaders

Not every successful business leader who is a Christian qualifies as a candidate for top-level leadership in a church. If a person's understanding of leadership has not been shaped by Scripture, a serious disconnect may occur as the person steps into a role in the congregation. Judy West recalls a pilot class she created for leadership development shortly after joining the staff of The Crossing. It seemed logical to recruit people who were marketplace leaders for this pilot, but West says the result was "a nightmare." Even though these individuals knew how to lead, they were not necessarily godly people, nor had they internalized The Crossing's vision and culture. After completing the class, none of these individuals moved into roles of serving in the church. Based on that initial experience, The Crossing refined its leadership development process considerably. Potential leaders are now required to go through three different sessions—"vision venues"—in which they learn more about the culture and direction of the church and what is required of leaders. Then they are expected to begin serving (not leading) in a ministry. When West needs someone to step into a leadership role, she looks for people who have gone through the vision venues, who are serving capably, and who have personal stories of The Crossing's impact on their lives. This process gives The Crossing a great pool to draw from to meet its key leadership needs.

Even if you recruit people who love God and are committed to the organization, the ways that they lead will be affected by the attitudes and behaviors of other leaders and the culture of the organization. When expectations are clear and match the culture, the right leaders will rise to the surface and thrive. The Church of the Resurrection (Methodist) is very intentional about its expectations for all its leaders. Staff members are asked to sign a covenant, which in turn sets the tone for those who serve in volunteer leadership roles. Volunteer leaders are held accountable for worship attendance, service, financial support, and personal spiritual growth. When leaders are accountable in this way and see their peers held to the same standard, it creates a virtuous cycle in which the positive, expected behavior is continually reinforced.

Unfortunately, many ministries suffer from the opposite, a vicious cycle in which unhealthy leaders create a negative environment that drives healthy leaders away. You may be in an organization where spiritual maturity is not a criterion for selecting leaders. Many churches have formal rules or informal traditions that place the wrong people in key leadership roles. These are often the people who have been members the longest or give the most money or have the loudest voices. If you find yourself in that situation, realize that it may take a long time to get the right people into key leadership positions. You may even need to amend the bylaws or make other procedural changes. But also realize that this is a high-leverage change. If the core leadership teams are not healthy and are filled with people who are not seeking God first, your organization will always struggle.

Finding the right people to serve on the board or in other key leadership groups raises one tricky aspect of diversity. I am not talking about ethnic or gender diversity but rather about diversity in backgrounds and experiences. Even though diverse gifts and perspectives are needed, it is very difficult to mix high-capacity leaders with people who are unaccustomed to making strategic decisions. The latter tend to obsess over smaller concerns, and the former want to focus only on the major issues.

Michael Lindsay found this to be a recurring theme in his interviews with high-level executives:

> Evangelical executives often had trouble serving in positions of responsibility in a church. James Unruh, who served as the chief executive of Unisys, also served at one time as an elder within his congregation. He has decided he will never serve again. Like other business leaders, the inefficiency of church meetings was too frustrating for Unruh. He said to me, "For most people, the biggest event of the month is coming to that meeting. . . . It's very frustrating to be patient and not to try to run things because that's what you're doing all day in your business."[8]

This dilemma is not easy to address. Some congregations have strong cultures of inclusiveness in their key leadership bodies, as opposed to a gift-based approach. This often creates the scenario described in Lindsay's interviews. Changing this culture will take time and may not be a price worth paying. But pastors need to be aware of a hidden cost: the loss of the wisdom of experienced leaders who may choose not to serve in this kind of setting.

Establishing Viable Structures

Getting the right people is vital, and having the right structures and processes is equally important. In fact, as already noted, the right structures and processes facilitate getting the right people. I was impressed in several of my interviews with how thoughtfully some leaders had developed this aspect of their organizations.

The process for selecting board members at HOPE International is a great example. Current board members are invited to submit formal, written recommendations for new board candidates. These nominees are then screened by a subcommittee of the board to assess whether they fit HOPE's needs and culture. Some are chosen, some are not, and some are invited to serve on one of the organization's regional boards, where their contributions can be observed first-hand. For the top-level board, new members serve an initial term of one year. This creates an easy exit point for anyone who is not a good fit.

A common organizational practice is to have limited terms for the members of a leadership group, after which time the person rotates off. But often the same person rotates back onto the group, almost automatically, after sitting out for a year. The members of Willow Creek Community Church's board serve for four years, and then they must rotate off. But Willow adds an interesting twist: a person can return to the board only by the unanimous vote of the current board members. If anyone on the board feels that the person did not make a positive contribution during his or her previous term, the person won't be invited to serve again. As Jim Mellado says, this is one significant way to "create intentional on-ramps and intentional off-ramps," which is a healthy practice for any leadership team.

Another interesting variation on structure is Cross Point Church, which has a board of elders and a separate board of directors. The former focuses on the spiritual health and wellness of the church and is the group to which Pastor Pete Wilson is accountable. The board of directors is appointed by the elders and is charged with the business of the church—policy, legal, and financial matters. Of course, you can't completely separate spiritual and business issues, so the two boards meet together periodically to form good working relationships and then at specific times on important decisions. Cross Point has made it clear, however, that the board of elders is the church's ultimate decision-making body and that the board of directors serves in an advisory role.

This points to one final aspect of structure that is extremely important: role clarity. Just as it is important for an individual staff member to be clear about the expectations for his or her job, leadership groups in your organization also need to be clear about their roles. Many organizations have never defined the expectations for these leadership groups or their purpose has drifted over time. When clarity is lacking, individual members will fill in their own definitions. This self-definition will often be shaped by a personal agenda or past experience in another ministry's leadership structure. How many times have you heard someone say, "At my former church, we did . . ."? If the leadership or advisory group lacks a clear understanding of its role, significant differences can emerge at the most inopportune times. For example, should the personnel committee set general policies for dealing with underperforming staff members and then let the pastor or executive pastor implement that policy? Or should the committee dive into a discussion on the performance of a specific employee? Should the church council focus on the broad strategic direction of the ministry or review every proposed initiative and program change? These are the kinds of struggles that arise from a lack of role clarity for leadership teams.

At a minimum, any organization should develop a simple, written description of the roles for each of its key leadership groups. The description should explain what they are expected to do and what is outside of their scope of responsibilities. The group's leader then has an opportunity—and an obligation—to enforce this in group meetings. If the agenda starts to stray beyond this scope, the leader can gently remind all participants that they need to get back to the things for which they have responsibility.

Beyond this, effective organizations regularly review these expectations. One of the best times to do this is when new members are added to the leadership team. The review can be done in the context of educating the newcomers, but it is also a great reminder for those members who are continuing to serve. At an earlier time in the history of the Church of the Resurrection (Anglican), Karen Miller realized that leaders were not in agreement on who was supposed to make which decisions. The congregation's leaders invested the energy to create clear role descriptions, and now each year, in separate off-site events, the vestry (lay leadership group), staff, and clergy are reminded of their specific responsibilities. This kind of clarity can reduce tension and help leaders stay on the same page.

The Hard Steps

Clearly defined roles, the right structure, and spiritually mature leaders are essential for healthy teamwork, but they are not enough. Another factor that is unseen and harder to describe is even more crucial: group chemistry. A trust-based environment in which people are able to engage in honest, open dialogue is the only way to tackle the real challenges confronting an organization. As Patrick Lencioni says, "Trust lies at the heart of a functioning, cohesive team. Without it, teamwork is all but impossible." He goes on to define *trust* as "the confidence among team members that their peers' intentions are good, and that there is no reason to be protective or careful around the group."[9]

Trust begins with the first chair leader. The pastor, president, or executive director sets the tone when it comes to building trust, because trust requires a level of vulnerability that does not come easily. Kouzes and Posner discovered how important this is: "If we could offer you only one bit of advice on how to start the process of creating a climate of trust it would be this: be the first to trust. Building trust is a process that begins when one party is willing to risk being the first to open up, being the first to show vulnerability, and being the first to let go of control."[10] If the leader of the group is not willing to be open and honest, the rest of the group will pick up on this and follow suit. If the leader is defensive when criticized, other members will tend to bottle up their concerns.

Rather than addressing the real problems, they may mirror the leader's defensiveness or make excuses if they are singled out.

Being vulnerable is a tough pill to swallow for many Christian leaders, especially pastors. On one hand, trust and vulnerability should come most easily to us. Scripture repeatedly directs us to be humble, trusting, and honest and to have confidence in God. On the other hand, some pastors have been attacked or betrayed when they have opened up and trusted others. Another obstacle to trust is when a spiritual leader believes that he or she belongs on a pedestal and should never admit to having feet of clay. These barriers to trust may not be easy to overcome, but a church will not accomplish what God wants unless it is led by a unified team that can deal with important matters in an environment of honesty and transparency.

The leaders I interviewed recognize the importance of a trust-based environment, especially in their top leadership body. Mitch Peairson uses words like *transparency* and *integrity* to describe interactions among Grace Fellowship's board, but he is quick to point out that this has been built over a number of years. Peairson is right: it takes time and intentionality to build this kind of environment.

Trust does not mean an absence of tension; it often means just the opposite. In describing leadership meetings at Healing Place Church, Dino Rizzo says, "There's tension all the time. You're making decisions about people and facilities and campuses. We have a healthy tension. There's nothing wrong with sitting in the room in a safe way, in an honorable way, and in respect saying, 'Walk me through this, Pastor.' It's hard to do that with people you don't trust. The starting point is making sure you have the right people at the table." In a trust-based environment, disagreement is allowed, and even expected, as spiritually mature people wrestle with how to best understand and follow God's will.

Spiritual leaders need to invite differing opinions, but that does not mean that the loudest voice rules the day. In fact, a healthy environment makes it easier for a leader to be confident in standing up to opposition. Peter Greer of HOPE International says, "I've grown in my realization that I don't have to say yes [to every request from a strong leader]. Just because someone is successful in business doesn't mean that the person knows the specific answer for every issue we face." But Greer also acknowledges an appreciation for the business leaders on HOPE's board because of their knack for asking the hard questions. This has forced him to sharpen his reasoning and has led to better decisions on strategic issues.

Disagreement in the process of discernment is normal, but too often this conflict becomes unhealthy. When major issues arise, the atmosphere can become toxic if a leadership team hasn't established norms for handling disagreement. Rodney Cooper says teams need to "storm together" to learn how to appreciate and work well with each other. It is in the midst of the tough challenges that people get beneath the superficial stuff to work on the serious matters, and in doing so, they build deeper relationships.

The concept of "storming together" is a great image, but two people see the same storm through different eyes. One sees a hurricane, and the other thinks it's a great day to fly a kite. This is another place where the differences between pastoral and business leaders can be quite pronounced. As we will explore in Chapter Eleven, many pastors think of themselves as "shepherds," people who should maintain peace as much as possible. Business leaders are not trying to cause conflict, but they are often much more blunt in the way they handle disagreements. They may get into a meeting and "cut to the chase." They may also seem to be "all business," as if the spiritual dimension does not exist.

What is a pastor to do if this happens? For starters, don't be afraid to emphasize God's presence, but also grow a little thicker skin. A pastor should not be surprised if the businesspeople behave in church meetings the same way that they do in their Monday-to-Friday jobs. If a person is rewarded professionally for making tough calls, getting to the bottom of issues, and strongly advocating for his position, you shouldn't be surprised if he or she does the same thing in a volunteer leadership role. The spiritual leader who encounters this behavior may be taken aback, but the wise leader discerns the difference between directness and disrespect, between a sharp difference of opinion and an attack. If the behavior truly becomes inappropriate, that is the point at which the pastor needs to confront it or redirect the conversation.

At the same time, business-minded leaders should remember that spiritual leaders are cut from a different cloth. The directness that is accepted and appreciated in the corporate arena can be offensive in ministry settings. Businesspeople should appreciate the weight their pastor carries in leading the congregation. They should realize that it takes a special gift to minister to a bereaved family or counsel a couple whose marriage is falling apart, all while preparing and delivering inspiring sermons and leading a complex organization. Rather than being frustrated with a pastor who approaches decisions differently, marketplace leaders should be thankful for someone who fears God more than people and who genuinely wants to discern God's will for the church.

Every time a leader stands up to a serious challenge, he or she takes a risk. Jan Davis of First United Methodist Church in Rowlett, Texas, describes the stewardship emphasis she led in her first year as pastor. The church had not done a stewardship campaign in five years, and several key leaders were opposed to doing one at that time. It was an agonizing season for Davis. She felt that the campaign was the right thing to do, but she also knew that a failed effort would hurt her credibility as a leader. Davis vividly recalls her fear and anxiety, and she also recalls spending a lot of time in prayer. In one pivotal moment as an associate prayed with her, Davis felt God directing her to move forward. She did so despite the concerns of other leaders, and the campaign exceeded her greatest hopes. Davis says, "I was still scared to death until the pledge cards started coming in, and then I couldn't believe it. I thought, 'I'm sorry, God, that I didn't trust you. How stupid I am thinking it's all about me.' God was there all along. It's not about me, it's not about my leadership. It's about the Holy Spirit working in me to do what God wants." In following God rather than backing down, Davis grew as a leader and the church grew as well.

Ultimately, a spiritual leader's ability to face challenges must come from his or her relationship with God. Gregg Matte was thirty-three years old and had never pastored a church when he was called to become the senior pastor of Houston's First Baptist Church. It was a huge step for Matte and for this prominent congregation. How did he earn the respect of the church's veteran lay leaders? Matte talks about the importance of building relationships with them, but he also says that he did not let himself get pushed around. He recalls one particularly tense moment: "I had a conversation with an older gentleman who told me I needed to remember who I worked for, that I worked for the congregation. And I said, 'No sir. I *work for* Jesus Christ, and I *serve* the congregation.' He said, 'Point taken,' and backed down." It's a bold answer, and a great way to put the discussion of teamwork in context. We need to strive for unity and getting our leadership teams on the same page, but great leadership does not mean abandoning our convictions about where God is leading.

INFLUENCING MORE THAN MINISTRY

This chapter has focused on the ways that diverse leaders can, and in fact must, work together to achieve all that God wants in their ministries. I can't end, however, without touching on one other important point. Earlier I said that we should not be surprised when business leaders bring their workplace mind-sets into the church. I want to conclude by considering the flow of influence in the opposite direction. Andy Doyle, bishop of the Episcopal Diocese of Texas, says, "I do not buy the business books that talk about Jesus as a great model for business, because Jesus is a great model for human relationships with one another and with God. Jesus offers us the opportunity to transform the world of business. At the end of the day, if we are not asking the question 'How does the church and the message of Christianity transform the way we do business in the world?' then we are missing our calling. I think we will know how well the church has been able to adapt and adopt the practices coming out of the business world when we, the church, begin to affect wholly the business community."

If you wonder why the church doesn't more significantly influence business leaders to transform their workplaces, Michael Lindsay again offers some potent insights. He reports that many evangelical business executives "talked about their pastor being completely removed from the working world they inhabit ... for preaching irrelevant sermons that fail to connect with the challenges faced by business leaders today."[11] I had a first-hand experience several years ago that brought this point home. I attended a seminar in Houston where the host church's pastor made a presentation on the need for Christian leaders to be different from the world. Nothing wrong with that. He then pointed to Enron

Corporation, which had recently collapsed in an epic financial scandal, as the counterexample. In his remarks, he made it sound as if every employee at Enron was unethical and driven solely by greed. As I sat in the audience, I fumed. I knew several people who worked for Enron, and I knew that many were honest, hardworking individuals, some of whom had lost their life savings when the company's stock collapsed. In trying to make his point and capitalize on a current event, this pastor made some gross generalizations that would have offended any businessperson in the audience.

Pastors who lack an understanding of the marketplace find it easy to vilify corporate managers. If you want to influence the business world, you need to get close enough to understand the everyday pressures that corporate executives face and the things that keep them awake at night. You may find that many of them agonize over decisions that could cost hundred of people their jobs or that may be within the law yet on the edge of what their consciences will allow. You may get a glimpse at how hard it is to practice humility and put others first in an environment where self-promotion is the norm. Likewise, if you are a businessperson, you can help build the bridge by inviting your pastor into the part of your life where you spend most of your waking hours.

I am not saying that biblical standards must be compromised in the marketplace. I am, however, saying that overly simplistic, black-and-white messages, like the one I heard, will alienate businesspeople. Instead, we need pastors who can relate to business leaders and offer godly counsel that they can use in their jobs. We desperately need men and women in the corporate and political arenas who are just as passionate about their faith as their pastors. This will only happen if the gap between them is closed. When that gap is closed, it will not only help leaders look more like Christ in their jobs but will also get them on the same page with their pastors in the leadership of the church.

What Are You Pursuing?

- Are you and other key leaders on the same page? Word for word? On the same page but not the same paragraph? In the same book but in different chapters? Not even in the same book?

- Be honest with yourself. Do you genuinely appreciate the people who have skills and perspectives that are very different from yours? Or do such differences frustrate you?
- Does your organization have the right processes to get the right people into leadership? Are those leadership groups structured in the right ways?
- Is there a trusted insider who can give you honest feedback on the positive and negative ways that you interact with other leaders?
- How vulnerable are you willing to be with your key leaders? What steps can you take to become more vulnerable?
- If you are a spiritual leader, make appointments to meet with some of your key leaders in their workplaces. Have no agenda other than to understand the leadership issues that they wrestle with and to learn from their experiences.

CHAPTER TEN

WHY IS CULTURE IMPORTANT?

To this point in the book, one word that I have used frequently but have never defined is *culture*. That is because culture is hard to pin down. Even though it is elusive, culture must not be ignored. Samuel Chand, in *Cracking Your Church's Culture Code*, says, "Culture—not vision or strategy—is the most powerful factor in any organization."[1] An even more colorful expression, attributed to Peter Drucker, is "Culture eats strategy for breakfast."

This point was driven home in my very first interview when Judy West of The Crossing said, "This culture spits people out. When you talk to Greg, ask him to explain what that means." A few weeks later, lead pastor Greg Holder described how The Crossing is intentionally fostering its culture. The church teaches that Christians are called to surrender their whole lives to Christ and emphasizes that this includes the ways in which people treat and talk to each other and how they resolve conflict. Through Bodylife, a class for people who are new to The Crossing, Holder teaches from John 17 that unity in the body is very important to God and that the way believers treat each other is how the world will know they belong to the Father. He remarks, "When the church shoots its wounded and eats its young, that's not just a bad thing. It's the exact opposite of what Jesus teaches."

So The Crossing consistently teaches and models unity, healthy conflict resolution, and forgiveness. As the leadership core has embraced and practiced this teaching, it has become normative. Invariably, some people do not understand or embrace this standard. If a person erupts in unhealthy conflict or gossip around others from the church, it is likely that someone will respond, "We don't do things like that here." At that point, the first person will need to decide whether to change his or her actions or find another church where such behavior is tolerated. Holder concludes that this kind of behavior-shaping "exclusivity" is what it means for a culture to "spit people out."

WHAT IS CULTURE?

If an art history expert could be dropped into the historical section of an unfamiliar city in Europe without knowing where she is, the buildings would give her plenty of clues. Where an untrained observer might simply see beautiful old structures, the expert can make an informed guess about the date of construction and the region in which it is located. A tourist might at best recognize generic styles of architecture, such as Romanesque, Gothic, Renaissance, or Baroque. The expert looks at a much finer level of detail in making her assessment. If examining a cathedral, she will look at the type of stones and mortar used, the level of detail and craftsmanship, the height of the roof, the length of the nave, the use or lack of flying buttresses, the style of steeple, the types of gargoyles, the colors and artwork in the stained glass, and much more. She will notice the influences from another designer or school of theory that will place the structure on a historical timeline. She may see clues from different eras that clearly indicate two stages of construction or many sporadic phases over a long period of time. All these bits of evidence, many of which seem insignificant on their own, are important puzzle pieces that fit together to tell the story of the building and the town as a whole.

In the same way, it would be simplistic to describe a church's culture in one or two words or to assess the culture based on a single piece of evidence. Every organization has its own unique culture, and there are countless internal clues that a wise leader will learn to recognize. Sometimes the culture is easy to read because it is clear and internally consistent, so that what is proclaimed to be important matches organizational behavior. Often it is much more elusive. People may make declarative statements about the organization's identity, but there is little evidence of that identity in what it does. Some organizations have multiple cultures, just as a building constructed in stages may show the influence of different artistic styles. Leaders who fail to understand the culture will be frustrated, because an organization's response to a leader is always a function of its culture.

I worked with one church that was seeking to develop a new long-range plan. The congregation, located in a fast-growing suburb, had outgrown its facilities and had ample land for expansion. Despite this, the leaders were unwilling to take the first steps toward launching a building campaign. Their reluctance was rooted not in a theological conviction (such as a belief that money should be given away rather than spent on buildings) but rather in their culture. At the risk of oversimplifying culture (which I just warned against), several deep-seated factors seemed to be at work. A previous building campaign had resulted in a beautiful sanctuary, but many leaders bore scars from the conflict that occurred in that era. The church had also had several incidents in which staff members had violated the trust of the people. On top of that, a significant contingent in the church seemed more concerned with their own comfort and well-being than with reaching into the community. The result was a culture that could not move forward despite a path that seemed clear.

A simple definition is that culture is "the way we do things here." Organization expert John Kotter goes a step further and defines culture as the "norms of behavior and shared values among a group of people." He then explains, "*Norms of behavior* are common or pervasive ways of acting that are found in a group. ... *Shared values* are important concerns and goals shared by most of the people in a group that tend to shape group behavior."[2]

As seen in Kotter's definition, behavior and shared values are closely intertwined, with each one influencing the other. Nevertheless, it may be helpful to describe each further. In the context of churches and other Christian organizations, think of behavior as the ways in which decisions are made, things get done, and people relate to each other. Are decisions made from the top down, by consensus, or by the power brokers in the parking lot after the meeting? Do people wait on staff to tell them what to do, or do things get initiated "from the bottom up"? Is there a sense of authentic community or just a pseudocommunity? When conflict occurs, is it handled in healthy ways, or does it go underground? "Shared values" relate to behavior, but they are rooted in the theological beliefs and the mission and purpose that drive the ministry. What do people truly believe about God and about Scripture? What is the real mission, as reflected in the congregation's priorities and resource allocations?

Notice that Kotter uses the phrase "shared values," not "stated values." Stated values are important only if they are lived out. When organizations talk about their values, they may be using the term in the same way as Kotter. If they have a small number of attributes that are widely shared, this describes the culture. In many other cases, the espoused values look like the list of everything your mother ever told you a person should be. Such a list is aspirational, and maybe even inspirational, but it does not describe the actual culture.

Culture Making, by Andy Crouch, adds an interesting twist to the discussion of culture. Crouch says that "culture is what we make of the world" and that it is also how we make sense of the world. The former is an act of creation and the latter an act of interpretation. Crouch explains the connection between these two acts when he says, "We make sense of the world by making something of the world."[3] A congregation that sees the world as being full of dangerous people who could corrupt the saints will tend to be legalistic and inward-looking. Another church looks at the same people with an attitude of "We are the same, but for the grace of God." This congregation will tend to be much more grace-filled and outward-focused. Each church is "making sense of the world" in its choice of theology, attitudes, and programs.

Crouch goes on to say that "culture ... defines for us the horizons of possibility and impossibility." In the first hypothetical church, it is possible for a member to feel smug and self-assured, and it is impossible (or at least difficult) for someone who is trapped in a cycle of "bad" sins to feel welcome and experience grace. Just the opposite is true for the second church, where all people truly feel that they belong.

The "horizons of possibility and impossibility" are evident at The Crossing, which has relational health as a central part of its culture. When church leaders teach unity and refuse to accept inappropriate behavior, this makes it impossible (or at least very difficult) for dysfunction to tear the relational fabric of the church. It makes possible a horizon where people experience emotional and relational healing and where authentic community is the norm.

Some cultures are exclusive and internally consistent, and others are weak or diluted. The former refers to a well-defined culture, one that "spits out people" if they don't fit. I worked as an engineer for Exxon for two years before going to business school, and my father spent his entire career in the organization. Exxon's culture is driven by an engineering, rational, quantitative mind-set. Engineers end up in senior management positions more frequently than individuals with financial, legal, or marketing backgrounds. Decision making is based on rigorous analysis, which makes it virtually impossible for people to "fly by the seat of their pants." The planning process is complex and lengthy, with lots of flowcharts. Some people fit in this culture and many don't, but few are left wondering if they belong.

Later in my career, I took a management position with a relatively small company that had been put together through a dozen different acquisitions. Each acquired business had its own culture. Some were very professional, and others were not. Some had a hard-driving work ethic, and others were laid back. Some were trusting and had high morale, and others had combative, poisonous atmospheres. One of our goals was to meld these pieces together into one company—one culture—which was a monumental challenge. We learned that the cultures of the acquired companies were much stronger than the desired corporate culture and that it takes a great deal of time and effort to reshape culture.

Like Exxon and The Crossing, some churches have well-defined cultures. In those cases, powerful momentum is created by a clear sense that "this is who we are." In others, the culture is like a soft drink that has been sitting in a glass too long. The ice has melted and the carbonation has escaped, leaving a lukewarm, flat, diluted beverage that should be poured down the drain. In my interviews, I didn't specifically ask the leaders to describe their ministry's culture, but it oozed out of everything they said. Here are a few glimpses of notable elements of culture in some of the organizations mentioned in earlier chapters:

- Healing Place Church has a strong identity in serving. From its beginning, the church has found ways to serve individuals in its community who are less fortunate. As Healing Place has grown, its ministry has expanded beyond Baton Rouge, but the culture of serving is still at the core.
- At Christ Fellowship, one aspect of the culture is a profound sense of seeking God in all major decisions and then stepping out in obedience, even when it seems crazy. The stories of the congregation's property acquisitions and new ministry launches give ample evidence of this.
- Financial integrity and generosity are a vital part of the culture at Church of the Highlands. This translates into transparency in the church's financials, a lean cost structure, and significant funds being sent out the door each year.
- Living Water's culture is defined by its name and history. The organization exists to lift the standard of living for the poorest of the poor by giving them access to clean water in the name of Christ. The fact that it took several years for Living Water to drill its first successful well is part of the lore that instills a persistence and "can do" attitude in its people.

Note that these examples show many different aspects of culture. For some organizations, it displays their mission. For others, it speaks to the way they make decisions. For all of them, it underscores their identity and grows out of their understanding of Scripture.

The concept of culture is not a human creation. The Exodus and the conquest and settlement of the Promised Land tell the story of God trying to mold a group of people to follow His ways. In other words, it is a story that reflects culture being created. The laws, the shared heritage, and the first-hand experiences in which God showed His love and power are interwoven to create the unique "norms of behavior and shared values" for the Israelites. This culture helped them "make sense of the world," using Crouch's terminology, in miraculous victories and unexpected defeats and in the course of their daily lives. However, the story also shows the difficulties of maintaining an exclusive, cohesive, God-focused culture. Even though God desired for the nation to be set apart and devoted to Him, the people allowed their culture to be diluted by others. As they intermarried, imported other gods, and changed the rules of community, the culture was reshaped into something other than what God had intended.

It would be easy, but wrong, to conclude that the Israelites just needed to be more exclusive. In Jesus' time, the Pharisees were diligently trying to create a strong, theologically sound culture, and they were having some measure of success in doing so. They were convinced that strict adherence to the Law would prevent them from reliving the horrors of the Babylonian exile and that their righteousness could actually open the way for the Messiah to come and usher out the Romans. In a sense, the Pharisees thought they were being godly and the Israelites wanted to be great, but neither culture was shaped as God intended.

WHY IS CULTURE IMPORTANT?

The biblical stories illustrate the importance of culture and some of the problems that can arise when the culture is defined poorly or inappropriately. In *Built to Last*, Jim Collins and Jerry Porras identify "core ideology," which is similar to Kotter's shared values, as a vital part of a visionary company. They explain, "Like the fundamentals of a great nation, church, school, or any other enduring institution, core ideology in a visionary company is a set of basic precepts that plant a fixed stake in the ground: 'This is who we are; this is what we stand for; this is what we're all about.'"[4]

In visionary companies, this core ideology is not "just a bunch of nice-sounding platitudes—words with no bite," according to Collins and Porras. These companies "take steps to make the ideology pervasive throughout the organization and transcend any individual leader."[5] In the exemplary organizations, everything—vision, management systems, hiring and employee development practices, and resource allocation—is driven by the core ideology.

Patrick Lencioni says that creating organizational clarity should be one of the "four obsessions of an extraordinary executive." He states, "An organization that has achieved clarity has a sense of unity around everything it does."[6] To create this clarity, the leadership team must wrestle with the question "What behavioral values are irreplaceable and fundamental?" Lencioni echoes Collins and Porras when he explains, "The key to answering this question lies in avoiding the tendency to adopt every positive value that exists."[7] Effective leaders make the hard choice between claiming a lot of good values and truly living a few culture-defining ones.

Southwest Airlines, consistently described as one of the best companies in the world, is a vivid example of a company that has organizational clarity. One of the values at Southwest is humor. The company's internal employee events are filled with humor, flight attendants and other customer-facing staff frequently tell jokes, uniforms are more casual than at other airlines, and its ads are always lighthearted. Anyone who flies on Southwest will notice the difference compared to other airlines. What about more serious values? Southwest certainly has others, but it is clear that a small number of values shape the company's identity and make it distinct. These values seep into everything Southwest does—that's the power of culture.

When a congregation's members are clear about their culture—who they are and how they make sense of the world—it becomes a powerful driver and filter. It's a driver because it helps direct resources and energy toward the things that are in line with the culture. It's a filter because it makes it easier to say no to good ideas that simply don't fit. The service-oriented, entrepreneurial culture at Healing Place church provided momentum for the creation of the Dream Center campus to serve the less fortunate in Baton Rouge. At Church of the Highlands, the culture of generosity drives church leaders to keep internal costs in check and helps them resist the pressure to add paid staff to run every program. Of course, there are plenty of examples of ministries on the other end of the spectrum. They say yes to every idea, especially ones that are promoted by influential members. Over time, this leads to an organization that feels like a cafeteria—lots of offerings that at best taste fair—rather than a fine restaurant that serves one type of food with excellence.

Perhaps the biggest reason that culture matters in churches is that it is too easy to drift away from God. The culture of every Christian organization should be shaped by dependence on and obedience to God. It seems obvious, but some people and organizations seem to lose sight of this in their pursuit of either greatness or comfort. They may declare, "We love God and others," but their actions may not match this claim. Reggie McNeal says, "The church world in North America ... has largely forsaken its missional covenant with God to be a part of kingdom expansion. It has, instead, substituted its own charter of church as a clubhouse where religious people hang out with other people who think, dress, behave, vote, and believe like them."[8] This drift away from the true heart of God is what happened both to the Israelites in the Promised Land and later to the Pharisees, and it is just as real a danger for the church today.

One other metaphor explains the importance and power of an organization's culture: a rubber band. You can stretch and twist a rubber band, but then it snaps back into place as if it had never been touched. In the same way, the culture of your church will keep pulling it back to a certain set of values and ways of doing things. In the best organizations, this can be a tremendous positive force. In other cases, leaders are faced with the challenge of reshaping the culture.

RESHAPING YOUR CULTURE

If you conclude that your culture needs to be reshaped, are there any bedrock principles for what the "right" culture is? The answer from business is surprising. Collins and Porras "did not find any specific ideological content essential to being a visionary company." As evidence, they point to Merck and Philip Morris. The former has the noble mission of making pharmaceuticals to improve human health, while the core business of the latter is cigarettes. Collins and Porras explain that "both Merck and Philip Morris—companies at opposite ends of the spectrum in terms of what their products do to people—show up as visionary companies guided by strong, yet radically different, ideologies."[9]

Of course, the Bible establishes some clear parameters that eliminate some of the norms and values of the marketplace. For example, a highly competitive culture that creates winners and losers within the church is contrary to the teachings of Scripture. So is a culture based on greed or one that is rigid and rule-oriented.

Even though you might find these elements in some successful companies, they do not fit in an organization that claims Jesus as Lord.

God's Word gives general boundaries, but it does not spell out the "right" culture for your church or mine. We are all to worship God, make disciples, use our gifts, minister to people in need, and be part of a genuine community. But in a biblical body of believers, these core practices come in many flavors—cultures—as seen in the earlier snapshots.

Consider two hypothetical churches about to celebrate their fiftieth anniversary, both located in neighborhoods that have changed dramatically over time. Both congregations recognize the needs and opportunities in their current communities and admit that they have not responded with effective ministries. As a result, each is debating whether to relocate to a more attractive and visible location outside of the neighborhood, closer to where many of its members now live. Regardless of the ultimate choice, this is a decision that will flow out of the church's culture and will define its culture in the future.

One church elects to move to the suburbs. The leaders, after much prayer, conclude that God is calling them to continue to reach people who are similar to their current membership and that they can do this better if they move. They also believe that God does not want them to abandon their old neighborhood, so they decide to donate their building to help start a new congregation, one that will better reflect the neighborhood and hopefully have more impact. The leaders of the second church, also after much prayer, conclude that God is calling them to stay in the community but to change their strategy in order to reach and minister to their neighbors. This requires significant changes in staffing and programming and in the attitudes of church members.

What does this scenario tell us about culture? Does one church have a "better" or "healthier" culture? Was one decision more godly than the other? Before we rush to judgment and pronounce one as more spiritual or a better steward or more strategic (or any other label we might want to use), we should admit that we can't see into the hearts of the leaders. If we interviewed them, each congregation's leaders might say that they deeply believe they are following God. If we look for fruit that validates the decision, we may not find it until months or years after the choice is made. Both churches could see God work in powerful ways—in terms of transformed lives and ministry results—through these very different culture-driven and culture-shaping decisions.

A common aspect of culture in these two congregations—and it's the most important one—is a deep commitment to seek God's guidance and obediently follow when His will is revealed. Of course, either could make the wrong decision as well. If church leaders didn't seek God, or if their choice was guided by personal motives under the guise of prayer, then whatever decision they made would be wrong. If the move to the suburbs was based on a fear of associating with people who are different, then the motivation wasn't biblical. If the second church's decision to stay in the neighborhood was driven by fear of change or attachment to a building, then this decision was equally nonbiblical, regardless of the pretty wrappings put around it.

This leads to another important aspect of culture. A leader cannot wake up one day and say, "Our culture needs to change and be . . . [more outward-facing, more evangelistic, more caring]. I will announce this to the church." Leaders need to be deeply aware of the existing culture and of how God may want to reshape shared values and behaviors, but they also need to know that changing a culture is the hardest and slowest kind of organizational change. Samuel Chand observes, "Changing a culture requires tremendous patience. We can rearrange boxes on an organizational chart in a moment, but changing culture is heart surgery. Culture is not only *what* we do but also *why* and *how* we do it. Culture is about the heart and head, and then it shapes what we do with our hands."[10]

In *Good to Great*, Jim Collins explains that moving an organization toward greatness is like pushing a giant flywheel. A flywheel is extremely heavy, and it takes many turns and tremendous effort to get it moving. But once it is spinning at a high rate of speed, it has enormous momentum. Collins says the leaders of great companies kept "pushing the flywheel" in a consistent direction over a long period of time. Their success was not due to one or two brilliant strategic decisions but rather, as Collins says, "it was a quiet, deliberate process of figuring out what needed to be done to create the best future results and then simply taking those steps, one after the other, turn by turn of the flywheel."[11]

GLIMPSES OF CULTURE CHANGE

The flywheel of culture is a powerful force in any organization, as seen in the incredible momentum it creates at Christ Fellowship, Healing Place Church, and others. Many of us, however, recognize that the culture of our organization suffers from one of the problems found in ancient Israel. Either the culture is weak and poorly defined, or it is sharply defined in ways that fall short of God's ideal. This raises the question "How can we reshape the culture so that it is more attuned to God and aligned with His will?" The stories of other Christian leaders who are in the midst of this kind of shift are informative.

With an average worship attendance over fourteen hundred people, a membership that includes many highly successful individuals, and a tradition of generously supporting a variety of outside ministries, Memorial Drive Presbyterian Church (MDPC) is one of the largest and most prominent churches in its denomination, the Presbyterian Church (U.S.A.). Nevertheless, senior pastor Dave Peterson is convinced that the culture needs to change. He describes MDPC and the other mainline churches in the Memorial area of Houston as being like "barkers on the midway." What does he mean? At the carnival, a few people are interested in the midway games, but the majority want to get to the rides. Peterson says that his church and others keep calling out to the Christian minority, trying to get them to "come to our booth" instead of finding a way to "go to the rides" where most of the people are. In other words, MDPC's culture is too focused on attracting people who are already churched rather than meeting the unchurched where they live and work and play.

How is culture change happening at MDPC? For Peterson, the first turn of the flywheel was his own awakening. The next turn was to find ways to articulate this reality to others. Using language such as "we need to get out of the aquarium and into the ocean," he began to paint the picture for other leaders. "We have an alarming habit of not facing reality," says Peterson, a habit that can quickly put the brakes on the flywheel when it is just beginning to turn.

One of the most important flywheel-turning steps was the development of partnerships in which members could have fresh encounters with the rest of the world. MDPC has developed significant relationships with local schools in which church members mentor children who come from disadvantaged homes. This has helped the church understand what it feels like to get "into the ocean." Another component of reshaping culture is the men's ministry, which uses a curriculum that challenges men to recapture a sense of adventure and apply this spirit to make a difference for the Kingdom. Peterson rejoices when guys tell him that they are bored with doing church as they've always done it because this opens the door to channel their energies into outward-facing ministries. Peterson has found that shifting the culture is a long-term, ongoing process that involves staff, elders, and the church as a whole, gradually moving the flywheel one turn at a time.

Culture change can also be focused on the mundane stuff, such as bringing more discipline to an entrepreneurial organization. Living Water International (LWI) is in the midst of major transition and growth, with Mike Mantel taking the reins from founders Gary Evans and Jerry Wiles and with its budget having nearly doubled to $18 million in just three years. As described earlier, LWI's mission is very clear: delivering clean water solutions in Jesus' name to people in need. Even though the mission is not changing, the way to accomplish its purpose as a larger organization is triggering an internal culture shift. LWI has had few standardized systems in place, but Mantel and LWI's leadership have begun formalizing a number of practices in areas such as personnel and decision making. These changes have been met with some resistance from employees who have enjoyed the sense of being a close-knit family and the ability to act quickly on an idea. If culture is "the way we do things here," Mantel knows that becoming more disciplined and structured is an important cultural shift that is necessary for LWI to continue to expand its ministry.

My own church has been a case study of reshaping culture with many turns of the flywheel. The congregation, founded in 1928, had grown to be a prominent congregation in the city of Houston in the 1970s and 1980s. Growth flattened during the final years of one senior pastor's tenure, but the church found renewed optimism under the energetic leadership of the next pastor.

Unfortunately, his pastorate ended abruptly in moral failure, and the church not only lost members but also lost confidence. When Barry Landrum arrived as senior pastor in 1996, average worship attendance had declined into the three hundreds and morale was low. The first several turns of the flywheel involved listening to the people and loving them, helping them heal from the disillusionment they felt while reminding them that God still had great plans for the church. At the same time, Landrum persistently reached out to anyone who visited the church, knowing that new families would bring new energy into the body and would lift the spirits of those who were already there. As that happened, a culture that had become downcast and inward-looking started to confidently turn outward again.

The next culture-defining issue was whether to start a contemporary worship service as a second offering on Sunday mornings. Two initial attempts at offering contemporary and blended worship were unsuccessful, but the third try was the charm. Though it might seem that the initial failures would slow the flywheel, momentum was actually built because Landrum demonstrated a humble willingness to reevaluate the specific plans while reinforcing the need to turn outward. During this season, we codified that value with the phrase "We do not just exist for ourselves; we exist for people that we have not yet met." In this case, adding the worship service enabled us to attract and meet a new group of people.

The flywheel continued to turn with several years of growth and a successful capital campaign. Then in 2004, the church was given the opportunity to buy the property of another church for use as a second campus. A decision that would have been impossible a few years earlier, due to both financial reasons and an inward-facing, pessimistic culture, was affirmed with a 96 percent positive vote, and West University Baptist launched Crosspoint Church as a second campus to reach people that we had not yet met.

BEFORE YOU TURN THE FLYWHEEL

I hope you agree that establishing a well-defined, biblical culture is a powerful foundation on which you can build. Before you start turning the flywheel, however, let me urge you to personally take stock of whether you are ready. Leaders who successfully reshape culture know the power that comes from clear norms of behavior and shared values. And they are prepared for the time and the cost it will take to get there.

As we have seen, reshaping culture is a lengthy process that will test any leader. Dave Peterson has been at Memorial Drive Presbyterian for sixteen years and has been intentionally driving toward an "out of the aquarium" culture for much of that time. At West University Baptist, attendance did not begin to grow until two years after Barry Landrum's arrival. It was three more years before the contemporary worship service was started and another four years before the second campus was launched. If you tend to become impatient, your desire for culture change may spill over into frustration or anger. If you do not have great stamina and conviction, your arm may wear out before you turn the flywheel enough times to create lasting momentum. And if you do not have a clear idea of where you are going, you will tend to jump from one great idea to another without changing the deeper culture.

In his research, Jim Collins found that the less successful companies suffered from this tendency to change directions frequently. The result was disastrous: "After years of lurching back and forth, the comparison companies failed to build sustained momentum and fell instead into what we came to call the doom loop."[12] Counselors know there is no "silver bullet" for a struggling marriage, for overcoming addictions, or for any of the other complex challenges people face in their personal lives. Cognitively, we know it's true for congregations as well, but far too many leaders grab one program after another, expecting that "this one will revolutionize our church." After a few months, they give up because they have found yet another sure solution, and ultimately they fall into the "doom loop."

Leaders pay a price in attempting to change an organization's culture, which is part of the broader dynamics of change that are explored in Chapter Eleven. But leaders also pay a price if they choose to accept a weak culture. When that happens, your congregation may begin to look like the church of Laodicea in Revelation 3, the one that Christ says he will spit out. My hope is that the Spirit's work in your life and in your church will create a culture that can never be described as lukewarm.

WHAT ARE YOU PURSUING?

- If culture is "the way we do things here," describe your current culture in a few words or phrases. Ask other key leaders to do the same. How similar or different are your answers?
- Does your organization have a written list of values? Are they simply espoused or truly practiced?
- What are the strengths of the existing culture? What most needs to change?
- Can you clearly describe the culture that you believe God wants for your organization?
- What is the most significant flywheel-turning step you can take to begin reshaping the culture?

CHAPTER ELEVEN

ARE YOU PREPARED TO CHANGE?

Change—it's a word that strikes fear in the hearts of many ministry leaders. They have either personally experienced or they know a close friend who has experienced the pain and disappointment of a well-intentioned change effort that ultimately failed. It may have been a relatively simple change—a modest reorganization or a shifting of resources to support a new priority—that was met with intense resistance. Or it may have been a much more sweeping effort that ended with a church split or the firing of the leader. Change is never easy. In churches and other Christian organizations, the difficulty and complexity of change seems to go up exponentially. That is why many Christian leaders shrink away from the challenge, even though they know their ministry is falling short of what God desires.

There is a great irony in this. At the heart of the gospel is the message of life-giving, supernatural change. Christ not only changes our eternal destinies, but the Holy Spirit also stirs in our souls to make us more and more like Jesus each day. It's the story of Paul, who was "a blasphemer and a persecutor and a violent man" (1 Timothy 1:13) before he was radically transformed by his encounter with Jesus. It is believing that God "is able to do immeasurably more than all we ask or imagine, according to his power that is at work within us" (Ephesians 3:20). If Christians have this divine source of power for personal transformation, why do they so often have a defeatist attitude about organizational change? And why is the corporate arena so much more successful at change than God's church?

Of course, some spiritual leaders have a Pollyanna attitude, not a defeatist one, and this can be equally damaging. These leaders seem to think that every Christian change story should have a happy ending. In essence, they say, "If we commit ourselves to the Lord and are doing our best to follow His will, then everything should turn out rosy every time." In reality, this theology is just as inadequate as the one that says change is impossible.

Applying the concepts from earlier chapters—planning, personnel management, measurement, culture—will involve change, which makes this a critical issue for every leader to understand. The leader who recognizes the complexities of change, particularly the inevitable obstacles, is better able to use all the other tools of leadership. Because of the dramatic shifts that have taken place in the business environment over the past three decades, there is a wealth of knowledge that we can and should tap into.

"THE HEART OF CHANGE"

Let me start with a confession. The right side of my brain has been playing catch-up with the left side for fifty years. The left side, of course, is the seat of analytical thinking and logic. The right side is where feelings and emotions and intuition come from.

As I worked with my two coauthors on *Leading Congregational Change* more than a decade ago, my contribution was 99 percent left-brained. I emphasized structure and process. I focused on the power of a logical, compelling argument and a clear vision. One of the first times that we presented the material in a seminar, I was amazed at the contrast between Jim Herrington's communication style and mine. We had a ton of information to cover, so I raced through my sections trying to convey as many facts and principles as possible. Jim seemed unconcerned about skipping material as he took time to tell stories of people and their struggles with change. By the end of the workshop, it was clear that Jim had connected with the hearts of the audience much more than I had. Today, when I make similar presentations, I don't neglect the facts, but I work hard to balance the right and left sides of my brain, perhaps communicating less information but doing it in a way that is more meaningful because it touches people's hearts.

I am not the only person who has learned this lesson. John Kotter is a professor at Harvard Business School and one of the world's leading experts on organizational change. Kotter's classic text, *Leading Change*, was a foundational resource in my earlier book. His clear, rational eight-step process for effective change efforts resonated with my left-brained temperament. Five years after *Leading Change*, a sequel, *The Heart of Change: Real-Life Stories of How People Change Their Organizations*, was released. In the introduction, Kotter and coauthor Dan Cohen write, "Our main finding, put simply, is that the central issue is never strategy, structure, culture, or systems.... The core of the matter is always about changing the behavior of people, and behavior change happens in highly successful situations mostly by speaking to people's feelings."[1] Kotter and Cohen explain, "People change what they do less because they are given *analysis* that shifts their *thinking* than because they are *shown* a truth that influences their *feelings*."[2] Kotter also discovered that the right side of one's brain must be engaged in any successful change effort.

One of the enduring characters from the television and movie industry is *Star Trek*'s "Mr. Spock." He is a Vulcan, a race of beings from another planet who have no emotions and are purely logical. One of the ongoing story lines in the *Star Trek* series is the conflicts that occur as pure logic (in Spock) interacts with human emotion (in the other characters). One of Spock's oft-repeated lines is: "That wouldn't be logical."

When it comes to leading organization change, whether in a business or a church, we need the cool, clear-headed logic of Spock. Leaders need to question whether the diagnosis of a problem is accurate or is being driven by emotion. They need to ask whether a proposed solution makes sense in light of the facts. But they also must realize that they are not leading a group of Vulcans. If they don't address the emotional and sometimes irrational side of change, they will never succeed.

DIAGNOSING HEART PROBLEMS

It is important but insufficient to know that change efforts evoke emotional responses. Effective leaders are aware of the many ways that these emotions spill out, and they seek to address them. On the surface, the most obvious reaction to a proposed change is active resistance. Kotter says, "Irrational and political resistance to change never fully dissipates."[3] A less obvious reaction is complacency. Complacency may seem preferable to resistance, but it can kill a change effort just as quickly. Kotter's original research found that "transformations always fail to achieve their objectives when complacency levels are high."[4]

Any leader who has attempted to initiate change knows that resistance and complacency are normal reactions. That is why Jim Collins and Jerry Porras say, "Comfort is not the objective in a visionary company. Indeed, visionary companies install powerful mechanisms to create *dis*comfort—to obliterate complacency—and thereby stimulate change."[5] Similarly, the first step in Kotter's eight-stage change process is "creating urgency." He understands that urgency—a deep sense that something is wrong and needs to be corrected—is the only thing that will motivate people to support a change effort.

Creating urgency is easier said than done. That's because human beings have a tremendous capacity to deny the need for change, especially when they dislike the implications. A left-brained leader cannot present a simple list of pros and cons to create urgency. After many years of doing research on great organizations, Jim Collins wanted to understand why companies stumble. In *How the Mighty Fall*, he describes five stages in the downfall of once successful corporations and explains, "One common behavior . . . is when those in power blame other people or external factors—or otherwise explain away the data—rather than confront the frightening reality that the enterprise may be in serious trouble."[6]

Robert Quinn, another noted change expert and author of *Deep Change*, echoes the same theme: "Our first inclination is always from a perspective that externalizes the problem, that keeps it somewhere 'out there.'"[7] Quinn later says, "Denial occurs when we are presented with painful information about ourselves, information that suggests that we need to make a deep change. Denial is one of several clear paths toward slow death. When we practice denial, we work on the wrong solutions or on no solutions at all."[8] There are no quick fixes to overcome denial. Rather, the wise leader knows that creating urgency takes time and is often a process of two steps forward and one step back.

Even in the face of overwhelming evidence, some people will deny the need for change because they are afraid of what lies ahead. Some of that fear is driven by an awareness that change is often painful. Jim Kouzes and Barry Posner say, "There's just no way you can make it perfectly safe to make a change."[9] Some fear is driven by uncertainty. Quinn explains that deep change "requires that we leave our comfort zone and step outside our normal roles,"[10] something people are very reluctant to do. Quinn later offers the memorable image that deep change requires us to "walk naked into the land of uncertainty."[11] Reluctance is a natural reaction when people are faced with a daunting process leading to an uncertain future.

Underneath fear and denial is an even more basic human response: self-preservation. When confronted with the need for change, the first question people usually ask is "How will this affect me?" Kotter and Cohen observe, "People eventually focus on self-preservation instead of organizational transformation."[12] When trust is high and people believe deeply in the organization's mission, they will be willing to make significant personal sacrifices, at least for a while. If the person doesn't understand the need for the change or doesn't trust the leadership, even the smallest changes may be met with resistance. As the personal cost increases, you can expect less support and more denial from those who are affected by proposed changes.

The challenges of widespread organizational change are evident in the story of Baylor University during Robert Sloan's tenure as president. When Sloan became president in 1996, the announcement that the regents had selected someone with strong academic credentials and deep Baylor ties was met with excitement. Over the next few years, Sloan led a process to define a sweeping new vision for Baylor, culminating in the fall of 2001 with the public release of "Baylor 2012." This ambitious ten-year plan called for Baylor to become a top-tier research university while at the same time strengthening the school's Christian roots. Sloan and the board saw Baylor as uniquely positioned to achieve this dual goal. The plan called for significant new construction and the aggressive recruitment of nationally recognized faculty. A capital campaign, a large bond program, and increased tuition were necessary steps to finance this vision.

Baylor 2012 was developed after extensive collaboration with key constituents and was fully endorsed by Baylor's board, and the initial response from the broader Baylor community was enthusi-astic. As often happens, however, serious resistance began to arise once implementation started. Baylor had the reputation of being an "affordable" Christian university, and some alumni objected to the dramatic rise in tuition. Faculty opposition to the plan grew as well. Some long-tenured professors resented the new attention to research-oriented faculty who were given endowed chairs and other preferential treatment. Others, fearing their academic free-dom would be stifled, were uncomfortable with Baylor's emphasis on reclaiming and proclaiming its Christian heritage.[13]

Sloan continued to lead the charge, and the board stood solidly behind him in the face of growing faculty and alumni opposition. But in 2005, the issue came to a head, and Sloan resigned from the presidency under pressure. One former regent said, "It's been too much, too fast. Too many people have been alienated." Shortly after announcing his resignation, Sloan himself said, "The natural side effect of change is conflict. We moved quickly and boldly to implement the vision and found that Baylor is not immune to the discomfort and insecurity generated by change."[14]

The hard work of leading large-scale change is not developing the plan; it is implementing it. Baylor 2012 was birthed out of prayer and extensive stakeholder involvement and seemed to have the right ingredients and the right support. When implementation began, however, the leader's interpretation of the vision and the full implications of the change effort became clear. The university continued to pursue Baylor 2012 after Sloan's departure, but at a slower pace and with several adjustments. It is hard to know if the real issue was a flawed plan, poor implementation by Sloan and the Baylor leadership team, a failure of nerve by the board, or just the normal human rejection of change. It is easy to see that change in any organization is a complex undertaking that is not for the faint of heart.

CHANGE IN THE CHURCH: IT JUST GETS MESSIER

Every one of the issues identified so far in this chapter is present in the church and other Christian organizations. On top of that, however, is another layer of organizational, theological, and personal factors that make change even more complicated.

A More Complex Organization

Churches have many unique characteristics compared to businesses, one of the most notable being their dependence on volunteers. When volunteers don't support a change, things get sticky. In business, the cooperation of employees is important for successful change, but at the end of the day, the employer holds the power of the paycheck. If corporate leadership decides to make a particular change (redesigning the information system, outsourcing the manufacture of a product), the rank-and-file employees don't have much choice. They may create some temporary obstacles, but in the end, those who don't like the change will usually find another job. Churches don't have rank-and-file employees—they have rank-and-file volunteers who are much harder to "fire."

It is not uncommon for volunteers to stay in place and resist change efforts, either overtly or subtly. For example, a church that is becoming more involved in its community asks each small group to serve in an outward-facing ministry such as a local soup kitchen or a school tutoring program. One of the most successful small group leaders feels that his group's sole purpose is to foster the spiritual growth of its members, so the leader never mentions the church's new emphasis. When a group member asks about getting involved, the leader answers that the group doesn't need to do anything different. In business, this leader would be reprimanded or let go for not following directions. Churches tend to ignore the issue because they are afraid or unable to "fire" the leader.

A related problem is the ability of church members to stay in place even when they are unhappy with organizational changes. Unhappy employees, if they have marketable skills, will generally leave a business. A church has strong relational bonds that tend to keep unhappy people from exiting. They may disapprove of the overall direction, but because "it's our family," they stay in order to be with friends they have known for years. An exacerbating factor is the short tenure of many pastors. Church members have learned from experience that if they don't like the current leader (and the direction being set by the leader), they just need to wait a couple of years and it will probably change.

One church developed an aggressive church-planting strategy. The senior pastor built a team and a culture that led to more than two dozen church plants during his long tenure. By all accounts, the church was highly successful and had a great impact for the Kingdom. Amazingly enough, some people in the congregation never accepted this strategy, and after the pastor's retirement, they helped shape a new direction in which church planting was deemphasized. The staying power of people is a powerful factor that can frustrate change efforts in any congregation.

Confusing governance structures are another obstacle to change in Christian organizations. I have seen all kinds of business structures—dotted-line reporting relationships, matrix structures, joint ventures, and task groups, to name a few. But none of these are as confusing as the typical congregation, where it is not clear what steps must be taken to obtain approval for major decisions. Much of this revolves around the real authority of the pastor versus the formal lay leadership group or groups. It becomes even more clouded when a small number of individuals "run" the church, irrespective of any formal roles. As noted in Chapter Nine, key leaders must be on the same page if the congregation is going to make any meaningful progress.

An even deeper factor is the congregation's unique way of making decisions and handling disagreements. Many churches have long histories of dysfunctional decision making, such as settling an issue after the meeting rather than in the meeting or resisting new ideas from the pastor. Once these patterns are established, they are hard to break. They become part of the culture, as noted in Chapter Ten. New members who bring a fresh perspective can help break the cycle, but many churches are so stagnant that they never hear these voices. Transformation efforts will never get off the ground as long as these patterns persist.

One final barrier to change in ministry is the lack of accepted measures for success. You have already seen the importance of measurement in Chapter Six and the reality that many Christian organizations struggle in this area. This has huge implications for change efforts. If the leadership does not see a gap between current results and an organizational goal, there is little urgency and even less impetus for change. Inadequate measurement also fuels the tendency toward denial. It is hard to create urgency simply by saying, "I think we're in trouble." If someone asks why and the leader answers that it's just a gut feeling, this response is easily dismissed. Even if there is an indicator of a problem—for example, baptizing only a few people each year—the leaders may not agree that this is the standard by which effectiveness is to be evaluated. Without useful metrics, churches may wait until a major indicator—such as giving—has gone into a steep decline, and they may miss the best window of opportunity for leading a positive change effort.

THEOLOGICAL FACTORS

Church of the Redeemer, an Episcopal parish in Houston, was a pioneer in the charismatic renewal movement in the 1960s. By 2011, the ninety-year-old congregation had declined to seventy members and needed $7 million in infrastructure repairs, so the diocese made the decision to close the doors. A newspaper article describing the closure included a picture of the church's well-known mural, called *Christ of the Workingman*, and concluded with the statement, "Members can't imagine worship without it."[15]

Is there something you can't imagine worshiping without? The story of Redeemer hints at the next layer of challenges that Christian organizations encounter. A person may "love" his or her job, but if the organization changes, it's just a job. If you try to change something in the church, however, you are stepping onto sacred ground.

The problem is that some churches act as if everything they do is sacred and therefore unchangeable. In contrast, one of the teachings of *Built to Last* is that visionary companies "preserve the core and stimulate progress." Collins and Porras explain, "It is absolutely essential to not confuse core ideology with culture, strategy, tactics, operations, policies, or other noncore practices.... Ultimately, the *only* thing a company should *not* change over time is its core ideology."[16] As noted in Chapter Ten, many experts teach that successful organizations have only a few core values. "Simulate progress" refers to the willingness to change anything that is not a core value or ideology. And yet the list of untouchables—beliefs, traditions, priorities, habits—in a typical church is several pages long.

How is this theological? Because underneath the long and inflexible list is the tendency for Christians to claim that each unchangeable item is biblically based and that it is vital to their relationship with God. If you come home to discover that your spouse has rearranged the furniture in the family room, you may not like the new layout. Perhaps you will discuss it, perhaps you won't, but you know that this doesn't fundamentally affect your marriage. But when a church changes its style of worship music, shifts from a Sunday school to a small group model, or moves from event-based to discipleship-based youth ministry, the outcry begins. People may turn to Scripture to support their position or argue that the change will inhibit spiritual growth for them and others. Because of the relationships in the church, even a leadership team that was unified around the decision may come unraveled under this kind of intense, "theological" pressure.

The theological overlay is complicated by the ways leaders describe God's presence in the actual decision. The leaders I interviewed spent significant time in prayer when they were facing important decisions. They often emerged with a sense of God's leadership, sometimes just an inkling and sometimes a deep conviction. But when should a leader say that a recommended course of action is "God's will"? Jim Leggett of Grace Fellowship described a spirited debate on whether to give away 10 percent of the church's capital campaign receipts to outside ministries. Leggett was inspired to do this, but his recommendation was turned down by the campaign leadership team. Leggett was disappointed in this decision, but he says, "It wasn't a burning bush. I'm not going to claim a burning bush unless there's been one."

Leggett shows great wisdom in this approach. If a leader has an unshakable conviction that God has spoken on a particular matter, he or she should say so. But often the leader doesn't have quite this level of clarity. In earlier chapters, we saw Todd Mullins of Christ Fellowship, Greg Hawkins of Willow Creek, and others express the importance of unity within their leadership teams and a confidence that God will speak with one voice. In Scripture, God communicates His plans in many ways: from the burning bush to Moses alone, through the prophet Nathan when David couldn't listen, and to the entire council in Jerusalem. Leaders must be careful about putting God in a one-dimensional communication box.

Leaders should also be mindful that the people with whom they are communicating may be jaded by past experiences with others who frequently declared, "Thus saith the Lord." As a result, a spiritual leader's genuine, heartfelt description of how he or she feels that God is directing a decision can trigger strong negative reactions among followers who have been hurt in the past. Leaders cannot erase this pain, but they can be mindful of the many ways that people's perceptions of God affect any proposed change. On top of this complex theological dimension, each leader brings his or her personality into the crucible of change.

The Leader's Temperament

The first chair leader in a Christian organization—pastor, executive director, bishop—is not the same as a CEO in business. Even though the role may have some similarities to that of CEO, there are many differences, one of the biggest being the leader's and followers' perceptions about the position. One of my favorite exercises in seminars is to ask participants to list different words and images that come to mind when they hear the word *pastor.* Inevitably, the word *shepherd* is listed. It's a great word that actually relates to the root meaning of *pastor.* It's a biblical concept. And ultimately, this image is a problem.

As shepherds, Christian leaders see "caring for the flock" as a primary responsibility. They remember the parable of the lost sheep in Luke 15 and Jesus' words about the good shepherd in John 10. Indeed, these are important and valid pictures. In the context of change leadership, however, they can be taken too far. When leaders believe that success means that no one will ever leave (losing a sheep) and everyone will always be satisfied, they are setting themselves up for failure. When they think of sheep as cuddly and cute animals that just need gentle coaxing, they are wrong about sheep and draw incorrect conclusions from the analogy.

Being an effective Christian leader does not mean an absence of conflict. Jan Davis of First Methodist in Rowlett, Texas, reflects that the story of Moses has taught her "God is calling me to lead people to places that are uncomfortable." Many spiritual leaders think that does not sound like being a good shepherd. These same leaders forget the many times that Jesus confronted his followers with hard sayings. Unfortunately, the shepherd image is deeply ingrained to the point that many pastors strive for peace at all costs and are unable to lead meaningful change.

In virtually any transformational effort, some people end up unhappy or angry. Ronald Heifitz, writing about this kind of leadership, says, "Leaders are always failing somebody. . . . Someone exercising leadership will be shouldering the pains and aspirations of a community and frustrating at least some people within it."[17] The fear of lost relationships and a disappointed community is daunting enough to stop some leaders. Quinn refers to this as a "peace-and-pay strategy"[18] in which leaders choose to not engage in deep change because of the personal cost.

Because they want the flock to be happy, pastors sometimes present a distorted picture of how their congregation is doing. Kotter identifies a number of sources of complacency in business, one of which is "too much happy talk from senior management."[19] Pastors are notorious for offering rosy descriptions that mask underlying problems. Whether they do so out of personal insecurity or habit or some other reason, this overly positive perspective contributes to a sense of complacency, which in turn hinders the very change that is needed. Christians should find hope in the gospel, but that does not mean that they should gloss over the real problems facing their ministries. Doing so only postpones the need to deal with the problem and often makes it worse.

A final reality is that success is not guaranteed. Quinn says, "The possibility of failure is a constant companion who walks beside every real leader."[20] As a result, some spiritual leaders choose not to initiate any change at all. Others may make a feeble attempt at change, encounter resistance, and then retreat into doing whatever is safe. Their tentativeness becomes a self-fulfilling prophecy of defeat that adds to the legacy of failed change efforts.

Though retreating may seem safe, it often leaves a deep, hollow place in the leader's soul. Quinn's thesis is that we only have two choices: deep change or slow death. While he recognizes the cost of change, he also appeals to leaders to not give up:

> Why, then, would anyone be willing to accept the pain that accompanies acts of transformational leadership? I suspect that such people have discovered that the pain of leadership is exceeded

only by the pain of lost potential. They understand that excellence is punished, but they have developed a value system that provides no acceptable alternatives. They are internally driven leaders who are committed to continuing deep change and the pursuit of excellence.[21]

Quinn appeals on a purely human level that drives toward greatness, but an even more important argument for courageous, godly change comes from Scripture.

A WORD FROM THE WORD

We know that God is unchanging. Psalm 102:25–27 says that God remains the same throughout all time, and Hebrews 13:8 tells us, "Christ is the same yesterday and today and forever." Hebrews 6:17 speaks of "the unchanging nature of His purpose." But God accomplishes His unchanging purpose by changing His people. You cannot read the stories in Scripture without realizing that change is an essential part of the journey for people of faith. God starts by changing an individual, stirring in his or her soul, and then using that individual to change something much larger. Young King Josiah's heart was pierced when the rediscovered Law was read to him, so he instituted massive national reform to remove the idols and restore the temple for the worship of the one, true God. Joseph of Arimathea took the simple but risky step of retrieving and burying Jesus' body, and his name is now a permanent part of the greatest story ever told.

God's plans often upend "organizations" just when things seem to be running well. The church in Jerusalem was growing by leaps and bounds, but the widespread persecution after the stoning of Stephen scattered the believers throughout the region. This caused the gospel to spread even more rapidly as a Jewish sect until Peter's dream and the resulting encounter with Cornelius opened the gospel to Gentiles. Paul's subsequent missionary work with Gentiles forced the church leaders to address an even more uncomfortable question: Which of the Jewish customs would believing Gentiles be required to follow? The answer, of course, paved the way for the rapid spread of the gospel throughout the Roman

Empire. These were massive changes, far more tumultuous than the ones that shake many churches today.

Clearly, God works through change, but it is equally clear that we cannot predict the outcome. Paul was a change agent. His ministry, empowered by the Holy Spirit, introduced dramatic change in the beliefs and religious practices of Jews and Gentiles. But the narrative of his work in Acts 17 shows the unpredictability of change leadership. In Thessalonica, most of the Jews rejected Paul's message and started a riot that forced him to leave town. At his next stop, in Berea, the Jews were "of more noble character" and "received the message with great eagerness" (Acts 17:11). Same message, same messenger, different results. One of the greatest mistakes spiritual leaders can make is to believe that the success of a God-inspired change effort is guaranteed. That simply does not square with the Bible.

Similarly, it is a mistake to think that God will unveil a complete plan before starting a process of transformation. Throughout the book of Acts, Paul and other leaders stepped out in faith without knowing where the journey would lead. Joshua is another vivid example of a change agent who led with an incomplete road map. He knew that the ultimate goal was the conquest of the entire Promised Land, but God guided him through the journey one step at a time. Frequently along the way, God came alongside Joshua and encouraged him to be strong and courageous. I believe that Christian leadership may be filled with even more short-term uncertainty than secular leadership because God wants us to learn to be dependent on Him, not on our own plans, and to demonstrate this dependence to others.

Perhaps the most important biblical message for Christian change agents is found in Romans 8:31: "If God is for us, who can be against us?" This is the message that sets us apart from non-Christian leaders in secular institutions. In the marketplace, leaders find it difficult to separate the end result from their personal identities. If the effort succeeds, they are heroes. If the effort fails, it reflects poorly on their competence. Christian leaders know that God doesn't guarantee a successful outcome, but they have great confidence that God is at work in the situation and loves them regardless of the end result. This should give them a boldness and a calm that is rarely found elsewhere.

One Church's Change Journey

In this chapter, I have focused on the barriers to change, because too many spiritual leaders neglect these challenges. We have seen the problems that occur when leaders ignore the emotional dimensions of change or fail to create urgency. But we have also seen that the transformational call comes from the heart of God and is something that leaders cannot avoid. So what does it look like when change is done well? As evidenced by the many references in this chapter, a number of resources look at this question. The ultimate answer will be unique for each organization, but Oak Hills Church in San Antonio is an instructive example.

Oak Hills is a fifty-three-year old congregation where Max Lucado served for twenty years as senior minister (and continues in a teaching role). When Randy Frazee stepped into the lead role in 2008, he had a clear vision to reshape the congregation even though Oak Hills was already one of the most vibrant churches in the city. Frazee says his "city-reaching vision [means] less time in the building and more time in the neighborhood, shifting from an attractional model to a missional model, leveraging the other six days of the week, and leveraging our people as ministers." That is the kind of change few leaders would attempt, especially when things are going well!

Frazee communicated this vision to the church's leadership before he was called to Oak Hills. He knew what God had put on his heart, but he wanted the congregation to decide: "Is my agenda an answer to your prayer?" They said yes, but Frazee didn't take for granted that they had a clear understanding of what this would mean. After arriving at Oak Hills, he led the elders and senior staff members through a six-month process to lay a biblical foundation for the vision. He wanted the leaders to have the conviction that the vision was God's call for the church so that they wouldn't reverse course when the implementation got tough. After this foundation was laid, the leadership team spent the next year in a highly collaborative, strategic planning process to develop specific plans that would move them toward the vision. Before approving the plan, the elders spent forty days in prayer, asking God to show them if this was His desire. Ultimately, the elders voted unanimously for the plan, and the church began to restructure staff and align resources.

The church's web site proclaims, "We are the body of Christ called to be Jesus in every neighborhood in San Antonio and beyond." The plans, which are now being implemented, involve doing more ministry in homes and local neighborhoods and less at the central campus. The biggest challenge is not structural but attitudinal. The new vision will challenge Oak Hills' members to have enough margin in their lives to be ministers in their own neighborhoods. It will push them to be not "consumers" of church programs ("I come to Oak Hills because it has the best ministry for my kids") but ambassadors of Christ in their communities.

One of the most interesting examples of the new strategy at Oak Hills involves the women's ministry. Like many churches, Oak Hills has offered several Bible studies for women at different times throughout the week. In the past, these Bible studies have been conducted at the main campus, with the church paying for child care, room setup, and administration. Not only is this approach costly, but it also has finite capacity limits and forces participants to come from all over the city to the one location. Under the new strategy, Oak Hills is emphasizing women's Bible studies in homes throughout San Antonio, launching twenty-five such groups in the first semester. This approach allows the church to exponentially increase its "capacity" for women's ministry and take a step toward being "the body of Christ in every neighborhood."

Frazee is quick to acknowledge that Oak Hills is a healthy congregation when it comes to making major decisions. He credits Max Lucado's leadership for creating an "environment built on humility and grace." Even in this environment, Frazee knows that the new direction is a substantial change and that some people will not be happy. Oak Hills is still in the early stages of making this shift, and time will tell whether it is successful. Irrespective of the ultimate outcome, the Oak Hills story illustrates several important principles that should undergird transformation in any Christian organization.

Start with a spiritual foundation. Even though this book is exploring ways to tap the wisdom of the business world, Christian leaders should never neglect the spiritual foundation. If they fail in this respect, the knowledge they gain is for naught. Randy Frazee started in the right place at Oak Hills. Even though he had communicated his vision before coming on board and it had been accepted by the church, he had not had time to lay the spiritual foundation to support that vision. He wanted the congregation's decisions to be based on biblical arguments, not pragmatic ones. Because Oak Hills spent time in God's Word and in prayer, the elders stood firmly on their convictions, even when some people questioned the new strategy.

This aligns with an experience that Jim Herrington, James Furr, and I describe in *Leading Congregational Change*. In the early years of our consulting work with congregations, our starting point was a strategic planning approach that assumed a strong foundation of "spiritual and relational vitality" in each congregation. We were surprised when serious conflict emerged in almost every case. We eventually learned that our assumption about the spiritual health of these congregations was incorrect and that we had overlooked the most important element for effective transformation.[22] Christian organizations that attempt deep change without a solid biblical and spiritual foundation will flounder.

Be patient and intentional. Once God has birthed a vision in a leader's heart, he or she feels a personal sense of urgency to make it a reality. Frazee's story is somewhat unique in the clarity of his vision before arriving at Oak Hills. He even developed a nine-page "memorandum of understanding" to communicate this to the church before accepting the call to serve as senior minister. With that kind of starting point, you might expect him to have swung into action quickly, but Frazee took a year and a half to develop plans.

His approach underscores an important truth about change leadership. People's heads start nodding yes long before their hearts assent. If a leader acts just because heads are bobbing up and down, he or she may discover that few people are following. Frazee's goal was to keep key stakeholders involved throughout the process so that they would not be surprised by major decisions. He believes that one reason pastors get into trouble "has less to do with the content than lack of good process." In other words, it's not the ideas that cause problems but the ways in which the ideas are developed. When pastors get impatient, they shortcut the process in their haste to make something happen.

Sociologist and leadership expert Michael Lindsay offers a helpful explanation that underscores this need for patience. Building on Gil Rendle's image that the emotions accompanying change are like a roller coaster, Lindsay adds, "Leaders must remember that they do not encounter these ups and downs at the same time as their followers. Leaders ride in the front cars of the roller coaster, which means they reach the peaks and the valleys before their followers. Sometimes the lag between the leader and follower can be so great that the leader is reaching the crest of a peak as the follower is just entering the valley before it."[23]

Selecting the right pace for a change effort is one of the greatest challenges of leadership. There is no formula to know when the organization is ready to move forward. The year-and-a-half process at Oak Hills may seem long, but Frazee actually had the advantage of a healthy congregation that knew his vision from the start. In many cases, it will take even longer to establish spiritual and relational vitality. In other cases, a deep and obvious organizational crisis will set the stage for change to happen much more quickly.[24] Just remember, your sense of "crisis" may not be shared by the congregation. The wise leader knows the importance of patience and persistence in leading change.

Share the leadership burden. The process of discerning God's vision at Oak Hills may have started with one person, but it didn't end there. Frazee involved the elders throughout the process, and this led to the unanimous vote in favor of a radical change for the congregation.

Sharing the leadership burden is a theme that appears throughout the literature on change management. Heifitz notes, "Each of us has blind spots that require the vision of others."[25] Kotter's second stage in the change process is "creating the guiding coalition."[26] In *Leading Congregational Change*, we refine Kotter's concept and refer to the coalition as a "vision community, ... a diverse group of key members who become a committed and trusting community in order to discern and implement God's vision for the congregation."[27]

Shared leadership is an important theme in many of the stories in this book. It is a powerful way to discern God's will and build consensus for change. It is also an important way to prevent leadership burnout. Leaders who truly share the burden of the role are following a model that can sustain them for the long haul.

Strive for clarity at every turn. An understated point in the Oak Hills story is Randy Frazee's drive for clarity throughout the process. Kotter says many visions "don't provide a clue as to how or why a transformation is feasible."[28] Frazee's initial declaration was an important first step, but each succeeding step brought a greater awareness of what it would actually mean for Oak Hills to be "the body of Christ in every neighborhood."

The clarity problem is especially pronounced in congregations. Some pastors think that they have been clear when they declare a high-level vision, but if the congregation doesn't know what to do, then clarity is still lacking. Frazee didn't offer concrete steps when he first described his vision for Oak Hills, but he was willing to engage other leaders to develop the next level of detail. Some pastors consciously (or unconsciously) avoid clarity because they are uncertain themselves. Others know that getting clear means saying no to some things so that they can say yes to others. That leads to the final characteristic of effective change efforts.

Change requires courageous leadership. Randy Frazee, and the abbreviated way I have told the Oak Hills story, makes change sound easy, but of course it never is. Even in Frazee's case, the journey has required courageous leadership that is driven by faith-filled conviction. It requires courageous leadership to be willing to walk away from an opportunity to lead a prominent church if its vision doesn't align with yours. It requires courageous leadership to enter into a significant and risky change process in an organization that is already experiencing great success. It requires courageous leadership to change well-established programs because they will get in the way of something even greater that God seeks to do.

Leading organizational change is hard. It's a path that is filled with uncertainty and risk. Quinn is right in saying that deep change "happens only when someone cares enough to exercise the courage to uncover the issues no one dares to recognize or confront. It means someone must be enormously secure and courageous."[29] It is why Heifitz says, "In exercising leadership, people often are drawn to taking courageous stands. Indeed, leadership may require the willingness to die."[30] Of all people, Christian leaders should have the courage to step out and lead. After all, it's the example of the leader that we all follow.

JOURNEY OR DESTINATION?

A final challenge for leaders who seek to bring about organizational transformation is the success-oriented mind-set that surrounds us. Don't get me wrong—the work we are doing is important, and we need to carry it out with great energy and diligence. But if getting to the final destination is all that matters, it can make for a very unpleasant and ultimately unsuccessful journey. Driving intently toward a destination can make leaders anxious about developing the perfect plan to get there. It can cause them to treat people as tools to be used to reach the objective.

Compare this destination mind-set with that of someone on a journey. If you are on a journey, the companions you choose and their well-being are important. Success is not defined strictly in terms of reaching a destination. You may not know exactly how you will get to your end point, so you are more willing to adapt and adjust to surprises along the way. That brings us back to two core concepts about leading change.

Enduring transformation requires touching the hearts of those who are being asked to change. No mater how compelling the logic for change may be, no matter how captivating the envisioned destination, a person's choice to support deep change is an emotional decision. I know of one church that was wrestling with whether to make several major changes in order to reach a younger generation. The pastor had plenty of facts to support the proposed changes—facts about the attitudes and spiritual beliefs of twenty-something adults and about the aging and declining status of the church—but the lay leadership was not motivated by this. The turning point was when one of the matriarchs shared her anguish that her twenty-five-year-old grandson was far from God. She concluded by saying, "I'd give anything for a church that would reach him. And I think we need to be that church for someone else's grandson." Her story touched hearts in ways that facts couldn't do, and it opened the church to a journey of change.

The other reality is that even if the final destination is clear (or at least somewhat clear), the complete map to get there rarely is. This can be difficult for leaders who are accustomed to providing confident answers. According to Heifitz, change leaders live with this tension: "Rather than fulfilling the expectation for answers, one provides questions; rather than protecting people from outside threat, one lets people feel the threat in order to stimulate adaptation."[31] Rodney Cooper of Gordon-Conwell says it succinctly: "If you can't live with ambiguity, you can't lead in the church."

One of my favorite images on the ambiguity of leadership comes from Robert Quinn, who says, "When we have a vision, it does not necessarily mean that we have a plan. We may know where we want to be, but we will seldom know the actual steps we must take to get there. We must trust in ourselves to learn the way, *to build the bridge as we walk on it*"[32] (italics added). To publicly acknowledge this is scary for leaders. It's even scarier to take the first step forward on an unfinished bridge. But that is what is required for leaders who want to see their organizations soar in an uncertain future.

WHAT ARE YOU PURSUING?

- What are the heart issues (your own and those of your leaders) that need to be addressed in order to navigate change successfully?
- What is the biggest obstacle to change that you can foresee?
- Are you personally prepared to lead organizational change? Do you have the conviction that is needed?
- Pick one Bible verse or story regarding change that is meaningful to you. Pick a quote from one of the experts in this chapter. Reflect on both, and let them guide and encourage you.
- Which people in your organization sense the need for deep change? Which people are not convinced but could become valuable allies if they were? How can you build relationships with them?
- Which of the change principles listed in the Oak Hills story is easiest for you? Which is hardest?

CHAPTER TWELVE

ARE YOU GUARDING YOUR HEART?

"What will it profit a man if he gains the whole world and forfeits his soul?" (Matthew 16:26, NASB). In this familiar passage, Jesus teaches his disciples about his upcoming death on the cross and the cost of following him. As Christian leaders, we know that this verse is important, but we also think it's behind us. After all, we have not only made a personal spiritual commitment to follow Christ as Lord and Savior, but we have also made a deep commitment of our lives, either in vocational ministry or as volunteers. We think, "I'm not trying to gain the world. I'm pursuing the things of God."

But what if the way that we are pursuing Kingdom-oriented success is a subtle, soul-sacrificing way of trying to gain the world? One of the darkest and most troubling aspects of Christian leadership is found in the pursuit of "success." The argument throughout this book is that God wants, and expects, the very best from us as leaders. Because of this, we should be willing to understand and adapt the best leadership practices that we can find in the secular arena. We should do this so that our churches and Christian organizations can have a greater impact for the Kingdom. In this pursuit, however, it is easy to cross the invisible line from pursuing success as directed by God and for His glory alone to pursuing things that appear godly but in reality are self-directed and self-glorifying.

My greatest fear about the use of secular leadership principles is at this fundamental level. The things that are proclaimed as business best practices do not have God at the center. The ultimate motivation behind these practices is to achieve success solely for the good of the organization and the individual. Even the most biblical-sounding principles from business—Level 5 leadership, caring for employees, pursuing a noble vision, making deep personal change—can have an underlying, self-serving drive. The marketplace leader who does these well will have greater success and will therefore be rewarded with promotions, pay increases, and recognition.

As ministry leaders, when we pursue "success" for the sake of success (under the guise of honoring God and building His Kingdom), we do so at the potential cost of our souls. I'm talking not about losing our salvation but rather about losing the sense of joy and purpose and fulfillment in ministry that God intends each of us to have. If you don't think that could happen to you, listen to the words of one of the country's most prominent pastors. At an earlier point in his long, successful career, Bill Hybels realized, "The pace at which I've been doing the work of God is destroying God's work in me."[1] His pursuit of success, all in the name of God, had begun to take a huge personal and spiritual toll. Because of this, Hybels had to step back and reorient his life.

The success trap can snare any leader, causing him to run at such a frantic pace that he never realizes he is out of step with God. Ruth Haley Barton, author of *Strengthening the Soul of Your Leadership*, says, "*Many* of us are choosing to live lives that do not set us up to pay attention, to notice those places where God is at work and to ask ourselves what these things mean. We long for a word from the Lord, but somehow we have been suckered into believing that the pace we keep is what leadership requires."[2]

In this final chapter, we need to step away from the advice and expertise of the business world. We need to stop and ask how we should define success. We need to explore how high-achieving spiritual leaders in a success-oriented society can stay spiritually renewed and refreshed. We need to consider how we can still pursue greatness but in doing so make sure that we are honoring God and not destroying our souls. We need to ask how to heed Proverbs 4:23, which says, "Above all else, guard your heart, for it is the wellspring of life."

At the close of most of my interviews, I asked two questions: "How do you define success?" and "What do you do to care for your own soul and keep it refreshed?" The responses from a variety of spiritual leaders and the wisdom from other Christian authors are instructive. Any leader who is pursuing greatness and godliness needs to reflect on these questions.

REDEFINING SUCCESS

Throughout this book, I have told the stories and philosophies of many "successful" spiritual leaders. They are viewed as successful because they lead large organizations that are making a difference in their communities and beyond. They pastor churches in which many people come to faith each year and in which ongoing spiritual growth is the norm. They lead ministries that offer physical and spiritual hope in the name of Christ. They have big visions that have been birthed by God's spirit in their own hearts and in the hearts of others. In that sense, these leaders define organizational success as diligently pursuing their visions and having greater Kingdom impact as they do so.

But how do they define success personally? Is their internal sense of worth and God's blessing tied up in the success of the organizations they lead? Or is it possible to separate the two? Ruth Haley Barton wonders, "Is it possible for a leader to have encountered God so richly that no matter what we are working toward here on this earth, we know we already have what we most deeply want—the presence of God, that which can never be taken from us?"[3] Barton contends that this reorientation is always possible but never easy.

Wrestling with the meaning and pursuit of success is one of the deepest tensions that Christian leaders will experience. On one hand is the assurance that God loves us and that we belong to Him. On the other hand is a dream that we believe, to our very core, is from God. Surely it must follow that achieving the dream is what God wants for us, and failure to achieve the dream represents some kind of personal failure. Our identity becomes completely enmeshed in the organization and its "performance."

As if this spiritual dynamic is not enough, our society makes it very clear that organizational success and personal success are inseparable. In the corporate world, promotions and salary increases are the indicators that a manager has succeeded, and these are based on the performance of that manager's business.

It is not enough to perform well; most executives are driven to outperform their peers. The obsession with comparison makes it difficult even for star performers to rest and feel satisfied in their results.

This mentality spills over into ministry, even though we should have different standards. One of my least favorite questions when pastors get together is "How big is your church?" There are *many* problems with this question. First, it is not "your" church; it is God's. Second, the question implies that there is only one way to measure organizational success. Third, it implies that the bigger number represents the better church. But the worst thing about the question is what it does in the souls of the leaders who are having the conversation. Regardless of their answer, the implicit message is that a congregation's size is the primary evidence of a pastor's own spiritual faithfulness. It allows an external standard to determine a person's internal definition of success.

In my interviews, when I asked, "How do you define success personally?" I was pleasantly surprised at the answers. Jim Leggett of Grace Fellowship has four questions that he periodically asks himself: "Am I still walking with God? Have I followed God's leadership in my life, which means have I been true and honest to the promptings He has given me in my life, personally and as a pastor? Third, I can't help but ask the question, 'Has the church grown?' I wrestle with the fact that I ask myself that question, but I can't help it. And then, is the staff team fulfilled?" Leggett does not deny that the congregation's numerical results are one reflection of his leadership and therefore affect his own sense of fulfillment. But he puts it in perspective. If he is not walking with God, the rest doesn't matter. If following God's leadership is more important than organizational growth, he can make Spirit-led decisions that may not be popular. Leggett also recognizes that shepherding the staff is a primary responsibility and that organizational success is not possible if the core leadership is struggling.

Greg Surratt of Seacoast Church explains, "My life verse is Galatians 6:9, which says, 'Don't become weary in doing good, for in due season you will reap a harvest if you don't quit.'" Surratt's personal commentary on this verse is, "We have to learn to do good. Then you have to learn to make good repeatable—that means systems to keep doing good. Then you have to learn how to encourage yourself in the time between harvests because that's the quitting part. Then God's responsibility is the harvest, both the timing and size of it. I have to tell myself over and over I'm not responsible for the [harvest]. I'm responsible for doing the right thing and not quitting."

Surratt's explanation strikes an important balance. We have been entrusted with a tremendous responsibility that we must carry out with diligence and persistence. We cannot slack off in "doing good," even when it is unpopular or difficult or when we are not seeing the results we hoped for. But God is responsible for the harvest. For spiritual leaders, the most dangerous message from secular experts is that the leader is responsible for the organization's results. That message simply does not square with the teaching of Scripture, which tells us that the leader is responsible for faithfully following God.

Surratt's comment about being encouraged between harvests is important for any Christian leader. Dry and difficult seasons are inevitable in ministry. The crowds turned away from the Messiah himself because his teaching was too hard. Spiritual leaders who expect continual growth set themselves up for disappointment. Not only that, they may also miss important lessons that God wants to teach them. Rodney Cooper of Gordon-Conwell teaches students to distinguish between the "redemptive journey" and the "missional journey" of a spiritual leader.[4] Cooper explains, "The redemptive journey is when God puts you in a place and allows you to fail and go through difficult times so He can redeem you. Through that redemption, you can go do the mission because you're prepared to do it." Far too often, leaders see setbacks as failures, not as opportunities to learn and grow and allow God to teach them something important for the next stage of their lives.

Greg Surratt experienced this kind of "failure" in the early years of Seacoast. The church had the typical surge of curious newcomers when it launched, followed by the normal decline in attendance. But it was five years before Seacoast grew back to its original size. Even though this was a season of discouragement for Surratt, he looks back on an important lesson he learned and continues to apply: "I have to remind myself to be real slow to put the good or bad tag on an event." In a world where many things can be measured instantly, it is difficult to take God's long-term perspective in assessing fruitfulness.

In many of my interviews, I heard definitions of success that were very personal. Peter Greer says, "When I look back at the end of the year, my number one measure of success is going to be, 'Is my wife a huge fan and supporter of HOPE International?' I see a lot of people that sacrifice so much for business and ministry, and that's one piece that keeps me grounded. Success cannot come at the expense of my family." Jeff Wells of WoodsEdge Community Church says, "Success is a lot harder to handle than failure. How can you live in this success-oriented culture and not be influenced by it? We have to redefine success. For me, the bottom line for success is not a large church, not a big budget, not books and fame. It's pleasing God and loving Jesus more. We have to constantly remind ourselves of this." Can these leaders quantify success numerically based on their definitions? Certainly not, but by clinging to these goals and listening to the Spirit, they create a buttress against the external forces that would define success for them.

Ruth Haley Barton cuts to the heart of the issue as she follows the story of Moses in her thought-provoking book. She takes her readers to that pivotal moment when the Lord tells Moses, "Go up to the land flowing with milk and honey. But I will not go with you, because you are a stiff-necked people and I might destroy you on the way" (Exodus 33:3). In the passage that follows, Moses pleads for God's reassurance that He will not abandon Moses or the people. Barton explains, "All of a sudden, this [God's presence] was more important to him than any promised land he had ever dreamed of." Then she drives home the application for every spiritual leader:

> This is a pivotal moment in the life of a leader. It is the moment when whatever the promised land is for us—a church of a certain size, a new ministry, a new building, writing a book, being sought out as an expert—pales in significance when compared with our desire for God. At this point we might realize that we are missing the presence of God for ourselves personally. We might look around at what we've done or built and wonder whether we have gotten where we are merely through our own effort and whether we

have somehow gotten out ahead of the very Presence that called us to this journey in the first place. . . . A great emptiness has opened up, and we realize, as Moses did, that there is no promised land we could ever envision that matters nearly as much as the presence of God in our life right here and right now.[5]

Leaders can guard their hearts only by defining success, first, as living in the presence of God and, second, as accomplishing the task God calls them to do.

Renewal for Leaders

This leads to an even more important question: How much do you experience the presence of God in your life? Some will answer, "We're Christian leaders. We are in God's presence and doing God's work all the time." But that's not my question. Spiritual leaders need to encounter God regularly in ways that are deeply personal. I am not talking about doing the work of ministry or even studying Scripture in preparation for teaching. I am talking about the intimate moments when you are alone with God and the only agenda is that of the Creator who wants to nourish and strengthen your soul. For many spiritual leaders, the honest answer is that this does not happen nearly as often as they need.

Why is it that pastors teach their congregations about the importance of "spending time with God" and yet fail to make this a daily practice of their own? One reason, as noted earlier, is that doing ministry can be treated as a surrogate for being in God's presence. We convince ourselves that spending sixty hours a week doing God's work is a valid substitute for an hour a day of personal devotional reading and prayer. Or we think that twenty hours of study for a sermon must mean that we have spent a lot of time in God's presence. Even those who recognize the difference between personal time with the Lord and doing ministry face the pressure to spend every waking minute on the job. The demands of ministry can be all-consuming—you can always spend more time preparing a sermon, counseling individuals in need, building relationships with key leaders, evaluating strategic decisions, and encouraging your staff. Far too many leaders know they need to create the time for their souls to be refreshed, but they put it off "until things slow down a little."

Reggie McNeal says, "Spiritual leadership is a work of heart. This truth escapes many spiritual leaders. Caught up in helping other people maintain their heart, they frequently ignore or neglect their own."[6] The pressure to neglect soul care exists for leaders in large churches and in small churches, for pastors and for other Christian leaders. The result of this neglect is often catastrophic. Bill Hybels says, "When leaders lead effectively, they tend to generate an increasing amount of velocity in their own lives and in the organizations they serve. . . . At a certain velocity, most speed-hungry leaders will run out of the wherewithal to lead well. At a certain velocity, the soul will simply dissipate."[7] None of us want our souls to dissipate, but we are the only ones who can prevent it from happening.

Personal Practices

The leaders I interviewed have a deep sense of calling and a relentless drive to do great things for God. So I was interested in understanding what they do to recharge and refresh their souls. A number of practices were described by these leaders, including regular exercise routines, submitting to spiritual directors, and periodic personal retreats. Most described a strong discipline of spending time with God on a daily basis.

Randy Frazee of Oak Hills Church says, "What replenishes me is a daily, weekly, and seasonal rhythm. I'm fairly religious about that."[8] Jeff Wells finds wisdom in Mother Teresa's words: "Jesus is the deep well, and every day I need to drop my bucket into the well." He devotes a significant amount of each morning to spending time alone with God in addition to several other practices. Wells says, "If you connect well with Jesus every day—in the Word and prayer and singing and just drawing close to Him—it's refueling." Tim Lundy reflects on the culture at Fellowship Bible Church and comments, "If you lean toward more of a corporate [environment], it can feel like a business all day." That's why Lundy finds it vital to spend "every day in the Word and journal out a prayer every day." He also knows that a pastor can become detached from the people in a large congregation, so he regularly looks for opportunities to hear "God stories" that are happening in the church's ministries and the lives of members.

It is not enough to set aside a daily time to spend with God if that time becomes too mechanical or hurried. During a recent season, Dan Reiland of 12Stone Church heard a distinct challenge from the Lord. Reiland explains, "I have a prayer room in my basement. I can't run down there and pray and then run out the door. God is saying, 'If you want to hear from me, I will not be rushed.'" Reiland has restructured his day so that he can have an unhurried time that allows him to slow down and listen to whatever God has for him.

In addition to a daily time with God, Greg Surratt says, "I make sure that once a week I have a Sabbath. I don't even call it a day off anymore because I can violate a day off but to violate a Sabbath is to do it to the Lord." Similarly, Chris Hodges of Church of the Highlands says, "I go to church on Mondays. I wake up first thing on Monday morning and watch online messages from some of my friends and take notes, just like I'm a member of that church. I'm real strict on my Sabbath. A ton of pastors would never dream of committing adultery, but they don't keep the Sabbath." Hodges then adds an important perspective: "The true principle of the Sabbath is to declare that nothing is accomplished by my own hands. It happens because I'm in relationship with God. We need to declare that at least weekly." Hodges makes an important point. The time that we spend with God, away from our jobs, not only refreshes us but also helps us have a proper understanding of our own significance. It weans us away from the addictive belief that the ministry won't survive without us.

My friends at Texas Methodist Foundation like to joke that I've spent enough time with them to become a Methodist. Though that may not be true, I have great respect for John Wesley. He is known for asking, "How is it with your soul?" That is the point of this section. Too many spiritual leaders rarely consider the question. I have not described the practices of other leaders to be prescriptive but simply to emphasize that every Christian leader needs to have deep, meaningful disciplines that will ensure that it is well with their souls.

SOUL RENEWAL IN COMMUNITY

Wesley's question is important for every leader to ask introspectively, but his movement found its strength in community. Wesley's "Sunday school" groups created environments where people knew each other intimately and loving accountability was the norm. In contrast, today's spiritual leaders are often the loneliest people in their ministries. They spend their days surrounded by friends who love God and who care for them and for the organization's success. And yet these leaders may not have anyone who truly knows what is happening in the depths of their souls or who can speak truth into their lives.

Reggie McNeal traces the reluctance of leaders to embrace community, at least in part, to the great American Western in which the "good guy" always operates alone. McNeal labels this a dangerous myth and says, "Leaders are not shaped in isolation. Leaders are shaped *in* community. And they are shaped *by* community. Leaders cannot be separated from the formative processes of community. Despite any claims to the contrary, leaders are not self-made people."[9] McNeal is right, both about the resistance to community and the importance of community in the process of shaping spiritual leaders.

Jim Mellado of the Willow Creek Association is no stranger to the pressures of leadership. As the head of a large and highly visible organization, Mellado has experienced the stress of pursuing a huge vision from God, the weight of making decisions to achieve that vision, and intense criticism from others. Mellado says one key to recharging his soul is being in the same trusted small group for fifteen years. "It's a group of folks that love me for who I am. What I do at the Association is irrelevant to our relationship." Mellado goes on to say, "I could not do what I do, could not have done what I've done here, I couldn't even be here had it not been for this group walking with me. I sometimes think, 'Can I make it to Saturday night?' [when the group meets]. It's been a safe place for me to process. If there's no safe place to process it will poison your soul."

Edwin Friedman says, "Living with crisis is a major part of leaders' lives."[10] When the crisis becomes intense and the criticism becomes personal, a leader can be deeply wounded. Robert Sloan of Houston Baptist University, who has experienced this kind of pain first-hand, reflects on how spiritual leaders can heal from these hurts: "Our typical answer, which I will agree with, is prayer and Scripture. But the way we typically interpret that is not good enough. Your private devotional life is important, but it must be a corporate devotional life as well. You need community worship and you need a small group. Even when you're getting beat to pieces, these will be the people who will understand and with whom you can share."

The kind of safe, supportive community described by Sloan and Mellado is rare for spiritual leaders, and it is generally not found within their ministries. Ruth Haley Barton notes, "Oftentimes a leader's soul is not strengthened in the community of those she or he is leading. In fact, life in the community of those one is leading often challenges and at times weakens the soul."[11] Because the source of trouble is usually within the organization or is a personal issue that insiders are not prepared to hear, ministry leaders most often find true community in an external group. Greg Surratt says, "I have friends in the ARC [Association of Related Churches] that I try to connect with regularly. We figure out ways to spend two or three days away just to be together." Intentionality, a common bond, and a safe place to share are the key ingredients for Surratt.

For the past four years, I have been privileged to be the facilitator for a group of executive pastors under the auspices of the Texas Methodist Foundation. I've seen participants come into our gatherings with heavy burdens, and I've seen them leave with a fresh perspective and a refreshed spirit. Even though I am the facilitator, I have experienced the same sense of renewal from being among these trusted friends. Every leader needs to have a place to retreat and recharge at times.

Another important dimension of community for spiritual leaders is accountability. A trusted group is not just a place for pouring out your heart so that others can encourage you and help you get back up. It should also be a place where the darker side of leadership can be exposed and where you can be appropriately challenged. Judy West of The Crossing admits, "I can lead my way through a day without including God, so it's a constant discipline of mine to be a servant of Jesus and not work for Jesus. I have to make constantly sure I'm on my knees because it's very easy for me to stand up and run on my own." I appreciate her candor—most spiritual leaders would not say this out loud, even if their lives give evidence of too much self-reliance and too little of the Spirit. West's awareness of this danger helps her recognize her need for accountability within community. According to West, The Crossing's senior leadership team is "constantly watching out for each other and figuring out, 'How do we make sure we're taking care of our souls?'"

Kouzes and Posner state, "You can avoid excessive pride only if you recognize that you're human and need the help of others. ... Exemplary leaders know that 'you can't do it alone,' and they act accordingly."[12] Even the secular experts know that effective leadership cannot be practiced in isolation, and the Bible clearly teaches the importance of community. So why do so many spiritual leaders try to go through the journey alone? Many factors may come into play—pride or insecurity, lack of healthy models, fear that confidential information will be "leaked." There may be many reasons that spiritual leaders avoid community, but the risks of leading in isolation are far greater.

Jim Mellado's earlier comment based on personal experience is reinforced by his broader perspective as leader of the Willow Creek Association. For years, the association has brought groups of pastors together in small gatherings to spend a couple of days with Bill Hybels and Henry Cloud. In this setting, pastors have an opportunity to recharge, reflect, and sharpen their leadership skills. Even these accomplished leaders, according to Mellado, consistently say they do not have anyone with whom they can have a safe conversation. This is a huge void and a dangerous reality for many spiritual leaders. Mellado explains, "Henry [Cloud] would say that one of the most common themes of leaders that end up in ditches is the fact that they do not have a single, [same-gender], fully disclosing relationship in their life that has no agenda other than their well-being and growth."

If you are relying on a solo practice of faith to stay out of the ditch, then think again. Consider the long list of people before you who thought the same thing but did not finish the race well. Whether you are at the top of your game or stuck in a valley that seems never-ending, you need those safe places of community and accountability. A deep personal walk with God is vital, but God created us to live in community, and we ignore this at our peril.

COMING FULL CIRCLE

"All exemplary leaders have wrestled with their souls. Such personal searching is essential in the development of leaders."[13] This is one of the themes of this chapter. But the source of this quote underscores one of the broader themes of this book. You may think these words come from a prominent pastor or a noted Christian leadership expert, but they actually come from Kouzes and Posner's *Leadership Challenge*.

Throughout this book, I have demonstrated the gap between the very best practices of leadership and the way leadership is often exercised in Christian organizations. Of course, in any endeavor, there is always a gap between the best and the rest. The problem arises when spiritual leaders refuse to acknowledge this gap or argue that business leadership principles cannot be translated into ministry settings. In light of all you have seen in these pages, it is hard to sustain this argument. Kouzes and Posner, Quinn, Kotter, Lencioni, and many other leadership experts offer wisdom that transcends the business realm. They support Jim Collins's assertion that "the critical distinction is not between business and social, but between great and good."[14]

At the same time, a single-minded pursuit of greatness is dangerous for Christian leaders. If we run only after greatness, we will end up running away from God. The divine element must be central as every Christian exercises his or her leadership gifts. God's presence will fundamentally reshape our attitude, our motivation, and our definition of success as leaders. Tim Lundy sums it up well: "God keeps teaching me that God does more in our churches despite us than because of us. It spurs me to want to do better and do it well, but it also frees me to know that He's going to do things despite me, not because of me."

That is the essential difference between Christian leadership and the leadership that is espoused by secular experts. We should work even harder, because we are "working for the Lord, not for men" (Colossians 3:23), yet the weight of responsibility *for the end result* should be as light as a feather on our shoulders. Bill Hybels is known for his intensity as a leader and for emphasizing the biblical admonition to "lead with all diligence" (Romans 12:8, NASB), yet he knows that the outcome is not in his hands. His axiom, "only God," makes this point: "We watch for our heavenly Father to move and stir and act and call. And when he does, we humbly thank him with the only two words that could even begin to give credit to the one to whom alone credit is due: 'Only God.'"[15]

Hybels's axiom highlights another theme that permeates this book. I have focused on identifying the places where the church falls short of the kind of excellent leadership that is found in business. But at the end of the day, leadership by non-Christians can only produce human results. Our ministries should be characterized by supernatural results that are explained by the phrase "only God."

At the end of my interview with Rich Stearns, he spoke of his aspirations for World Vision: "I dream of the day when we will be on the cover of *Forbes* or *Fortune* or *Business Week* because when they think about excellence, World Vision comes to the top as an example. We should be more excellent than the secular world because we serve a great God and we have a great mission."

Is that a preposterous dream? I don't think so. In fact, I think it is a noble goal for any Christian leader. Not that Stearns or any of the rest of us want to be on the cover of a magazine for our own notoriety, but we should aspire to a kind of leadership that the outside world will notice. It is leadership in which Christian organizations become known for a level of excellence that businesses cannot achieve. It is evidenced by the unity of their leadership teams. It is seen in personnel practices that blend compassion with high expectations so that staff members soar in their performance. It becomes apparent not only in the clarity and size of their vision but also in their ability to achieve that vision.

When the table is turned, and Christian organizations become the standard setters for excellent leadership, we will know that we are truly practicing great *and* godly leadership.

What Are You Pursuing?

- How do you define success personally? How do the standards of the world influence your definition?

- How often do you experience God's presence in a deeply personal, sustaining way? What do you need to do to care for your soul and keep it refreshed?
- When is the last time you unplugged and spent significant time in God's presence?
- What will keep you from ending up in a ditch? Are you in at least one fully disclosing relationship with someone of the same gender? If not, with whom can you develop such a relationship?
- What is the next step you need to take on the journey toward great *and* godly leadership?

THE PEOPLE BEHIND THE STORIES

Alan "Blues" Baker serves as the directional leader at Menlo Park Presbyterian Church in the San Francisco Bay area. This new role was created to complement the teaching gifts of senior pastor John Ortberg. Prior to Menlo Park, Baker spent more than twenty years in the U.S. Navy, culminating in his appointment to rear admiral and assignment as the 16th Chaplain of the U.S. Marine Corps.

Greg Brenneman is the chairman of CCMP Capital Advisors, an international private equity firm. Prior business experience includes chairman and CEO of Burger King and Quiznos, CEO of PricewaterhouseCoopers Consulting, and president and COO of Continental Airlines. Brenneman also serves on the boards of Home Depot, ADP, Edwards Group, Francesca's Collections, and Quiznos. Brenneman is a lay leader at WoodsEdge Community Church in The Woodlands, Texas, and also serves on the advisory board of the New Canaan Society and World Vision.

Jenni Catron is executive director of Cross Point Church in Nashville, Tennessee, an eight-year-old multisite congregation. She is also the founder of Cultivate Her, a leadership environment for women. Catron previously spent nine years as an artist development and brand manager in the Christian music industry.

Rodney Cooper is the Kenneth and Jean Hansen Professor of Discipleship and Leadership Development at the Charlotte, North Carolina, campus of Gordon-Conwell Theological Seminary. He is an internationally known speaker and is the author of several books, including *Shoulder to Shoulder* and *Double Bind*. His prior experience includes positions at Denver Seminary, Western Seminary, and Promise Keepers.

Scott Cormode is the Hugh DePree Professor of Leadership Development at Fuller Theological Seminary in Pasadena, California. Cormode is the founder of the Academy of Religious Leadership and the creator and editor of the *Journal of Religious Leadership*. He is also the author of *Making Spiritual Sense: Christian Leaders as Spiritual Interpreters*. Cormode previously served on the faculty of Claremont School of Theology.

Jan Davis is the senior pastor of First United Methodist Church of Rowlett, Texas. She has been in local church ministry for more than eighteen years, most recently as executive pastor of Christ United Methodist in Plano, Texas. She serves on the board of ministry for the United Methodist Church's North Texas Conference. Before entering seminary, Davis had a career in sales and marketing for Texas Instruments.

C. Andrew Doyle was seated as the ninth bishop of the Episcopal Diocese of Texas in June 2009. Before his election, he served for five years as the canon to the ordinary under Bishop Don Wimberly. Doyle previously served as a priest in local parishes and a school in the diocese, and has a particular interest in reaching younger generations.

Dan Entwistle is the managing executive director for programs and ministries at the United Methodist Church of the Resurrection in the Kansas City area, where he serves alongside senior pastor Adam Hamilton. Entwistle oversees the church's ministry teams and the implementation of the church's strategic direction. In his nearly twenty years on staff, he has helped create the structure and systems that have helped Resurrection become one of the largest Methodist churches in the country.

Dave Ferguson is a founding pastor of Community Christian Church, an innovative missional church with eleven Chicago locations that have grown in average attendance from five people to more than fifty-five hundred since its beginning two decades ago. He is also the visionary and movement leader for the NewThing Network, a catalyst for a movement of reproducing churches. Ferguson is the coauthor of three books, including *The Big Idea: Focus the Message, Maximize the Impact* and *On The Verge: The Apostolic Future of the Church* with Alan Hirsch.

Randy Frazee is senior minister of Oak Hills Church in San Antonio, Texas. Prior to Oak Hills, Frazee served as a teaching pastor at Willow Creek Community Church and as senior pastor of Pantego Bible Church. Frazee is the author of several books, including *Making Room for Life: Trading Chaotic Lifestyles for Connected Relationships* and *The Connecting Church: Beyond Small Groups to Authentic Community.*

Peter Greer is president of HOPE International, a Christian microfinance organization based in Lancaster, Pennsylvania, that seeks to offer a "hand up" rather than a handout to alleviate poverty in the poorest places on the globe. Greer has been involved in microfinance at the ground level in Zimbabwe, Cambodia, Rwanda, and the Democratic Republic of Congo and is the coauthor of *Let the Poor Be Glad: Joining the Revolution to Lift the World out of Poverty.*

Alistair Hanna is the executive director of Alpha International's regional arm in Latin America and the founding chairman of Alpha North America. Hanna's passion for Alpha grew out of his experience with the Alpha course at Holy Trinity Brompton in London, which led him to this "second-half" involvement, after a successful corporate consulting career with McKinsey & Company.

Greg Hawkins is executive pastor of Willow Creek Community Church in South Barrington, Illinois, where he has served on staff since 1991. He oversees the staff, has guided several strategic planning processes, and has been the staff leader for the church's capital campaigns. Hawkins is the point leader for Reveal, an initiative that uses research tools to help churches better understand spiritual growth. Hawkins started his career in the marketplace as a consultant for McKinsey & Company.

Chris Hodges founded Church of the Highlands in Birmingham, Alabama, in 2001, and he continues to serve as the church's senior pastor. In the decade since its inception, Highlands has expanded to seven campuses and eighteen worship services. Hodges is also a cofounder of the Association of Related Churches, a church-planting network, and he serves on the board of John Maxwell's EQUIP ministry.

Greg Holder has served since 1997 as lead pastor at The Crossing, a fast-growing church in the Saint Louis, Missouri, area. He is a cocreator of the Advent Conspiracy and coauthor of a book by the same name that describes a global initiative challenging churches and individuals to celebrate Christmas with simplicity while giving outrageously to people in need. Holder is also a contributing writer for *The Voice*, a new translation of Scripture that tells the beautiful story of God's love and redemption of creation.

Janice Riggle Huie has served as the bishop of the Texas Annual Conference of the United Methodist Church since 2004 and has led the conference to adopt a new missional strategy aimed at making disciples of Jesus Christ for the transformation of the world. She served for two years as the president of the Council of Bishops. Huie previously served as president of the General Board of Higher Education and Ministry of the United Methodist Church and currently serves on the boards of several colleges, a hospital, and other denominational agencies.

Kevin Jenkins is president and CEO of World Vision International (WVI), a Christian relief, development, and advocacy organization dedicated to working with children, families, and communities to overcome poverty and injustice. Jenkins came to WVI's London headquarters in October 2009 after a successful business career that culminated in his role as the president and CEO of Canadian Airlines and a similar role at Westaim Corporation. Jenkins was previously involved with World Vision as a sponsor, volunteer, fundraiser, and board member through World Vision Canada.

Jim Leggett is the founding pastor of Grace Fellowship United Methodist Church in Katy, Texas. During the fourteen years since Grace was planted, attendance has grown from twenty-two people to twenty-seven hundred, and the church has started two daughter congregations. Leggett, a self-described "chemical engineer nerd" by training, subsequently returned to seminary and now leads a church whose vision is to be a house of prayer for all nations.

Terry Looper is the founder, president, and CEO of Texon, an energy service company headquartered in Houston. Looper is a member of Grace Presbyterian Church and has served in leadership or advisory roles at the church, Houston Christian High School, Younglife (Houston), and other ministries.

Al Lopus is the president and cofounder of the Best Christian Workplaces Institute (BCWI) in Mercer Island, Washington. BCWI provides measurement tools and advisory services to help Christian organizations set the standard as the best, most effective workplaces in the world. BCWI's survey has been used in more than four hundred Christian organizations. Lopus is also on the board of directors of the Christian Leadership Alliance and is active at the Mercer Island Covenant Church.

Tim Lundy formerly served as the directional leader and a teaching pastor at Fellowship Bible Church, a multisite congregation with the vision to be a church of irresistible influence in Little Rock, Arkansas, and beyond. Lundy's previous experience includes ministry roles served in Memphis; Dallas; and Bangkok, Thailand. He has recently moved to Los Gatos, California, to serve as teaching pastor at Venture Christian Church alongside Chip Ingram.

Mike Mantel serves as president and CEO of Living Water International, which exists to show the love of God by helping communities acquire desperately needed clean water and to experience "living water"—the gospel of Jesus Christ, which alone satisfied the deepest thirst. Mantel joined Living Water, headquartered in Houston, in September 2008 after seventeen years in various leadership roles with World Vision.

Gregg Matte has served as senior pastor of Houston's First Baptist Church since 2004. Prior to coming to Houston, Matte founded and led Breakaway Ministries, a weekly worship gathering that grew to more than four thousand students on the campus of Texas A&M University. He is also the author of *Finding God's Will: Seek Him, Know Him, Take the Next Step* and is the first pastor to receive the outstanding alumnus award from the Mays Business School at Texas A&M.

Jim Mellado is president of Willow Creek Association (WCA), where he is responsible for providing overall leadership to accomplish WCA's purpose of maximizing the life transformation effectiveness of local churches around the world. While at Harvard Business School, Mellado wrote a case study on Willow Creek Community Church and subsequently joined WCA at its Chicago-area headquarters. He competed in the decathlon in the 1988 Olympics as a member of El Salvador's Olympic team.

Brent Messick serves as managing executive director and CFO of the United Methodist Church of the Resurrection in Leawood, Kansas. His responsibilities span the business and operations of the church, including stewardship and generosity, finance and accounting, facilities, technology, and human resources. Messick came to Resurrection in 1995 with a finance background in the corporate arena.

Karen Miller is executive pastor at the Church of the Resurrection, an Anglican congregation in Wheaton, Illinois. Prior to joining the staff of Resurrection in 2003, she worked as a clinical social worker and therapist. Miller, along with her husband, Kevin, has written a book on marriage titled *More Than You and Me.*

Todd Mullins has served on the senior leadership team of Christ Fellowship in Palm Beach, Florida, for more than twenty years and has recently succeeded his father, Tom Mullins, in the role of lead pastor. Christ Fellowship was founded by the senior Mullins in 1984 and has grown from living room to school cafeteria to horse barn to four vibrant campuses today.

Debi Nixon is managing executive director of regional campuses and Catalyst for the United Methodist Church of the Resurrection in Leawood, Kansas. In this role, she serves on the church's senior leadership team, oversees its regional campuses, and coordinates its leadership development for leaders from other churches. Nixon was the church's first children's ministry director, starting as a volunteer and then joining the staff in 1994.

Mitch Peairson has called Grace Fellowship United Methodist Church in Katy, Texas, his church home for fourteen years and has served as executive pastor for more than eight. He has oversight for ministry and operations staff, has been a key leader on two capital campaigns (one as a volunteer and one as staff), and has served on the praise team. Ministry was a later calling for Peairson, who spent more than twenty years in commercial real estate.

Dave Peterson has served as senior pastor of Houston's Memorial Drive Presbyterian Church since 1995 and has been in ministry since 1972. Beyond his local church role, he has been a trustee for San Francisco Theological Seminary, Whitworth College, and Houston Christian High School; cochairs a Presbyterian Church (U.S.A.) campaign to raise $40 million for missionaries and church planting; and is actively involved in the Presbyterian Global Fellowship.

Rob Pettigrew has twenty years' experience as a hydrogeologist and manager at URS Corporation. Rob served as a journeyman for two years with the Southern Baptist International Mission Board. He has led numerous short-term mission trips and volunteered on water development and disaster relief projects with several mission organizations. Pettigrew currently serves on the board and executive committee of Living Water International and is a member of Crosspoint Church in Houston.

Dan Reiland is executive pastor at 12Stone Church in Lawrenceville, Georgia. He previously partnered with John Maxwell for twenty years, first as executive pastor at Skyline Wesleyan Church in San Diego, California, and then as vice-president of leadership and church development at INJOY. Reiland is widely known as the author of INJOY's newsletter, *The Pastor's Coach.*

Dino Rizzo, with his wife, DeLynn, started Healing Place Church in Baton Rouge, Louisiana, in 1993 with the single focus of being a healing place for a hurting world. The church has grown to eighteen worship services in eleven locations as far away as Mozambique. The story of Healing Place Church and its passion to serve the poor and hurting is described in Rizzo's book, *Servolution: Starting a Church Revolution Through Serving.* Rizzo is also a cofounder of the Association of Related Churches.

Robert Sloan is the third president of Houston Baptist University, where he has served since the fall of 2006. Sloan previously served as the president and chancellor of Baylor University and prior to that as the founding dean of George W. Truett Theological Seminary at Baylor. Sloan has published extensively and has pastored churches throughout Texas and beyond.

Rich Stearns is the president of World Vision, based in the Seattle area and serving the needs of the poor throughout the world. Stearns has been in this role since leaving the business arena in 1998. He has extensive corporate experience and has held the position of president at both Parker Brother Games and Lenox Inc. Stearns is the author of *The Hole in the Gospel.*

Geoff Surratt has recently moved across the country to become the pastor of church planting for Saddleback Church in Orange County, California. He previously served in a second chair role as the pastor of ministries for Seacoast Church in Mount Pleasant, South Carolina, where he was on staff for fourteen years. Surratt is the coauthor of *The Multisite Church Revolution, Multisite Road Trip,* and *Ten Stupid Things That Keep Churches from Growing.*

Greg Surratt planted Seacoast Church in Mount Pleasant, South Carolina, in 1988 and continues to serve as the church's senior pastor and directional leader. Seacoast is one of the early adopters of the multisite model and has grown to twenty-nine weekend worship experiences in thirteen separate locations. Surratt is also a founding board member of the Association of Related Churches.

Greg Wallace is the senior pastor of Woodridge Baptist Church in the northeast suburbs of Houston. He took the reins of this struggling church plant (Sand Creek Mission at the time) in 1992 as a bivocational pastor while continuing a very successful business career and has seen the church grow steadily throughout his tenure.

David Weekley founded David Weekley Homes in 1976 at the age of twenty-three and now serves as chairman of this company, the third-largest privately owned homebuilder in America. He gives generously of his time and financial resources to a variety of nonprofit organizations. Weekley has been involved as a board member or adviser for HOPE International, Saint Luke's Episcopal Hospital, Metro Houston Young Life, and other organizations and is a member of Memorial Drive Presbyterian Church in Houston.

Jeff Wells is the founding and senior pastor of WoodsEdge Community Church, a fifteen-year-old congregation in The Woodlands, Texas, with a strong emphasis on encountering God through biblical teaching and giving generously to external ministry projects. Wells has also served in ministry in Oregon. He was a collegiate all-American athlete and the American record holder for the marathon.

Judy West is one of the pastors at The Crossing in the Saint Louis, Missouri, area, where she oversees staff and leadership development and leads many classes and teams. West started attending The Crossing in 1994 and joined the staff in 1998. Previously, she was an elementary school guidance counselor and NCAA Division 1 track and cross-country coach. She also leads Team Living Water, one of the largest running groups in the nation, which has raised close to $200,000 for the drilling of fresh-water wells.

Ken Williams is the former executive pastor of WoodsEdge Community Church in The Woodlands, Texas. Williams was a member of this growing congregation when he was asked by senior pastor Jeff Wells to use his leadership and administrative gifts to help the church go to the next level. Williams previously worked in the energy industry and has returned to the marketplace with Simplify Corporation.

Charles Zech is director of the Center for the Study of Church Management at Villanova University in Villanova, Pennsylvania, where he has been a professor of economics since 1974. The center was created to serve the Catholic Church in the United States by helping individuals in church leadership and administrative roles become better stewards of church resources by improving their business and management skills. Zech is also the author or coauthor of over seventy-five books and articles.

PRACTICAL TIPS FOR MANAGING PEOPLE

Any leader wants high morale and outstanding performance from every person on the staff. Many leaders struggle to accomplish this goal. This appendix is not a comprehensive list, but it does offer a number of practical ideas to supplement the concepts discussed in Chapter Five.

General
- If you can't afford a human resource (HR) professional, have one person (usually an executive pastor or business manager) serve as the point person for HR issues. Invest in seminars or other training for this person.
- Leverage the knowledge of members with HR experience by asking for their advice on general policies and specific issues.
- Understand and comply with the laws, particularly the ones that could cause major problems. Compliance is not just a legal issue; it also sends an important message to employees that you care and intend to treat them fairly.
- Develop a personnel policy manual, and be consistent in administering the policies. If you don't have written policies, start with the basics and add over time. Review and update the policies periodically.

Hiring
- Cast the net as wide as possible in looking for candidates.
- Be clear about the duties and expectations of the position. A written job description is the best way to do this.

Without this clarity, it's hard to determine who might be a good fit.

- Prepare for the interview. Don't walk in cold and ask questions off the cuff and then make a decision based on whether you "like" the candidate. Decide in advance what you need to know to evaluate if this person fits your needs.
- In the interview, know what questions are out-of-bounds legally. Other than that, don't be afraid to ask hard questions that help you dig beneath the surface.
- Always conduct more than one interview using different interviewers (staff or volunteer). Getting other perspectives is vital.
- Listen for subtle clues that give you insights into candidates, and listen also for what they *don't* say.
- Remember that the interview process is a two-way street. You want candidates to make well-informed decisions, so give them time to ask questions, and give honest answers about the good and bad of the organization and the job.
- Go beyond the résumé and the interview. Check references and any other sources. Always ask, "Would you hire this person again?"
- Be clear with candidates about the next steps in the process and the timing. Don't leave them hanging.
- Document the terms of an employment offer in writing to avoid later confusion.

Performance Evaluations
- Adopt a "no surprises" mentality. The criteria against which employees are being evaluated should be known in advance, and any significant concerns should have been voiced long before the formal appraisal.
- Treat the evaluation as a developmental tool designed to help employees perform at their full potential in the coming year. Look back to identify areas for improvement and forward to establish specific steps to be taken.
- "Speak the truth in love." Evaluations should accomplish both—truth and love. Love does not mean positive platitudes that leave people wondering if they did a good job. Truth does not mean beating them up.

- Listen. Some of the best evaluations are those where employees reflect on their own performance and create their own development plans for the coming year.

Compensation

- Don't make decisions in a vacuum. Look for comparables, either in published reports or informal surveys, to determine the appropriate pay rate for positions. Likewise, make sure that the compensation is internally consistent. (Two people doing similar jobs should receive similar salaries.)
- A person's financial "need" should not be the driving factor for setting compensation.
- Don't be surprised if details of a staff person's compensation leak out, even if they are supposed to be confidential. Handle compensation in such a way that if it becomes public, there is no embarrassment.
- Pay increases in Christian organizations tend to be very small, so don't be surprised if someone leaves for better pay or if the cost for replacing a person is much higher. For long-tenured staff, benchmark their pay against an outside standard to make sure it is fair.
- Benefits (medical insurance, vacation time, child care, and so on) should be awarded consistently, not as an "extra" to attract or retain a key person. Be aware that there are a number of legal issues related to the administration of benefits.

Terminations

- The "no surprise" rule carries over to performance-related terminations. This should be the final step in a process in which employees have been given clear feedback on their shortfalls and opportunities to improve. The best practice is to document these conversations along the way.
- Be a stickler in following internal procedures and any applicable laws. Failure to do so is unfair and may expose the organization to unnecessary lawsuits. When in doubt, seek outside legal advice.
- Prepare exactly what you plan to say in advance. This is not the place to ad lib. At the same time, it is a Christian organization, and this is not the place to be cold and detached.

- Define the severance package. Know in advance what will be provided and be consistent with the way that other severances have been handled.
- Don't fly solo. The direct supervisor and one other managerial-level person should be in the meeting, especially if you expect the conversation to be contentious.

PRACTICAL IDEAS FOR MEASUREMENT

The theme of Chapter Six is that measurement matters. When measurement is done well, it focuses the attention of the leaders and the organization on the key indicators of progress toward the vision. This appendix offers some ideas that go beyond the typical metrics of attendance and budget. The suggestions are geared for congregations, since there are an endless variety of measures that can apply to other kinds of Christian organizations. Because each organization needs to develop its own unique metrics, let this be a starting point for a healthy discussion of what truly matters.

General Recommendations
- *Start from the vision.* The key organizational metrics should always tie to the vision. If people wonder how a key measure relates to the vision, you may need a better metric. Similarly, every major element of the vision should have a metric associated with it.
- *Focus on just a few things.* It takes time and effort to do measurement well, so don't try to measure too much. When too many metrics are used, organizational leaders will be confused about what is most important.
- *Capture information whenever reasonably possible.* This may seem inconsistent with the advice to focus on just a few things, but there is a difference between capturing information and creating metrics. Think about data that might be useful in the future and then capture them.

- *Measure what's important.* It is better to attempt to measure an important factor in an imperfect manner than to measure an unimportant factor that is easily quantified or measure nothing at all. Do your best to measure the things that matter, and continue to refine the measurement process.
- *Agree in advance on your standard for success.* Not only does this give you a target, but the conversation may also help you refine the metric.
- *Be consistent.* Confusion occurs when organizations frequently change their metrics. Pick the key metrics, and stick with them.
- *Look at trends.* A static metric (such as number of baptisms in a year) is interesting, but a trend is much more useful. For whatever metrics you choose, pay attention to the trends over multiple years.
- *Communicate the results.* Measurement is powerful only if it is used to guide and motivate leaders. Once metrics are developed, be sure to communicate results regularly.
- *Get help from others.* If measurement is not your expertise, others in the congregation can help. There may also be great ideas from other similar organizations. Don't try to do it all on your own.

Evangelism

Spreading the gospel and reaching people for Christ is one of the core purposes of any congregation. The easy measures for evangelism are the number of baptisms or professions of faith. What measures inform a more complete understanding of evangelistic effectiveness?

- *Number of first-time visitors.* Since evangelism is a process and worship attendance is often an important step in the process, quantifying the number of first-time visitors is one indicator of effectiveness.
- *Source of new visitors.* Survey new visitors (by e-mail or letter) to seek their feedback. Ask how they heard about the church. If you are counting on members to invite friends or using an advertising campaign, this will help measure the effectiveness of your strategy.

- *Percentage of new visitors who return.* No church gets 100 percent of first-time visitors to return, but tracking the percentage who come a second time gives insights into the first impressions that are created.
- *Membership distribution.* Of the people who join the church in a year, measure the distribution between children, teens, and adults. Of the adults, measure the distribution between new Christians, unchurched people (who have not been active in any church for at least a couple of years), and transfer members.

Assimilation

Assimilation is the continuation of the process that starts with evangelism and outreach. A church is not successful if a person becomes a Christian or joins the church but never plugs in. What are the indicators of effective assimilation?

- *Percentage of new visitors who become members.* This metric straddles the line between evangelism and assimilation. In a culture where membership is often seen as unimportant, a person's decision to become a member can be an important step in assimilation.
- *Participation in small groups.* This is a standard measure in many congregations, whether "small group" is defined as Bible study or Sunday school classes or home groups. People who are involved at this level tend to find meaningful community that helps them assimilate.
- *New member snapshot.* Develop an aggregate profile of all the people who joined over a period of time (say, between twelve and eighteen months ago). Measure the percentage that are attending regularly, participating in some type of small group, or serving in a ministry. High percentages point to effective assimilation.
- *Dropout rate.* Measure the number of people who have left the church (moved membership or stopped attending) over the past year in comparison to the total members and new members. Calculate the breakdown between those moving out of town, moving to another church, or dropping out.

Spiritual Growth

"Making disciples" means much more than seeing people profess their faith in Christ, yet spiritual growth is extremely difficult to assess. Too often we have assumed that participation in church activities automatically leads to growth. Willow Creek's work in *Reveal* clearly shows that this is not the case. Congregational surveys seem to be the best way to get a handle on this important dimension of effectiveness. Be aware of the self-reporting bias in a survey. People will tend to report more positively on themselves than is actually the case. This makes it even more important to observe trends rather than static numbers when using surveys.

- *Reveal.* This is the most sophisticated and widely used survey tool available today. A number of related resources to explain and supplement the survey are also available at www.revealnow.com
- *Create your own survey.* If you have the expertise in-house and have specific outcomes in mind, you can develop your own survey. It is best to test (and debug) a survey with a small group before launching with the entire congregation.

Deployment into Ministry

Every Christian is called to use his or her gifts in ministry and in service to others. Effective churches expect people to be deployed in ministry and create the opportunities for them to do so.

- *Involvement in ministry.* Measure either the number of people or the percentage of members who are serving in some capacity.
- *Depth of ministry involvement.* There is a considerable difference in the amount of time and energy required for someone to serve in an annual event versus a weekly or other high-level commitment. Consider assigning a value (such as A, B, or C or estimated number of hours) to each type of ministry involvement to create a more refined measure than the simple "involvement in ministry" metric.
- *External versus internal ministries.* If a congregation wants to make a difference in its community, the proportion of people who are serving in an outward-facing ministry (such as a thrift

shop, medical clinic, or ESL program) versus those serving in ministries for members (youth Bible study teacher, office volunteer) is an indicator of effectiveness.

- *Ministry impact.* In addition to measuring involvement by members in ministry, measuring the number of nonmembers who have been ministered to is another way to assess ministry reach.

Ministry Effectiveness

Every congregation consists of multiple ministries. These may be for particular age groups (children, youth, senior adults) or specific areas of interest (women's and men's, recovery, singles, music). Evaluating the effectiveness of individual ministries is another fruitful area for measurement.

- *Attendance trends.* The overall trends, and the trend relative to the church's total attendance, give an indication of the attractiveness of the ministry.
- *Surveys.* An annual survey that invites the congregation to rate each ministry can give valid feedback into how each ministry is viewed. In designing a survey, adding a simple line for "comments" can yield valuable information.
- *Outcome-based measurement.* Ask each ministry leader to answer the question "How will you know that your ministry has been successful?" and then develop one or more metrics related to this outcome. For example, a small group ministry might say, "We will be successful if half of our groups multiply within the next twelve months." The measurable outcomes can then be tracked.

Giving

Every church measures giving, but many do not understand the financial patterns and trends. Contributions by members are a strong indicator of their support for the church's leadership and vision and of their own spiritual growth. Analysis of segments and the trends within each segment can be insightful. When doing contribution analysis, using a minimum threshold (for example, exclude any household that gives less than $500 or $1,000 per year)

will paint a clearer picture. Following are some specific segments
and questions to consider.

- *Top contributors.* How has their total giving changed? Have any
  new people stepped up to this level of giving (based on a
  defined threshold such as $10,000 or $20,000 per year)?
- *Other contributors.* Is the number of contributing households
  growing or shrinking? How is the amount given in this
  category changing?
- *New contributors.* How many new contributors are there? How
  does this compare to the number of new members?
- *"Lost" contributors.* How many households that gave the
  previous year did not give this year? Are there any insights as to
  why (relocation, loss of job, dissatisfaction, other)?

NOTES

CHAPTER ONE: IS GREAT THE ENEMY OF GODLY?

1. Jim Collins, *Good to Great: Why Some Companies Make the Leap . . . and Others Don't* (New York: HarperCollins, 2001), p. 1.
2. Bill Hybels, *Courageous Leadership* (Grand Rapids, Mich.: Zondervan, 2002), p. 27.
3. James C. Collins and Jerry I. Porras, *Built to Last: Successful Habits of Visionary Companies* (New York: HarperCollins, 1994).
4. This portion of Collins's presentation ended up in *Good to Great* in a chapter titled "First Who . . . Then What."
5. Jim Cymbala, *Fresh Wind, Fresh Fire* (Grand Rapids, Mich.: Zondervan, 1997), p. 134.
6. Collins, *Good to Great*, p. 21.
7. Jim Kouzes and Barry Posner, *The Leadership Challenge*, 4th ed. (San Francisco: Jossey-Bass, 2007), p. 16.
8. Dale Buss, "Life Lessons," *Forbes*, Dec. 21, 2007, www.forbes.com/2007/12/21/churches-executives-lessons-lead-manage-cx_db_1221 megapastors.html
9. Collins and Porras, *Built to Last*, p. 84, emphasis in the original.
10. Dino Rizzo, *Servolution: Starting a Church Revolution Through Serving* (Grand Rapids, Mich.: Zondervan, 2009), pp. 63–64.
11. This phrase was first used by Origen (A.D. 235) and in recent times was applied by Larry Crabb to advocate the use of secular psychological principles in Christian counseling.
12. Jim Collins, *Good to Great and the Social Sectors: A Monograph to Accompany* Good to Great (New York: HarperCollins, 2005), pp. 1–2, emphasis in the original.
13. Hybels, *Courageous Leadership*, pp. 69–70.
14. Dallas Willard, *The Divine Conspiracy: Rediscovering Our Hidden Life in God* (New York: HarperCollins, 1998), p. 1.
15. Ibid., p. 10.
16. Kouzes and Posner, *Leadership Challenge*, p. 50.

17. Ibid., p. 53.
18. Willow Creek Association, "Creating a Leadership Development Engine," *Defining Moments* audio journal, Sept. 2010.

CHAPTER TWO: WHERE SHOULD YOU BEGIN?

1. Kouzes and Posner, *Leadership Challenge*, p. 344.
2. Reggie McNeal, *A Work of Heart: Understanding How God Shapes Spiritual Leaders* (San Francisco: Jossey-Bass, 2000), p. xv.
3. Robert Quinn, *Deep Change: Discovering the Leader Within* (San Francisco: Jossey-Bass, 1996), p. 156.
4. Ibid., p. 9.
5. Ibid., p. 165.
6. Ronald A. Heifitz, *Leadership Without Easy Answers* (Cambridge, Mass.: Harvard University Press, 1998), p. 235.
7. McNeal, *Work of Heart*, p. 25.
8. Collins, *Good to Great*, p. 27.
9. Ibid., p. 35.
10. Kouzes and Posner, *Leadership Challenge*, p. 347.
11. Ibid., p. 348.
12. Collins, *Good to Great*, p. 21.
13. William Willimon, "Ambitious Like Jesus," *Leadership Weekly*, Oct. 12, 2010, www.christianitytoday.com/le/currenttrendscolumns/leadershipweekly/ambitiouslikejesus.html
14. Reggie McNeal, *Practicing Greatness: 7 Disciplines of Extraordinary Spiritual Leaders* (San Francisco: Jossey-Bass, 2006), p. 3.
15. McNeal, *Work of Heart*, p. 27.
16. Ibid., p. 27.
17. Quinn, *Deep Change*, p. 127.
18. McNeal, *Work of Heart*, p. 60.
19. Ibid., p. 59.
20. Heifitz, *Leadership Without Easy Answers*, p. 273.
21. Edwin H. Friedman, *A Failure of Nerve: Leadership in the Age of the Quick Fix* (New York: Seabury Books, 1999), p. 14.
22. McNeal, *Work of Heart*, p. 41.

CHAPTER THREE: IS GOD IN YOUR PLANS?

1. Patrick Lencioni, *Silos, Politics, and Turf Wars: A Leadership Fable About Destroying the Barriers That Turn Colleagues into Competitors* (San Francisco: Jossey-Bass, 2006).

2. Peter Senge, *The Fifth Discipline: The Art and Practice of the Learning Organization* (New York: Doubleday, 1990), p. 208.
3. Hybels, *Courageous Leadership*, p. 31.
4. Ibid., p. 144.
5. Collins and Porras, *Built to Last*, p. 141.
6. Reggie McNeal, *The Present Future: Six Tough Questions for the Church* (San Francisco: Jossey-Bass, 2003), p. 93.
7. Three books that offer different perspectives and approaches for congregational planning are Jim Herrington, Mike Bonem, and James H. Furr, *Leading Congregational Change: A Practical Guide for the Transformational Journey* (San Francisco: Jossey-Bass, 2000); Will Mancini, *Church Unique: How Missional Leaders Cast Vision, Capture Culture, and Create Movement* (San Francisco: Jossey-Bass, 2008); and Gil Rendle and Alice Mann, *Holy Conversations: Strategic Planning as a Spiritual Practice for Congregations* (Herndon, Va.: Alban Institute, 2003).
8. McNeal, *Present Future*, p. 99.
9. Ruth Haley Barton, *Strengthening the Soul of Your Leadership: Seeking God in the Crucible of Ministry* (Downers Grove, Ill.: InterVarsity Press, 2008), p. 144.
10. Bill Hybels, *Axioms: Powerful Leadership Proverbs* (Grand Rapids, Mich.: Zondervan, 2008), p. 155.
11. Barton, *Strengthening the Soul of Your Leadership*, p. 198.
12. Patrick Lencioni, *The Five Dysfunctions of a Team: A Leadership Fable* (San Francisco: Jossey-Bass, 2002), pp. 195–196.

CHAPTER FOUR: ARE YOUR PLANS FRUITFUL?

1. Collins and Porras, *Built to Last*, pp. 92–94.
2. Ibid., p. 101.
3. Kouzes and Posner, *Leadership Challenge*, p. 191.
4. Rick Warren, *The Purpose-Driven Church: Growth Without Compromising Your Message and Mission* (Grand Rapids, Mich.: Zondervan, 1995), p. 43.
5. Houston Baptist University, "Ten Pillars: Faith and Reason in a Great City," Feb. 19, 2008, www.hbu.edu/images/hbu/publications/presidents_office/The_Ten_Pillars_HBU_Vision.pdf
6. Hybels, *Axioms*, pp. 49–50.
7. Collins, *Good to Great*, p. 139.
8. Andy Stanley, *Visioneering: Fulfilling God's Purpose Through Intentional Living* (Sisters, Ore.: Multnomah, 1999), p. 204.
9. Senge, *Fifth Discipline*, p. 154.

CHAPTER FIVE: WHO IS ON THE BUS?

1. Kouzes and Posner, *Leadership Challenge*, p. 24.
2. Collins, *Good to Great*, p. 41.
3. Hybels, *Courageous Leadership*, p. 173.
4. Collins, *Good to Great*, p. 53.
5. Ibid., p. 57.
6. Patrick Lencioni, *The Three Signs of a Miserable Job: A Fable for Managers (and Their Employees)* (San Francisco: Jossey-Bass, 2007), p. 221.
7. Kouzes and Posner, *Leadership Challenge*, p. 24.
8. Ibid., pp. 294–295.
9. Collins, *Good to Great*, p. 121.
10. Lencioni, *Three Signs of a Miserable Job*, p. 237.
11. Marcus Buckingham and Curt Coffman, *First, Break All the Rules: What the World's Great Managers Do Differently* (New York: Simon & Schuster, 1999), p. 33.
12. Ibid., p. 149.
13. Hybels, *Axioms*, p. 75.
14. Collins, *Good to Great and the Social Sectors*, p. 15.
15. Buckingham and Coffman, *First, Break All the Rules*, pp. 33–34.
16. Kouzes and Posner, *Leadership Challenge*, p. 293.
17. Buckingham and Coffman, *First, Break All the Rules*, p. 177.
18. Kouzes and Posner, *Leadership Challenge*, p. 282.
19. Buckingham and Coffman, *First, Break All the Rules*, p. 200.
20. Ibid., p. 206.
21. Ibid.
22. Ibid., p. 207.
23. Ibid., pp. 209–210.
24. Willow Creek Association, "Handling Staff Reductions Well," *Defining Moments* audio journal, June 2009.
25. Lencioni, *Three Signs of a Miserable Job*, p. 253.

CHAPTER SIX: DO YOU MEASURE WHAT MATTERS?

1. McNeal, *Present Future*, p. 106.
2. Greg L. Hawkins and Cally Parkinson, *Reveal: Where Are You?* (South Barrington, Ill.: Willow Creek Association, 2007), p. 14.
3. Reggie McNeal, *Missional Renaissance: Changing the Scorecard for the Church* (San Francisco: Jossey-Bass, 2009), p. 16.
4. Christian Schwartz, *Natural Church Development: A Guide to Eight Essential Qualities of Healthy Churches* (St. Charles, Ill.: ChurchSmart Resources, 1996), p. 19.

5. Thom Rainer and Eric Geiger, *Simple Church: Returning to God's Process for Making Disciples* (Nashville, Tenn.: Broadman & Holman, 2006), pp. 13–14.
6. United Methodist Communications Office of Public Information, "New Study Identifies Key Factors Impacting Vital Congregations," press release, July 12, 2010, www.umc.org/site/apps/nlnet/content3.aspx?c=lwL4KnN1LtH&b=2454759&ct=8519227
7. McNeal, *Missional Renaissance*, p. 16.
8. Elevation Church, *2009 Annual Report: The Year in Numbers*, 2010, www.elevationchurch.org/2009annualreport
9. Robert S. Kaplan and David P. Norton, "The Balanced Scorecard: Measures That Drive Performance," *Harvard Business Review*, Jan.–Feb. 1992, p. 71.
10. Lencioni, *Three Signs of a Miserable Job*, p. 237.
11. "Oil Spill Report Card: Scientists Give Gulf a D," Associated Press, October 19, 2010.
12. Collins, *Good to Great and the Social Sectors*, p. 5.
13. Ibid., p. 8, emphasis in the original.
14. Hawkins and Parkinson, *Reveal*, p. 7. More information is available at www.revealnow.com
15. Ibid., p. 29.

CHAPTER SEVEN: HOW WILL YOU FINANCE THE DREAM?

1. Patrick Lencioni, *Death by Meeting: A Leadership Fable About Solving the Most Painful Problem in Business* (San Francisco: Jossey-Bass, 2004), p. 229.

CHAPTER EIGHT: ARE "ALL SYSTEMS GO"?

1. Norman Shawchuck and Roger Heuser, *Leading the Congregation: Caring for Yourself While Serving the People* (Nashville, Tenn.: Abingdon Press, 1993), p. 206.
2. Daniel Stid and Jeffrey L. Bradach, "Strongly Led, Undermanaged: How Can Visionary Nonprofits Make the Critical Transition to Stronger Management?" Bridgespan Group, Aug. 1, 2008, www.bridgespan.org/LearningCenter/ResourceDetail.aspx?id=312&itemid=312&linkidentifier=id
3. Collins, *Good to Great*, p. 121.

CHAPTER NINE: IS EVERYONE ON THE SAME PAGE?

1. Kouzes and Posner, *Leadership Challenge*, p. 347.
2. Heifitz, *Leadership Without Easy Answers*, p. 268.
3. Jon R. Katzenbach and Douglas K. Smith, *The Wisdom of Teams: Creating the High-Performance Organization* (New York: HarperBusiness, 1993), p. 45.
4. Ibid., p. 235.
5. Senge, *Fifth Discipline*, p. 221.
6. D. Michael Lindsay, *Faith in the Halls of Power: How Evangelicals Joined the American Elite* (New York: Oxford University Press, 2007), pp. 194–195.
7. Ibid., p. 197.
8. Ibid., p. 195.
9. Lencioni, *Five Dysfunctions of a Team*, p. 195.
10. Kouzes and Posner, *Leadership Challenge*, p. 224.
11. Lindsay, *Faith in the Halls of Power*, p. 195.

CHAPTER TEN: WHY IS CULTURE IMPORTANT?

1. Samuel R. Chand, *Cracking Your Church's Culture Code: Seven Keys to Unleashing Vision and Inspiration* (San Francisco: Jossey-Bass, 2010), p. 2.
2. John P. Kotter, *Leading Change* (Boston: Harvard Business School Press, 1996), p. 148, emphasis in the original.
3. Andy Crouch, *Culture Making: Recovering Our Creative Calling* (Downers Grove, Ill.: InterVarsity Press, 2008), pp. 23–24.
4. Collins and Porras, *Built to Last*, p. 54.
5. Ibid., p. 71.
6. Patrick Lencioni, *Four Obsessions of an Extraordinary Executive: A Leadership Fable* (San Francisco: Jossey-Bass, 2000), p. 153.
7. Ibid., p. 157.
8. McNeal, *Present Future*, pp. xv–xvi.
9. Collins and Porras, *Built to Last*, p. 69.
10. Chand, *Cracking Your Church's Culture Code*, p. 59.
11. Collins, *Good to Great*, p. 169.
12. Ibid., p. 178.

CHAPTER ELEVEN: ARE YOU PREPARED TO CHANGE?

1. John P. Kotter and Dan S. Cohen, *The Heart of Change: Real-Life Stories of How People Change Their Organizations* (Boston: Harvard Business School Press, 2002), p. x.

2. Ibid., p. 1.
3. Kotter, *Leading Change*, p. 132.
4. Ibid., p. 4.
5. Collins and Porras, *Built to Last*, p. 187.
6. Jim Collins, *How the Mighty Fall: And Why Some Companies Never Give In* (New York: HarperCollins, 2009), p. 78.
7. Quinn, *Deep Change*, p. 33.
8. Ibid., p. 52.
9. Kouzes and Posner, *Leadership Challenge*, p. 205.
10. Quinn, *Deep Change*, p. 9.
11. Ibid., p. 10.
12. Kotter and Cohen, *Heart of Change*, p. 28.
13. Mark Wingfield, "Baylor Vision Sparks Changes and Questions," *Baptist Standard*, July 11, 2003, www.baptiststandard.com/index.php?option=com_content&task=view&id=503&Itemid=131
14. Marv Knox, "Sloan to Step Down as Baylor President, Assume Chancellor's Role," *Baptist Standard*, Feb. 4, 2005, www.baptiststandard.com/index.php?option=com_content&task=view&id=3083&Itemid=133
15. Kate Shellnut, "Joyful Noise Is Going Silent," *Houston Chronicle*, Feb. 25, 2011, www.chron.com/disp/story.mpl/metropolitan/7445234.html
16. Collins and Porras, *Built to Last*, p. 82.
17. Heifitz, *Leadership Without Easy Answers*, p. 235.
18. Quinn, *Deep Change*, pp. 20–22.
19. Kotter, *Leading Change*, p. 40.
20. Quinn, *Deep Change*, p. 158.
21. Ibid., p. 177.
22. Herrington, Bonem, and Furr, *Leading Congregational Change*, pp. 7–10.
23. D. Michael Lindsay, *Rev*, Jan. 2007. The roller coaster analogy is based on Gil Rendle's *Leading Change in the Congregation: Spiritual and Organizational Tools for Leaders* (Herndon, Va.: Alban Institute, 1998).
24. Randy Frazee also has experience with this kind of rapid, crisis turnaround, described in *The Comeback Congregation* by Randy Frazee and Lyle E. Shaller (Nashville, Tenn.: Abingdon Press, 1995).
25. Heifitz, *Leadership Without Easy Answers*, p. 268.
26. Kotter, *Leading Change*, pp. 20–22.
27. Herrington, Bonem, and Furr, *Leading Congregational Change*, p. 41.
28. Kotter, *Leading Change*, p. 75.
29. Quinn, *Deep Change*, p. 103.
30. Heifitz, *Leadership Without Easy Answers*, p. 246.

31. Ibid., p. 126.
32. Quinn, *Deep Change*, p. 84.

CHAPTER TWELVE: ARE YOU GUARDING YOUR HEART?

1. Hybels, *Courageous Leadership*, p. 193.
2. Barton, *Strengthening the Soul of Your Leadership*, p. 62.
3. Ibid., p. 215.
4. The concept of redemptive and missional journeys comes from Lee B. Spitzer, *Endless Possibilities: Exploring the Journeys of Your Life* (Mercerville, N.J.: Spiritual Journey Press, 1997).
5. Barton, *Strengthening the Soul of Your Leadership*, p. 159.
6. McNeal, *Work of Heart*, p. ix.
7. Hybels, *Axioms*, p. 166.
8. Randy Frazee's book *Making Room for Life: Trading Chaotic Lifestyles for Connected Relationships* (Grand Rapids, Mich.: Zondervan, 2003) makes a compelling argument for resisting the frenetic pace of society, which pressures people to always do more. He advocates spending less time at work and in activities and more time with family, in community with others, and with God.
9. McNeal, *Work of Heart*, p. 115, emphasis in the original.
10. Friedman, *Failure of Nerve*, p. 27.
11. Barton, *Strengthening the Soul of Your Leadership*, p. 170.
12. Kouzes and Posner, *Leadership Challenge*, p. 347.
13. Ibid., p. 346.
14. Collins, *Good to Great and the Social Sectors*, p. 2.
15. Hybels, *Axioms*, p. 62.

ANNOTATED BIBLIOGRAPHY

Barton, Ruth Haley. *Strengthening the Soul of Your Leadership: Seeking God in the Crucible of Ministry*. Downers Grove, Ill.: InterVarsity Press, 2008.
Far too many spiritual leaders focus on improving their leadership while ignoring their souls. Barton's work is a powerful counterbalance to this dangerous tendency. It is very readable, but take your time to reflect on her rich insights.

Buckingham, Marcus, and Curt Coffman. *First, Break All the Rules: What the World's Greatest Managers Do Differently*. New York: Simon & Schuster, 1999.
Based on eighty thousand interviews conducted by the Gallup organization over twenty-five years, Buckingham and Coffman's work is full of practical insights on getting the best performance from the people you manage.

Collins, James C., and Jerry I. Porras. *Built to Last: Successful Habits of Visionary Companies*. New York: HarperCollins, 1994.
Built to Last is the first of Jim Collins's remarkable research-based works on organizational effectiveness. Leaders of Christian organizations who sift through the business terminology will find plenty of nuggets that are applicable.

Collins, Jim. *Good to Great: Why Some Companies Make the Leap . . . and Others Don't*. New York: HarperCollins, 2001.
Good to Great remains at the very top of my recommended reading list for any leader. Since most leaders inherit organizations that are not "great," Collins's basic question ("How can we make the leap from good to great?") is essential to their success. His research is packed with memorable phrases and practical principles that any leader can use.

Collins, Jim. "Good to Great and the Social Sectors: A Monograph to Accompany *Good to Great*." New York: HarperCollins, 2005.
This short monograph helps bridge the gap between Collins's business-based research and the unique challenges faced by nonprofit organizations. It is best read in conjunction with *Good to Great*.

Collins, Jim. *How the Mighty Fall: And Why Some Companies Never Give In.* New York: HarperCollins, 2009.

Collins's most recent research project looks at the other side of organizational effectiveness: the reasons that some companies fail to sustain success. As in his other books, many of the key findings are readily transferrable to Christian organizations.

Friedman, Edwin H. *A Failure of Nerve: Leadership in the Age of the Quick Fix.* New York: Seabury Books, 1999.

I wish I had read Friedman's work much earlier in my career. His diagnosis of the "failure of nerve" by many organizational leaders is right on the mark. As a rabbi and psychologist, Friedman brings an interesting perspective to the complex leadership challenges facing businesses, governmental entities, and religious institutions.

Hawkins, Greg L., and Cally Parkinson. *Reveal: Where Are You?* South Barrington, Ill.: Willow Creek Association, 2007.

The groundbreaking research by Willow Creek, first within the congregation and subsequently with a number of other churches, offers a fresh perspective on the ways that congregations can evaluate and facilitate spiritual growth. It also shows the power of survey-based tools in measuring congregational effectiveness. Hawkins and Parkinson have written three subsequent books in this series: *Follow Me: What's Next for You?*; *Focus: The Top Ten Things People Want and Need from You and Your Church*; and *Move: What 1,000 Churches Reveal About Spiritual Growth.*

Heifitz, Ronald A. *Leadership Without Easy Answers.* Cambridge, Mass.: Harvard University Press, 1998.

Like Friedman, Heifitz argues that the challenges faced by today's organizations require a different kind of leadership than the kind that was successful in earlier generations. He describes the importance and difficulty of leading in situations when the solution cannot be determined through available information, which he calls "adaptive change."

Herrington, Jim, Mike Bonem, and James H. Furr. *Leading Congregational Change: A Practical Guide for the Transformational Journey.* San Francisco: Jossey-Bass, 2000.

This book grew out of our work with congregations that were struggling to achieve meaningful and lasting change. It adapts the work of John Kotter, Peter Senge, and others to the unique dynamics of local churches.

Hybels, Bill. *Axioms: Powerful Leadership Proverbs.* Grand Rapids, Mich.: Zondervan, 2008.

This short book is filled with axioms that Hybels has used during his years of leading Willow Creek Community Church. Each axiom is only two or three pages long but full of wisdom.

Hybels, Bill. *Courageous Leadership.* Grand Rapids, Mich.: Zondervan, 2002.

Hybels speaks from the depth of his heart and his years of experience as he offers an inspiring blend of biblical and practical advice for church leaders. Each chapter addresses a different dimension of leadership.

Katzenbach, Jon R., and Douglas K. Smith. *The Wisdom of Teams: Creating the High-Performance Organization.* New York: HarperBusiness, 1993.

This is still one of the best resources that I have found on the subject. Katzenbach and Smith give a clear definition of *team*, explain the power that can be unleashed when teams are working well, and describe what it takes to make this happen.

Kotter, John P. *Leading Change.* Boston: Harvard Business School Press, 1996.

Kotter is one of the world's foremost experts on the subject of organizational change, and this is his classic text. Based on his work with a number of organizations, Kotter describes an eight-stage process that guides successful change efforts. He also describes many of the pitfalls that can undermine change efforts.

Kouzes, James M., and Barry Z. Posner. *The Leadership Challenge*, 4th ed. San Francisco: Jossey-Bass, 2007.

This is one of the best general leadership books on the market. Kouzes and Posner write in a style that is very accessible and encouraging. They show that you don't have to be at the top of the organization to lead and that anyone can grow as a leader. They don't just inspire; they provide concepts and tools to facilitate this growth.

Lencioni, Patrick. *The Five Dysfunctions of a Team: A Leadership Fable.* San Francisco: Jossey-Bass, 2002.

Lencioni's fable-style business books are some of the most popular and insightful resources on the market. This one gives a compelling diagnosis of the problems that many business (and churches) have with teamwork and then offers a prescription to address the problems.

Lencioni, Patrick. *Silos, Politics, and Turf Wars: A Leadership Fable About Destroying the Barriers That Turn Colleagues into Competitors.* San Francisco: Jossey-Bass, 2006.

Another of Lencioni's very readable fables, the title does not quite capture the full impact of this book. While it does address organizational barriers, the thrust is a different approach to setting organizational priorities that not only overcomes silos but can also reshape typical planning processes.

Lencioni, Patrick. *The Three Signs of a Miserable Job: A Fable for Managers (and Their Employees)*. San Francisco: Jossey-Bass, 2007.
This fable will challenge any boss to rethink his or her approach to managing and motivating employees (or volunteers).

Lindsay, D. Michael. *Faith in the Halls of Power: How Evangelicals Joined the American Elite*. New York: Oxford University Press, 2007.
If you have ever been curious about the mind-set of Christians who are highly successful leaders in business and politics, Lindsay's book is packed with insight. Based on interviews with 360 of these leaders, Lindsay describes their faith practices, philanthropy, attitudes toward the church, and more.

McNeal, Reggie. *The Present Future: Six Tough Questions for the Church*. San Francisco: Jossey-Bass, 2003.
McNeal paints a compelling picture that the church must change if it is to follow God's call to change the world. This is a great resource to help pastors and lay leaders recognize how much the world around them has changed.

McNeal, Reggie. *A Work of Heart: Understanding How God Shapes Spiritual Leaders*. San Francisco: Jossey-Bass, 2000.
McNeal's book is divided into two parts: the first examines the heart-shaping influences in the lives of four biblical characters, and the second unpacks the six categories of influence. *A Work of Heart* challenges leaders who are at the top of their game and encourages leaders who are in the deepest valley to see God's heart-shaping work in all their circumstances.

Quinn, Robert E. *Deep Change: Discovering the Leader Within*. San Francisco: Jossey-Bass, 1996.
Quinn is another of the world's leading experts on organizational change, and I have recommended this book countless times. He challenges leaders to recognize their potential to be agents for change and forces them to confront the risk of settling for the status quo, which in Quinn's words leads to "slow death."

ACKNOWLEDGMENTS

You may think that writing a book is a lonely endeavor, but that perception is only partly true. This project has been a rich experience that I have been able to share with many old and new friends, people who have been a blessing every step along the way.

It always starts with family for me, because they are the ones who are deeply involved from start to finish. Thank you, Bonnie, for saying yes to this endeavor, even though you knew the sacrifice it would require of you. Thanks for believing in me, encouraging me, and loving me. But mostly, thanks for being a great and godly wife who is always at my side and always making me better. Our children also give up a lot when I submerge myself in the world of words. Thanks to Matthew and Jonathan for helping with the research and to David and Hope for giving up time to let me do this. My mom and dad have always been in the stands cheering for me, literally at countless track meets and figuratively in every other adventure of life, and I'm deeply grateful for their enduring love and support.

I have once again been privileged to work with the outstanding publishing team at Jossey-Bass and Leadership Network. Thanks to Sheryl Fullerton for her excellent editorial guidance and wise counsel and to Mark Sweeney, Greg Ligon, and Stephanie Plagens for their encouragement and attention to the things that matter. I can't mention Leadership Network and OneHundredX without also expressing my appreciation to Bob Buford. His vision and passion have inspired and encouraged countless leaders, and I'm grateful to be one of them.

You have already met the men and women who are striving to be both godly and great leaders, and they are introduced further in Appendix A. Some are old friends and others are new relationships, but each of them made a contribution to this book far beyond the quotes and stories that appear on the printed pages.

Tom Billings, executive director of Union Baptist Association, has also been a champion of this project and a great friend to me for many years. As I struggled with earlier concepts that didn't work, Tom gently nudged me to not give up. Once the first draft was complete, his feedback strengthened the final product. In addition, I appreciate the valuable input I received from Robert Creech, Phil Taylor, Jim Turley, and Jon Stouffer. Even though their names don't appear in the text, their insightful comments have left an imprint on these pages.

A special word of appreciation is due to Greg Hawkins, executive pastor of Willow Creek Community Church. Not only did my interview with Greg provide insights into leadership at this great church, but he also offered feedback that shaped the final product. I am thankful to have enjoyed the friendship and encouragement of such a humble and capable servant over many years.

Another group of individuals gave me just the right help at just the right times. Thanks to Marshall Shelley at *Leadership Journal* for publishing the article that started the ball rolling; to Kimberly Wolfe for helping me understand art history; to Michael Lindsay, Sherry Surratt, and Fred Oaks for helping me make valuable connections for interviews; and to Dougal and Kathy Cameron for also helping arrange interviews and for the blessing of the perfect writer's retreat where much of this material was composed.

For the past four years, I have been privileged to serve as the facilitator for a group of executive pastors through the Texas Methodist Foundation. They've been remarkably open to allow a Baptist into their midst, but more than that, they've been a tremendous encouragement for me as a leader and a writer. Thanks to Bob, Cathy, David, Debra, Ferel, Holly, Jan, Jim, Judy, Lyle, Mike, Mitch, Peter, Philip, Rebecca, Sharon, Susan, and Susan.

Finally, my church, West University Baptist (and its sister campus, Crosspoint Church), is a vital part of my leadership journey. It's where I have learned and applied many of the leadership concepts described on these pages. But much more than that, it's a place where I am encouraged to encounter God and pursue His plans. I have been privileged to serve under two godly senior pastors in my ten years: Barry Landrum, who took a chance in bringing me onto the staff and helped me transition from marketplace to ministry leader, and Roger Patterson, whose friendship and partnership in ministry have made a deep, lasting imprint on my life. I am blessed to serve with and be loved by a great pastoral and program staff—Aaron, Barbara, Dave, Doug, Jeff, Jennifer, Lance, Lee, Robby, Ronny, and Shannon—and a great support staff. Liana Fairbanks and Laura Hatfield deserve special thanks for lifting my load so capably as I have worked on this project. And thanks to all the people of our congregation for allowing me to use my gifts in this way. My prayer is that you will pursue greatness and godliness and in doing so will hear the Master say, "Well done, my good and faithful servants."

M.B.

THE AUTHOR

Mike Bonem is a consultant, coach, pastor, author, and leader. For more than twenty years, he has assisted congregations, judicatory bodies, and other Christian organizations and their leaders in discerning God's vision and unlocking their full potential for the Kingdom. Mike brings a diverse mix of experiences to this work. He has served in vocational ministry for more than a decade as executive pastor of West University Baptist Church in Houston, and he began his career in the marketplace, first as a consultant with McKinsey & Company and later in senior leadership roles with two small businesses. He received a master's degree in business administration from Harvard Business School and a bachelor of science degree in chemical engineering from Rice University. Mike is the coauthor of two previous books, *Leading from the Second Chair: Serving Your Church, Fulfilling Your Role, and Realizing Your Dreams* and *Leading Congregational Change: A Practical Guide for the Transformational Journey*. He has spoken on leadership issues at conferences throughout the country and internationally. Mike and his wife, Bonnie, have been married for over twenty-five years and have four children.

For more information, go to www.mikebonem.com

INDEX

Chand, S., 168, 178
Change: in the church, 189–196;
clarity, striving for, 202;
communicating, Scripture on,
193–194; courageous leadership
required for, 202; destination
mind-set, 203–204; emotional
responses evoked by change
efforts, 186–187; failure, and
leaders, 195–196; God's presence
in decisions, 193; God's role in,
197; heart of, 185–186; leadership
burden, sharing, 201; preparing
for, 184–204; Scripture on, 184,
196–197; selecting the right pace
for, 201; spiritual foundation,
starting with, 199–200
Christ Fellowship (Palm Beach, FL),
38, 91–92, 101–102, 117–118,
120–121, 123, 153–154, 179;
culture, 173; hiring practices, 87;
Place of Hope, 118
Christ United Methodist Church
(Plano, TX), 132
Christian leadership, 3, *See also*
Biblical leadership; Leadership;
business principles in Scripture,
9–10; business thinking as
antithesis of, 8–9; "caring for the
flock" as primary responsibility,
194; church as organism versus
organization, 12–13; and conflict,
194–195; and corporate principles,
13–19; dilemma for, 19; and
failure, 73; dry and difficult
seasons in ministry, 209; pastor/
ministry leader training or
experience in leadership, 16; as
pastors and managers, 79–80;
personal practices, 212–213;
personnel decisions, 75; and
single-minded pursuit of
greatness, 217–218; soul care,
neglect of, 212; and vision, 55;
weaknesses, understanding, 22–23

Christian organizations: and "best
places to work" standard, 84;
financial management tools, 129;
financial systems in, 130; job
responsibilities and criteria for
success in, 90; measurement in,
99–100; need for effective
management in, 90; praise for
good work/caring for staff, 90;
systems in, 137–138
Church databases, 103
Church of the Highlands, 105, 118,
122–123, 213; budget, 122;
conservative budgeting approach,
122; culture, 173; generosity of,
122; measurement metrics,
110–111; philosophy, 122
Church of the Redeemer (Episcopal),
192
Church of the Resurrection
(Anglican), Wheaton, IL, 45, 125
Church of the Resurrection
(Methodist). *See* United Methodist
Church of the Resurrection
(Leawood, KS)
Church splits, 8
Churches: change in, 189–196;
change journey, 198–203; as
complex organizations, 190–192;
core values, 192–193; decision
making, 191; governance
structures, 191; lack of accepted
measures for success, 191–192;
organism versus organization,
12–13; resistance to change,
192–193; temperament of leader,
194–196; theological factors,
192–194; volunteers' resistance to
change, 190–191
Clarity: creating, 85–86; drive toward,
53; striving for, 202
Cloud, H., 216
Coaching mind-set: adopting, 89–92;
employee accountability, 90
Coffman, C., 85, 87, 89, 90, 92–93